Tim Keller has been an immensely wise mentor for many of us. This book is a rich account of the sources of his spiritual formation, of the people who helped lead him to them, and of the dynamics contributing to the successes of Redeemer Presbyterian Church in New York City.

GEORGE MARSDEN, AUTHOR OF *JONATHAN EDWARDS: A LIFE*

Collin Hansen brilliantly examines the story behind one of the greatest thinkers, teachers, and writers of our time. If you've been as blessed as I have by Tim Keller's work and ministry, you must read this book.

JOHN THUNE, US SENATOR FROM SOUTH DAKOTA

As a Tim Keller admirer I was eager to read this biography, and Collin Hansen did not disappoint. In his marvelously written narrative, we learn much about the people, experiences, and struggles that have shaped Tim's amazing ministry. I can add that I found this book inspiring—but with the awareness that saying so does not do justice to the profound ways it also spoke to my soul!

RICHARD J. MOUW, PRESIDENT EMERITUS,
FULLER THEOLOGICAL SEMINARY

Here is the story of a man possessed of unusual native gifts of analysis and synthesis, of the home and family life that has shaped him, of people both long dead and contemporary whose insights he has taken hold of in the interests of communicating the gospel, and also of the twists and turns of God's providence in his life. These pages may well have been titled *Becoming Tim Keller*. That "becoming" has been neither a quick nor an easy road. But Collin Hansen's account of it will be as challenging to readers as it is instructive.

SINCLAIR FERGUSON, AUTHOR OF *THE WHOLE CHRIST*

Tim Keller is a spiritual father to me and to so many through his teachings. No one has shaped my view of God and Scripture more, so what a treasure to be able to read all that has shaped his! This is the story of a faithful, imperfect man and the God he so loves and has given his life to serving.

JENNIE ALLEN, AUTHOR OF *GET OUT OF YOUR HEAD* AND
FOUNDER AND VISIONARY OF IF:GATHERING

Collin Hansen's informative study of Tim Keller explains how this traditional Calvinist became so effective as a minister in New York City despite that city's reputation for ignoring anything traditionally Christian. Especially important have been diverse influences that included well-known authors and preachers, but also lesser-known Bible teachers and pastoral exemplars as well as fellow Presbyterians who combined cultural, biblical, and pietistic emphases with the doctrinal. Under God, this mixture has not only worked, but also shown others the staying power, even in a hypermodern world, of what might be called soft-shell Calvinism.

MARK NOLL, AUTHOR OF *AMERICA'S BOOK: THE RISE AND DECLINE OF A BIBLE CIVILIZATION, 1794–1911*

Tim Keller's sermons and books have influenced me greatly, but I believe his curiosity has influenced me most. To now have insight into the people and places that cultivated his *brilliance*—a dramatic yet suitable word—feels like a gift I didn't know I needed.

JACKIE HILL PERRY, BIBLE TEACHER AND AUTHOR OF *HOLIER THAN THOU*

Tim Keller has done the hard work of being a faithful servant in our fractured world. His love of neighbor and consistent witness to the gospel are both inspiring and humbling. Even those of us who've earmarked his many books and listened to scores of his sermons will learn a lot about the ideas, people, and events—from the tumult of the 1960s counterculture to the terrorist attacks of 9/11 to the polarized times in which we live today—that shaped Tim's life and ministry. Collin Hansen's book is a special treat.

BEN SASSE, PRESIDENT OF THE UNIVERSITY OF FLORIDA

Like millions of others, I have been deeply impacted by Tim and Kathy Keller's ministry. In recent years, as I've gotten to know them, I have an even deeper appreciation for their abiding faith in Jesus. I think all of us who have benefited from their ministry will be intrigued to learn more about the events and decisions that have shaped their lives.

BILL HASLAM, FORTY-NINTH GOVERNOR OF TENNESSEE

My faith in God was challenged daily in front of millions while cohosting *The View*. That same decade, my pastor, Tim Keller, taught the facts of the Bible to unbelievers without judgment. His teaching deepened my understanding of shedding shame and prepared me to live out the truth and grace of the gospel while sharing the gospel. This book will illuminate the "why" behind the "who" of Tim Keller.

ELISABETH HASSELBECK, EMMY AWARD–WINNING DAYTIME COHOST OF *THE VIEW* AND *NEW YORK TIMES* BESTSELLING AUTHOR

In our time, few Christian leaders have a vision of the faith that is as recognizable—and as globally influential—as Tim Keller. In this engaging book, Collin Hansen charts the fascinating range of figures whose writings and examples influenced that vision and guides the reader through a life spent exploring and distilling the best of the Christian tradition. By humanizing a towering figure, Hansen challenges his own audience to learn from the deliberateness that marks Keller's own journey in the faith. Quite simply, I could not put this book down.

JAMES EGLINTON, MELDRUM SENIOR LECTURER IN REFORMED THEOLOGY, NEW COLLEGE, UNIVERSITY OF EDINBURGH

I'm so grateful for this well-written and expertly researched work. Collin Hansen reveals things that many of us never knew about Keller. This is a book about Tim Keller of course, but in the end, it is a book about Jesus Christ. I'm fairly sure this was intentional, or at least instinctive, and as a result it is a delight.

TIM FARRON, MEMBER OF THE BRITISH PARLIAMENT AND FORMER LEADER OF THE LIBERAL DEMOCRATS

TIMOTHY KELLER

His Spiritual and Intellectual Formation

COLLIN HANSEN

ZONDERVAN REFLECTIVE

ZONDERVAN REFLECTIVE

Timothy Keller
Copyright © 2023 by Collin Hansen

Requests for information should be addressed to:
Zondervan, *3900 Sparks Dr. SE, Grand Rapids, Michigan 49546*

Zondervan titles may be purchased in bulk for educational, business, fundraising, or sales promotional use. For information, please email SpecialMarkets@Zondervan.com.

ISBN 978-0-310-12868-7 (hardcover)
ISBN 978-0-310-12871-7 (international trade paper edition)
ISBN 978-0-310-12870-0 (audio)
ISBN 978-0-310-12869-4 (ebook)

Cover design: Micah Kandros Design
Cover photo: © Arianne Ramaker
Interior design: Sara Colley

Printed in the United States of America

23 24 25 26 27 28 29 30 31   /LSC/   14 13 12 11 10 9 8 7 6 5 4 3 2 1

To my grandfather, William,
who proclaimed the gospel before me,
and to my son, William,
who will proclaim the gospel after me, I pray.

CONTENTS

Part 3: Trial by Fire (1975 to 1989)

Part 4: From Gotham to Globe (1989 to Present)

PREFACE

W hen he walks out the door, the first ten thousand people he sees will have no idea who he is."

That's how Kathy Keller described her husband, Tim, walking down the sidewalks in New York. Tim's longtime assistant Craig Ellis has walked with him on countless streets in New York, and they've ridden together on innumerable subway rides. No one ever recognizes Keller.[1] It's not like Tim Keller blends into the crowd. Standing six foot four with a bald crown, he's one of the few people you'll see walking down the street reading an open book.

He's more likely to be recognized in London than in New York, where he has lived for more than thirty years. When Billy Graham hosted evangelistic meetings in New York in 1957, Graham sought publicity through association with the rich and famous to build a bigger platform for preaching the gospel. When Tim Keller started Redeemer Presbyterian Church in 1989, he deliberately avoided publicizing the church, especially to other Christians.[2] He wanted to meet skeptics of religion on the Upper East Side more than he wanted to sell books in Nashville. Whether they visited occasionally or joined as members, celebrities such as Jane Pauley, Elisabeth Hasselbeck, Robin Williams, and Diane Sawyer discovered a church that wouldn't exploit their fame to garner attention.

So why write about someone so uninterested in publicity? Because it's not really about him. Unlike a traditional biography, this book tells Keller's story from the perspective of his influences, more than his influence. Spend any time around Keller and you'll learn that he doesn't enjoy talking about himself. But he does enjoy talking—about what he's reading, what he's learning, what he's seeing.

The story of Tim Keller is the story of his spiritual and intellectual influences—from the woman who taught him how to read the Bible, to the professor who taught him to preach Jesus from every text, to the sociologist who taught him to see beneath society's surface.

With free access to Keller's family, friends, and colleagues, we visit the childhood home where he battled wits with bullies. We return to the small Southern church where he learned to care for souls. And we explore the city that lifted him to the international fame he never wanted. A child of the 1960s, student in the 1970s, church planter in the 1980s, and leader of one of New York's largest churches on September 11, 2001, Tim Keller's life spans many of the last century's most tumultuous events.

This is the story of the people, the books, the lectures, and ultimately the God who formed Timothy James Keller.

PART ONE

HONEST TO GOD

1950 to 1972

ONE

MOM COMPETITION

Allentown, Pennsylvania

1950 to 1968

Tim Keller's grandmother forbade her two sons from fighting in World War II. One son's fiancée was so ashamed that she broke off the engagement when he registered as a conscientious objector. The other son, William Beverly Keller, met his wife in the violent men's ward of a mental institution.

William, known as Bill Keller, always loved to tell the story that way. Louise Anne Clemente worked as a nurse, and Bill needed to fulfill his draft service. When they were both twenty-two, they married in Wilmington, Delaware, on May 24, 1947. The marriage between Keller and Clemente represented changing social norms across the United States following World War II. As young couples married across religious and ethnic lines, they upended denominational loyalties and contributed to the growth of an evangelical movement. The Kellers' oldest child would be baptized as a Roman Catholic, confirmed as a Lutheran, enrolled in seminary as a Wesleyan Arminian, and ordained as a Presbyterian.

Bill Keller was born in 1924 in Quakertown, Pennsylvania. His mother came under the influence of Mennonite pacifists in the area. A teetotaler who loathed the policies and programs of President Franklin Delano Roosevelt, she belonged to the Church of God (Holiness). The Keller family, however, claimed several veterans of the American Revolution in their family history. The first Keller in America brought his wife and four children to Philadelphia from Baden, Germany, in 1738. They settled down to farm in Bucks County, Pennsylvania, and built their lives around the Lutheran church and school. For two hundred years, generations of Kellers didn't stray far from home.

Meanwhile, Tim Keller's Clemente grandfather, James, was born in 1880 near Naples, Italy, and came to America at age eighteen. His Clemente grandmother was born to Italian immigrants in the United States, just before the turn of the twentieth century. Her parents arranged the marriage.[1] When Bill Keller and Louise Clemente wed in 1947, they were required to hold the ceremony in the priest's home instead of at the church, because Bill was a Lutheran. Louise never forgave what she perceived as a slight. She had her eldest son baptized Catholic, but she left the church and raised her children as Lutherans.

Louise gave birth to Timothy James Keller in Allentown, Pennsylvania, on September 23, 1950. Bill taught art in a small school district south of Allentown, and they lived in an apartment. Bill didn't enjoy the work and abandoned teaching for a career in advertising so that he could provide a more stable income for his family. He began designing kitchens for Sears. The family moved into Allentown and built a new house across the street from Bill's parents, on a plot that had been Grandmom Keller's garden. Bill Keller eventually took a job with a retail store called Hess Brothers and climbed the corporate ladder from advertising manager to sales promotion manager. As an executive, Bill spent long hours out of the home away from his family. Louise didn't expect him to cook or clean or change diapers—really, to do anything to help her in raising the children.[2] Tim Keller's friends remember Bill as a "shadow," sitting silently in his chair.[3]

Everyone knew who ran the household.

Who's Boss

Two more Keller children followed—Sharon Elizabeth in 1953 and William Christopher in 1958. Tim dedicated his book *Walking with God through Pain and Suffering* "to my sister Sharon Johnson, one of the most patient and joyful people I know, who has taught me much about bearing burdens, facing grief, and trusting God."[4]

Tim led the way for his younger siblings. He taught his younger sister, nicknamed "Shu," to ride a bike by sending her into a pile of boxes. He taught her how to keep her thumb out of her fist when punching so she wouldn't break it. He wrote the stories for their puppet shows, where they sold tickets and snacks. Shu remembered listening to Tim as he climbed to the top of a small tree and told stories down to her through the leaves. Tim composed a comedy routine about the early years of American history. Using their parents' record albums, they acted out *The Music Man* and sang Stan Freberg tunes. Later in life, when he wanted to impress his future wife, Kathy, he had a whole catalog of musicals to draw from, since they were some of the only music Louise allowed in the home other than opera.

Living on the second-to-last street in Allentown, with no branch library and one family car, the Keller children made the most of the books their mother accumulated. And it wasn't like 1950s America, with fuzzy reception on small black-and-white TVs, would have given him many alternatives. Tim was reading by age three, even without an unusual amount of help from his parents. The Keller children developed love for history and nonfiction in general by reading *The Rise and Fall of the Third Reich* by William Shirer and especially the *Funk & Wagnalls Standard Reference Encyclopedia*. When they saw something on TV, Tim wanted to look it up in the encyclopedia. No matter the article's subject, it all fascinated him. He seemed to retain everything he learned and lectured his younger siblings. The family didn't have much money for books, but they owned a collection of Rudyard Kipling's works. The Kellers also kept copies of *Jane Eyre* by Charlotte Brontë, along with *Wuthering Heights* by her sister Emily Brontë.

Tim may have played the ringleader for his younger siblings. But everyone knew who was boss. Visitors couldn't even walk down the hallway without Louise asking where they were going.[5]

"My mom had a huge need to control," Sharon said. "The trouble was, being raised by her, it was like there was one way to do it—her way. And if you were different, you were wrong. There was no such thing as, 'There is more than one way to skin a cat, and if you can't find a door, open a window.'"

Louise Keller's Italian Catholic upbringing demanded that her oldest son would make her proud and her oldest daughter would make her happy. All three children developed an intuitive gift for discerning displeasure from others.

"I think she was hardest on Tim, for sure," Sharon said. "She would have weeks where it's like, 'I'm going to teach Tim who's boss this week.'"

Each child coped differently under the pressure. Sharon escaped into daydreaming. Billy and Tim adopted her bent toward works-righteousness, but developed secret interior lives. Tim pushed back. He defied. He argued. He didn't—couldn't—win her affection and approval. Many years later, when Tim married his wife, Kathy, she noticed what she would later dub the "Mom Competition" between Louise and her older sister Angela. Tim's cousin graduated from college at age fifteen and went on to become a chemical engineer. But Tim couldn't match his brilliance, so he failed to earn his mother any points in the all-important sibling rivalry.[6] Sharon saw her mother as insecure, as someone who needed to be seen as the best in her role to show her worthiness.

"Tim's intelligence was so widespread," Sharon said. "I don't think my mom quite understood that as we were growing up. Tim's a global thinker. She wasn't."

An accelerated learning program, later abandoned by the school, left emotional scars on young Tim. In third grade, he entered the "opportunity class" for gifted Allentown youth. These "best and brightest" students didn't attend class with their neighbors but instead met together inside a school located in one of the city's poorer neighborhoods. It's not hard to see why the district changed this plan even before Tim had graduated from high school. These "egghead" students were marked for bullying, mocking, and teasing. School contributed to Tim's childhood feeling of loneliness. He grew up socially awkward, a wallflower who didn't know how to make or sustain friendships. He retreated into reading as a way to control his environment and affirm his own worth. Still, between loneliness and the relentless perfectionism of his mother, Tim became prone to constant internal self-criticism.

Shu, however, remembers how her older brother adapted to adverse conditions. Tim and his younger brother Billy both attended the opportunity class and became targets for neighborhood bullies. Perhaps recalling how and why she met their father, Louise banned the boys from fighting. Out of sheer survival instinct, Tim developed a skill for talking himself out of tight corners with bullies. And he further developed that skill in frequent arguments with his mother, who didn't shy away from telling her children how often they disappointed her.

"One of the reasons why I think he does so well with talking to people is the result of how he had to handle our mother," Sharon said. "And he did. If it wasn't for him we'd never have seen *Star Trek*. He was the one who would have to offer the argument in order to watch this or do that. She was pretty ruthless when it came to getting what she thought. To her, she was just helping us, giving us social graces."[7]

Under the weight of guilt at home, Tim found some refuge in activities. He tried wrestling, but he excelled at playing the trumpet in the marching band.[8] Tim valued his experience with Boy Scouts so much that one of his sons made Eagle Scout even while living on Roosevelt Island in New York. Tim's wife, Kathy, would later nickname Tim "Boy Scout" because his commitment to doing the right thing would never even allow him to park in front of a fire hydrant in the city.[9]

Evangelical Congregational Church

Even within her Italian immigrant family, Louise Keller stood out for her high moral standards, and she judged other Catholics for falling short. Later in marriage, Louise Keller faulted her husband for abdicating his leadership in the family's religious life. So Louise assumed responsibility. As a nurse during the war, Louise had a Protestant friend who read the Bible and prayed for herself, which was foreign to her Catholic experience. Louise was fascinated to see that she could interact personally with God. After Tim's baptism, she concluded that the Catholic Church didn't line up with Scripture.

So she took the family to the Kellers' ancestral Lutheran church, which at that time was part of the Lutheran Church in America—a denomination that would later become part of the Evangelical Lutheran Church in America. The Kellers attended worship every Sunday and even had Tim baptized again as a Lutheran. Louise became a Bible study teacher and a pillar of the church, which was located only a mile from their home. While Louise didn't put much emphasis on theology, she frequently played Bible trivia with her kids. Tim memorized the names of every king of Israel and Judah.

As a teen in the early 1960s, Tim attended confirmation classes in the Lutheran church. In this small congregation, pastors didn't stay around for long. His first teacher, a retired minister named Rev. Beers, offered his parishioners an orthodox take on Christian history, practices, and theology. He required students to memorize the outline of the Augsburg Confession and taught about judgment and belief in Jesus alone for salvation through the acronym SOS: the law shows our sins, the gospel shows our Savior. It was 1963, and it was the first clear presentation of the gospel of grace that Tim Keller had ever heard.

At this time in his life, however, Tim didn't grasp the message as anything more than another interesting idea he needed to master to pass a class. And yet a seed had been planted. Later another pastor, Jack Miller, would water that seed when he cited Martin Luther. And from that seed of the gospel emerged the power that eventually transformed Tim's life, helping define his communication of the gospel as liberation from two kinds of legalism.

The first kind of legalism—salvation through good works—he learned from his second confirmation teacher, a recent graduate of the Lutheran seminary in Gettysburg, Pennsylvania. Frustrating Tim's mother and grandmother, this minister advocated for the civil rights movement at the height of social activism in 1964. Similar to the professors Tim later encountered in college, this minister also cast doubt on biblical authority and what he considered to be outdated doctrines. He spent little time talking about doctrine or the church. Christianity was a matter of political activism, an effort to make the world a better place.

The juxtaposition between his first and second year of confirmation jarred Tim:

> It was almost like being instructed in two different religions. In the first year, we stood before a holy, just God whose wrath could only be turned aside at great effort and cost. In the second year, we heard of a spirit of love in the universe, who mainly required that we work for human rights and the liberation of the oppressed. The main question I wanted to ask our instructors was, "Which one of you is lying?" But fourteen-year-olds are not so bold, and I just kept my mouth shut.[10]

After a decade with the Lutherans, Louise Keller found a more congenial match for her own view of religion in the Evangelical Congregational Church, which emphasized human effort in maintaining salvation and achieving sinless perfection. Both at home and in church, Tim Keller learned this second form of legalism—that of the fundamentalist variety. By the time Tim was leaving home to attend college, he didn't just know about Martin Luther; he could personally relate to Luther, who had been afflicted with a pathologically overscrupulous conscience that expected perfection from himself in seeking to live up to his standards and potential.

Those external standards only increased as his parents befriended Bishop John Moyer, a minister in their small denomination, which had German-speaking roots in the Methodist tradition. When Tim graduated from Louis E. Dieruff High School and set off for Bucknell University in 1968, his mother envisioned that he would return one day to lead the Evangelical Congregational Church. Perhaps such a lofty religious position would prove her worth as a mother.

But Tim wasn't so sure he wanted anything to do with Christianity. A cycle of shame had left him starved for a community where he could be included and accepted, even admired. And if that meant he needed to abandon the church, so be it.[11]

TWO

THE ABSURD MAN

Bucknell University

The 1968 incoming class at Bucknell University would graduate 650 students four years later in 1972. From their senior year of high school to the day they graduated from college, the world transformed before their eyes.

As they prepared to graduate from high school, Martin Luther King Jr. was assassinated in Memphis, Tennessee, on April 8. Less than two months later, Robert Francis Kennedy was assassinated in Los Angeles, California, on June 6. As they headed off to college, the Soviet Union suppressed a reform movement and invaded Czechoslovakia on August 20. And the nation watched in horror and fascination as Mayor Richard Daley's Chicago police brutalized protesters outside the Democratic National Convention between August 26 and 29.

Bucknell, a small liberal arts school in rural Lewisburg, Pennsylvania, remained largely traditional and conservative. Some

2,800 students lived within short walking distance of each other in three dorm groupings. Throughout much of the 1960s, students were still expected to abide by curfews, and women's dress lengths were regulated. Dorms required men to be announced and escorted in to visit women in their rooms.

The counterculture arrived with Tim Keller's freshman class in 1968. Students divided in easily recognizable ways—long-haired hippies flaunted drug use and sexual liberation on one side, while traditional students sported the Greek letters of their fraternities and sororities on the other. As a wallflower, Keller never risked rejection from the business, engineering, and science students in fraternities. But he didn't fit with the hippies either, even though they took many classes together in the humanities.

In Keller's view, the hippies postured just as much as the jocks.[1] The local chapter of Students for a Democratic Society was relatively small. Philip Berrigan, a Roman Catholic priest and anti-war activist, was held in federal prison in Lewisburg after he conspired to burn draft records with homemade napalm. But no mass movement of nearby students would protest his incarceration in this small central Pennsylvania town of fewer than six thousand people.

Lewisburg may not have been the center of anti-Vietnam protests, but Bucknell kept pace with many of the day's fashionable academic trends. Bucknell's roots stretch back to 1846, when the school was founded by Baptists. But by the time Keller arrived, the administration no longer encouraged traditional expressions of Christian faith. This was the era of mainline Protestantism, when dogma took a back seat to doing good, when the campus Christian Association changed their name to Concern for Action. The psychology department had long since moved on from Sigmund Freud. But the religion department still assigned his teachings regularly. Only two years earlier, *Time* magazine asked, "Is God Dead?," spurred by the publication of Thomas J. J. Altizer and William Hamilton's *Radical Theology and the Death of*

God.[2] Bucknell's religion faculty advanced Altizer and Hamilton's cause across their courses.

Another popular course assignment was John A. T. Robinson's *Honest to God*. When the book was rereleased in 2013 on its fiftieth anniversary, the publisher contended that the book had been described as the "most talked-about theological work of the twentieth century." Existentialists such as Martin Heidegger, Jean-Paul Sartre, and Albert Camus were considered the cutting-edge thinkers of the era. Robinson, an Anglican bishop, argued for realigning concepts of God along existentialist lines and rejecting any notion of God as "out there." Robinson saw himself drawing together the work of Paul Tillich, Dietrich Bonhoeffer, and Rudolf Bultmann to recast Christianity for the nuclear age. Looking back fifty years later, the publisher explained why *Honest to God* created such a stir:

> It also epitomized the revolutionary spirit of a fresh and challenging way of looking at the world, which, throughout the 1960s, was to bring about the disintegration of established orthodoxies and social, political and theological norms. It articulated the anxieties of a generation who saw these traditional givens as no longer acceptable or necessarily credible.[3]

As a religion major, Tim Keller read all of these texts and many more. In a course on the Bible as literature, he heard the standard liberal narrative that the Gospels had been compiled as oral traditions from communities scattered around the Mediterranean. Keller's professors taught that the communities weren't so much trying to attest to historical reality as crafting an original narrative that addressed their own situation and solidified their own leadership. Over the years these stories, transmitted orally, took on even more fanciful dimensions. Only then were they written down and standardized. The notion of a historical Jesus, according to this understanding, is but a fable. Most mainstream religion scholars of the twentieth century cast the historical Jesus in their own image—an especially dynamic teacher full of wisdom, who demanded justice and offended authorities.[4]

The history and sociology departments at Bucknell were no less radical, as they were committed to Herbert Marcuse and the neo-Marxist critical theory of the Frankfurt School. Keller agreed with aspects of their critique of the American bourgeoisie society that had reared him in Allentown, but the philosophy behind this form of Marxism baffled him as a teen. He couldn't see how the pursuit for social justice coincided with an understanding of morality as relative. Intellectually, he couldn't align with the odd fusion of Freud and the modern therapeutic with Marxist cultural analysis.

His confusion further intensified because Keller failed to see much concern for social problems from the Christians who advocated for personal morality. He knew he couldn't settle for a Christianity that would mandate apartheid in South Africa or segregation in the American South.[5] He was appalled at the violence he saw waged in the name of Christ against Blacks and their allies in the civil rights movement across the South. Particularly harrowing for Keller as a young teen was a photo of James Meredith, who was shot while he was marching for civil rights in 1966. The shooter demonstrated no concern for Meredith or for the consequences of his crime. Keller struggled to believe that an entire society, especially one so pervasively Christian, could rationalize the evil of racial segregation.

> It marked the first time I realized that most older white adults in my life were telling me things that were dead wrong. The problem was not just a "few troublemakers." Black people *did* have a right to demand the redress and rectifying of many wrongs.
>
> Although I had grown up going to church, Christianity began to lose its appeal to me when I was in college. One reason for my difficulty was the disconnect between my secular friends who supported

the Civil Rights Movement, and the orthodox Christian believers who thought that Martin Luther King, Jr. was a threat to society. Why, I wondered, did the nonreligious believe so passionately in equal rights and justice, while the religious people I knew could not have cared less?[6]

During these college years, so different intellectually and morally from the Evangelical Congregational Church of his youth, Tim began to doubt Christianity. But it wasn't just an intellectual problem for him. He just couldn't sense anything real to Christianity. For two years he struggled between the rigid evangelical faith of his mother, which he could not feel, and the progressive existentialist theology of his professors, which he did not find intellectually satisfying.

Born Again

As a religion major, Keller took courses that covered Judaism, Islam, Hinduism, Confucianism, and Buddhism. He especially wanted to find an alternative to Christian views of eternal judgment, of damnation and eternal conscious torment in the fires of hell. He searched for a religion that would not judge anyone, whatever they might do or believe. He knew he believed in a God of love. He just didn't know which religion, or whether any religion at all, could best introduce him to that God.

Keller appreciated the Buddhist emphasis on selflessness and detached service to others, but Buddhism didn't allow for any kind of personal God, and he concluded that love is something only a person can do. Pagan religions didn't offer this loving God, with their creation myths full of capricious and even malicious gods fighting each other. Only in the Bible did Tim encounter a God who created the world for his own enjoyment, for the sake of love. Studying other religions helped Tim see that not all religious views include a loving God.[7]

So he turned his attention to the historical arguments against Christianity and, in particular, in the trustworthiness of the New Testament. He realized that Christianity is rather unusual in its assertion that its core beliefs stand or fall on the historical accuracy of its claims.[8] As Tim investigated what he was learning in class, he wasn't persuaded by the evidence against the earliest written accounts of Christianity. He concluded that his Bucknell professors and the revolutionary books they assigned were wrong.[9]

Keller may have disagreed with *Time* magazine's assertion that God was dead, but he didn't yet feel as though Jesus was alive. Years in church had not led him to a personal experience of God. He didn't pray with any sense of God's presence and felt trapped in a crisis of identity. He sensed the intense expectations of his mother but lacked the desire to fulfill them. Long before the days of the smartphone, Tim spoke to his parents no more than once or twice per month. And when his mother sent him letters, he typically didn't respond. He felt little personal attachment to the Christianity he knew in his teen years and was still searching for a place to fit, a place to belong. He valued the philosophical objectivity of the classroom, but it was only in hindsight that he could recognize his true need—that he cared less about truth and more about belonging. At the time he just felt lonely and unloved.[10]

During their sophomore year, Tim's friend Bruce Henderson lived off campus on the third floor of an apartment with low ceilings. They were so low that Tim, because of his height, couldn't stand comfortably. So he often lingered outside the apartment at the top of the stairs with his back against the wall. Tim, described by Bruce as "master of the pop in," often engaged him in heated debates, even growing animated to the point that Bruce feared Tim's large arms and hands would dent the apartment hallway's walls. Bruce, working three jobs as a student, often backed down because he didn't want to pay for the damage. But he didn't back down from the fight entirely, as the two young men debated identity in ways that only college sophomores can—discontented with authority but not experienced enough to find their own way forward.

Bruce and Tim had met and become friends through InterVarsity Christian Fellowship. Tim had attended the spring retreat in 1969 during his freshman year. Jim Cummings, a student on the same floor in Tim's freshman dorm, had invited Tim to the InterVarsity meetings. With his Lutheran background and his study as a religion major, Tim was an inviting contact for these evangelistically minded students. Tim could speak the language of InterVarsity because of his experience in the Evangelical Congregational Church. He would even act like a Christian because he so desperately wanted friends. It wasn't long before the InterVarsity students got a copy of some C. S. Lewis books into his hands. Soon after, the works of John Stott brought Tim back to Martin Luther's distinction between law and gospel, between saving oneself through good works and receiving salvation as a gift of grace. What Tim had previously recited for a confirmation exam at age fourteen now appeared revolutionary at age twenty. He began to see that the rigid religion of his mother wasn't the only path to being an orthodox, Bible-believing Christian.

Even though Keller had participated in several InterVarsity events, he wasn't part of the chapter's inner ring during the spring retreat, held at a barn converted into a Bucknell faculty member's summer home. Not that InterVarsity had much of an "outer" ring. There were no more than fifteen active students in the Bucknell chapter in the spring and fall of 1969. And even that small group was never all together at one time. Tim wasn't yet ready to join the group, but he had found a community that would help him in his search for answers to his many questions. At the very least, these were students willing to debate him, helping him refine his own beliefs. As older students took interest in him, Tim reciprocated. But he didn't tell them that outside InterVarsity he was living another life—a life apart from the Christianity he adopted for the InterVarsity crowd.

By January 1970, during his sophomore year, Tim knew he could no longer continue his double life. He'd been reading the InterVarsity books and befriending InterVarsity students. Only one hurdle remained. What if he met someone he loved—someone who made life worth living—but Christianity said they couldn't be together? Wouldn't that rejection make a lonely young man somehow even lonelier?

Bruce Henderson remembers a decisive moment on his twentieth birthday, April 21, 1970, when he woke up to find Tim sitting on the floor at the foot of his bed, silently waiting for him. Bruce knew something was different, that something significant had changed in Tim. His wrestling was over. Tim had repented of his sin and believed in Jesus. He had put his heart's faith and trust in Christ alone for salvation.

So, what happened? Why did he change? His intellectual concerns about evil, suffering, and judgment didn't suddenly disappear. But after looking for answers in other religions and after debating with Christians, Tim finally came to experience his personal need for God. It wasn't a new method of spiritual enlightenment. Instead, he finally reached the end of himself. Overwhelmed by his sin, face-to-face with his failures and flaws, Tim found the God of love who revealed himself in Jesus Christ and his Word.[11] No longer would he presume to judge God. Now he would follow the God who is just and at the same time is the one who justifies sinners. The Just One had forgiven his sin. The student of religion had become the disciple of Jesus.

"During college the Bible came alive in a way that was hard to describe," he remembered in his book *Jesus the King*. "The best way I can put it is that, before the change, I pored over the Bible, questioning and analyzing it. But after the change it was as if the Bible, or maybe Someone through the Bible, began poring over me, questioning and analyzing me."[12] He'd been taught by his mother and the church of his youth that the Bible is God's Word. But until this personal encounter, the good news of the Gospels didn't strike him as the ultimate reality.[13]

Keller doesn't recall any dramatic changes accompanying his

conversion. He sensed a new reality in his prayer life, though, and he gave up his double life of "freedom"[14] without God. But his friends certainly witnessed a change.

"If you ask about whether there was a change in Tim, there sure was in college," Bruce Henderson said. "He was a heck of a lot kinder, and you could reach him emotionally. All of a sudden he was present. He was there."[15]

Intellectually Credible and Existentially Satisfying

Keller didn't keep this experience to himself either. InterVarsity became not only his source of spiritual nourishment but also his outlet for Christian activism. Over the next two years at Bucknell, the InterVarsity students would help him develop a zeal for evangelism. They would teach him to study the Bible and then teach it to others. They would help him ground his beliefs and actions in God himself and not in a subjective or fleeting sense of the world.[16]

Less than two weeks after Bruce Henderson woke up with Tim at the foot of his bed, InterVarsity students were huddled together amid a national crisis. It was the end of April 1970 and the height of the protest movement against President Richard Nixon's expansion of the Vietnam War by invading Cambodia. On May 4, 1970, National Guard soldiers opened fire against student protesters on the campus of Kent State University, killing four people. Students across US campuses, including Bucknell, responded by striking and refusing to attend classes. Keller and the other InterVarsity students at Bucknell, no more than fifteen altogether, prayed and debated whether they should participate in the strike, which remained peaceful. Classes had been canceled, and most Bucknell students were gathering on the open quadrangle every day. An open mic invited diverse perspectives, which favored more liberal and progressive views. The InterVarsity students weren't sure how best to contribute to the conversation on campus.

Eventually one of the students made a sign—white letters on a black background—and posted it on the outskirts of the crowd. For the next day or two, Tim and another student engaged anyone who approached the sign, which read, "The Resurrection of Jesus Christ Is Intellectually Credible and Existentially Satisfying." They didn't get much of a response—mostly mocking and eye rolls. One student, a friendly acquaintance, surprised Keller by yelling, "Tim! F*** Jesus Christ." But Keller remembered many substantial conversations with confused students too. He observed that every person considering Christianity brought rational objections and questions—as well as personal ones—just as he had done before his personal encounter with God.[17] Manning the InterVarsity book table, Tim handed out many of the same books that had helped him on his own faith journey.

Keller threw himself wholeheartedly into InterVarsity leadership. He and Bruce, incoming officers for InterVarsity at Bucknell, traveled that summer of 1970 to Upper Nyack, New York, for a weeklong training session with legendary InterVarsity staffer C. Stacey Woods. The Bucknell students were an answered prayer for Woods. InterVarsity had wanted to open a chapter in Lewisburg but had been thwarted for years by a hostile chaplain.

Bruce doesn't remember much of what they learned at the retreat. But he remembers that during the six-hour round-trip drive and time spent together on the banks of the Hudson River, he and Tim worked out an entire year's worth of activities for InterVarsity. They planned retreats. They identified guest speakers. They organized small groups— all in a week's time.

Those plans included a rock concert with evangelistic aims. Bruce knew about a group back in Pittsburgh called John Guest and the Exkursions. That fall of 1970, the group performed three concerts at Bucknell, which included brief evangelistic sermons by Guest, an Episcopal priest. Born in Oxford, England, Guest had committed his life to Christ at age eighteen in 1954 during a Billy Graham sermon. He would eventually become a renowned evangelist in his own right and go on to help found Trinity Episcopal School of Ministry and serve on the board of the National Association of Evangelicals.

Guest's rock concerts at Bucknell didn't yield immediate evangelistic results. But they resulted in more than one hundred three-by-five-inch index cards from students expressing interest in spiritual conversations. The small cadre of InterVarsity students at Bucknell now had work to do—following up with interested students.

"This was in Tim's wheelhouse," Bruce said. "He took those cards, and he would visit, one-on-one, with every one of those people. I don't know how he ever got any schoolwork done. He really thrived on taking these young people under his wing. He loved it."[18]

His GPA was suddenly lower on the priority list for Tim. Bruce remembers taking a social psychology class with Tim, who didn't demonstrate any great zeal or proclivity for writing in those student days. But it didn't matter. Tim had found his true calling to public ministry.

Small groups overseen by Keller and the other InterVarsity officers proliferated across campus. The first chapter meeting had seventy students instead of the customary ten or so they had seen the previous year. Tim's own faith blossomed in the spiritually charged environment of those growing InterVarsity meetings. His roommate for all four years, Frank King, didn't profess faith in Christ until their senior year and, in fact, had grown frustrated with the steady stream of students stopping by and calling on Tim at all hours. Younger students at Bucknell were eager for Tim's spiritual counsel. And he often connected personally with their heartfelt hopes and fears.

"Out of his own life experience, he has a depth of feeling that comes through in his preaching that sounds authentic to people," said

Janet Essig, an incoming Bucknell freshman in the fall of 1970. "He wasn't talking at people. He was really listening to people, and they felt encouraged."[19]

Essig grew up in Summit, New Jersey, about twenty-three miles east of Manhattan. She chose Bucknell because she considered it a haven from the unrest on so many other campuses she had considered.[20] This was a turbulent time on many colleges, and not until December 1972, the year Keller graduated from Bucknell, did the Vietnam draft end. Sue (Kristy) Pichert, in the same incoming class as Essig, remembers Bucknell a bit differently—as a sorority school prone to partying. She chose Bucknell because she knew they had a thriving group of Young Life leaders. She had become a Christian through a Young Life camp at age sixteen.

Sue first heard of Tim Keller when she received a handwritten note from him the summer before she enrolled. The InterVarsity officers divided all eight hundred incoming freshmen between them and wrote notes welcoming them to check out the chapter. In this era before smartphones, emails, and texts, she was the only freshman who wrote back—and only after her sister, Kathy, had perused the letter and pronounced the group okay. Two years older, Kathy was a junior at Allegheny College and had already run the gamut of religion classes with unbelieving professors and chaplains who supported everything but genuine Christianity.

During freshman week, Sue (Kristy) Pichert was getting settled on the fourth floor of the girls freshman dorm when two upperclassmen called on her. This wasn't all that common, and the other women were impressed. One of her visitors was Tim.[21] Since students lived in such close proximity, Tim could follow up with his list of interested freshmen without much trouble.

During the John Guest concert, many freshmen sensed that God was working in unexpected and powerful ways. Janet Essig remembers the concert held right outside her freshman dorm. Sue met another freshman believer in Christ, and they would later wed. Her husband, Jim Pichert, remembers Guest emphasizing the difference between knowing Jesus and knowing about Jesus.[22] Hundreds turned out for the event. The freshmen couldn't believe how many other Christians were on campus, all raising a finger to point the "one way" to God through Jesus. That year, InterVarsity at Bucknell exploded from just ten or fifteen students to more than a hundred, largely fueled by zealous believers in this incoming freshman class. Many students professed new faith in Christ despite no organized evangelistic program. For Tim and his friends, it was all shocking and wonderful.

The Jesus Movement had come to Bucknell.

Life Together

Tim's final two years at Bucknell would be characterized by intense and frequent discussions about Jesus with students considering the Christian faith.[23] This experience and the constant expectation of revival would remain with Keller the rest of his life.

The spring of 1971, acting on behalf of InterVarsity, Tim invited Ed Clowney, the first president of Westminster Theological Seminary, to visit Bucknell and give a special evangelistic talk. Given the popularity of existentialism, Keller asked Clowney to address "The Christian and the Absurd Man" and engage with Albert Camus and Jean-Paul Sartre. Camus was so popular with professors at the time that in the same semester, Tim was assigned his novel *The Stranger* in three separate courses. He had asked the right person to speak. Clowney had studied the Danish Christian and existentialist Søren Kierkegaard for his Master of Sacred Theology degree at Yale.

Clowney expected a small gathering of ten students to greet him after his three-hour drive from Philadelphia. Instead, about 150 showed up. The event was standing room only.

Keller remembers the talk as one of the best he'd ever heard. Clowney affirmed Camus's description of the alienation that afflicts humans. Compared to optimistic liberals, Camus was far more realistic about life. Then Clowney argued that the "absurd existence" is not noble but is instead cursed. Alienation is not just an arbitrary reality but is our sentence, our curse, for seeking to live apart from God. He showed how Christianity offers a better explanation for why this world does not satisfy. And he progressed through the biblical story from creation to fall before pointing toward redemption.

InterVarsity invited the crowd that attended the talk to join them on their spring retreat the following weekend. But Tim didn't think anyone would come. Why? Clowney planned to speak about the church, with five long expositions from 1 Peter 2:9–10. Tim, who still believed a person needed to leave the church to find vibrant spiritual life, only signed up for the retreat because he was a chapter officer. To his surprise, about twenty students attended. And one woman professed new faith in Jesus after talking with Clowney.[24]

"It just blew me away," Keller said of Clowney's teaching on the church. "I never forgot it."[25]

Bruce Henderson, Tim's friend and the InterVarsity chapter president, was likewise impressed with Clowney.

"Clowney was wonderful. He was just fantastic," Bruce said. "He could talk to you. He could talk at your level. He took genuine interest in every single person. He was one of those guys who, once you heard him, you could be in a town fifty miles away, but you'd drive to hear him."[26]

In addition to Clowney's talk and retreat, InterVarsity students at Bucknell led evangelistic Bible studies. And they hosted a book table outside the cafeteria in the student union. Keller in particular loved managing the book table. "He was always pushing books, as you might imagine," Sue Pichert said.[27] The books provided fodder for discussion and debate with Christians and non-Christians alike, and Tim was happy to engage with anyone willing to talk.

InterVarsity Press books were prominently featured at chapter meetings and freshman activity fairs. F. F. Bruce's *The New Testament Documents: Are They Reliable?*, originally published in 1943, countered the prevailing thinking of the Bucknell religion department. Colin Brown's *Philosophy and the Christian Faith* came out in 1969 from InterVarsity and covered the writings of Thomas Aquinas, René Descartes, David Hume, Immanuel Kant, Georg W. F. Hegel, Søren Kierkegaard, Friedrich Nietzsche, Ludwig Wittgenstein, Karl Barth, and Francis Schaeffer. Brown, a professor at Fuller Theological Seminary, summarized their positions but also offered Christian responses. Other InterVarsity Press authors prominently featured were Paul Little, Francis Schaeffer, J. I. Packer, and John Stott.

Packer's *Knowing God*, which Keller read in 1971, gave him a taste of Reformed theology. He learned that doctrine and devotion should walk hand in hand on the Christian journey. Of course, C. S. Lewis's *Mere Christianity* was perhaps the most popular title recommended by Keller at the book table. As much as the content, Keller admired Lewis's unique style—his ability to weave together clear prose with memorable illustrations and convincing logic. Imagination and reason could be combined in a compelling, beautiful way.

For a precocious student such as Keller, the high-level philosophical engagement of these InterVarsity authors showed him you could be intellectually serious and also a Christian. Indeed, Keller represented the fruit of InterVarsity's labors on college campuses since the 1940s. If evangelicals had struggled to evangelize college students before World War II, and thus suffered from a reputation of anti-intellectualism, that's not what greeted Keller at Bucknell in the late 1960s.[28] For the rest of his life, Keller's ministry would never stray far from what he learned while standing behind the book table—especially from British authors such as Stott, Lewis, and Packer.

"Tim thrived in that situation," Bruce Henderson said. "His extroversion would come out. His arms would start moving. He loved the debate. He loved to talk. I think that was really important to the intellectual development of many of us."[29]

InterVarsity introduced Keller to an especially thoughtful stream of evangelical Christianity. To authors such as Packer, who shaped his theological emphases, and Stott, who gave him his first model for preaching. To the practice of a daily quiet time of prayer and reading Scripture. To the priority of closely reading biblical texts in small groups that met weekly for sharing and worship. And to the enduring value of deep Christian friendships—the kind of "life together" extolled by Dietrich Bonhoeffer. Inspired by the communal living of Bonhoeffer's underground seminary during wartime Germany, the InterVarsity students met in small groups every day at 5:00 p.m. to pray and then eat. This spiritual regimen resembled a monastic order. Never would Keller know a more intense, formative Christian community.[30] Before social media and answering machines, the students relied on one another through the vulnerable and intimate moments of these transitional years.

Bruce Henderson's friendship and leadership stood out to Tim in these initially confusing but ultimately clarifying times, and he would later serve as the best man in Tim's wedding. Keller remembered, "Bruce was also a giver of tough love, and I remember that he supported me fully as a friend even as he sometimes confronted me about issues in my life he believed I had not fully faced."[31]

Bucknell, along with its network of alumni, would remain a lifelong influence on Keller. Mako Fujimura, an early elder at Redeemer Presbyterian Church in New York, was another Bucknell graduate, and he credits the school's emphasis on interdisciplinary education as formative for Keller's ministry success.[32] Bucknell alumnus Dick Kaufmann would later serve alongside Keller as executive pastor of Redeemer during a crucial transition for the church as it grew in size and complexity.

Keller didn't stay in touch with many of his classmates for very long after Bucknell, mainly because he and his future wife, Kathy, would form such strong friendships with couples in seminary and in their first church. But Tim would always recall what he learned about the Christian life as a new believer from the Bucknell crew that included Jon Voskuil, Betsy Hess, Bob Pazmiño, David Reimer, Janet Kleppe, and Lora Graham.

Way Over Our Heads

His friend Bruce Henderson remained in Lewisburg three years after they graduated and even served in leadership at First Presbyterian Church, the most popular congregation among Bucknell students, including Keller. First Presbyterian Church dates back to the Second Great Awakening of 1833, and in that long and venerable history, the Rev. Richard (Dick) Merritt receives only an obligatory mention alongside other pastors in the official church history. But Bucknell alumni see plenty of Merritt in Keller's ministry, all the way through his time pastoring in New York.[33]

Before coming to central Pennsylvania, Merritt graduated from Princeton Theological Seminary, where he had studied with renowned professor Bruce Metzger. For those who've heard both Keller and Merritt preach, the similarities are obvious in several key ways.

"Dick Merritt was a very sophisticated person. He read widely," Bruce Henderson remembered. Merritt peppered his sermons with literary references. "He was probably as sophisticated as anybody I've ever met in terms of the breadth and depth of his readings. He's probably the single best preacher of any kind I've ever heard. Here he was this unknown in this little college town in central Pennsylvania. He could've been a national figure. He was that good. I think that much of Tim's style reflects Dick Merritt's approach."[34]

Whether from Clowney or Merritt, Keller heard at Bucknell the kind of approach to evangelical preaching that he would himself embody in future decades. No bells and whistles. Always present the basic gospel message—Christ is in charge of the world, and he is the way to God, because he alone can redeem us from our sins.

"That was common in both Dick Merritt and Edmund Clowney—the ability to tell you that you are a sinner, and you believe that, but there's a way out, and that way is Christ," Henderson said.[35]

Merritt's preaching wasn't his only contribution to the spiritual growth of Bucknell students, however. He also prayed with the InterVarsity upperclassmen for the incoming 1970 freshman class. During finals week, Merritt opened up First Presbyterian Church and his office at the church to students looking for a quiet space. On Sunday nights, when Bucknell served its worst meal, First Presbyterian hosted a student dinner. Church families rotated cooking responsibilities, and Keller was a regular. Merritt didn't plan any formal program with the students. He just answered questions and spent time with them.

Merritt's style and substance were both formative for Keller. Along with InterVarsity, First Presbyterian Church offered a spiritual haven from the religious establishment of Bucknell, which students such as Bruce Henderson regarded as actively hostile to evangelicals.

Several years ago, Henderson hosted Scottish theologian Andrew Purvis, chair in Reformed theology at Pittsburgh Theological Seminary and an advocate for evangelical renewal in his denomination. While his son was attending Bucknell, Purvis was invited to campus to preach at Rooke Chapel.

"That would have been unthinkable in our day," Henderson said. "Looking back, God clearly blessed us, despite the fact that we were in way over our heads."[36]

THREE

THE WOMAN WHO TAUGHT HIM TO STUDY THE BIBLE

InterVarsity Christian Fellowship

No one would have confused Barbara Boyd with a hippie.

Intense and disciplined, she stood tall and straight. She dressed conservatively with a preference for clothing on sale at Talbots. Some would describe her as rigid. Everyone could agree she led an especially self-controlled and organized life.

When Janet Essig visited her later in life, Boyd was upset that she showed up late. Boyd, a former elementary school teacher, still valued punctuality. Essig had gotten to know Boyd in Summit, New Jersey, a little more than ten miles southeast of Morristown, where George Washington twice encamped his army for the winter during the Revolutionary War. One day near the end of the 1960s, Essig was reading David Wilkerson's mega-bestseller *The Cross and the Switchblade* in the public library when a woman approached her and invited her to a Bible study.

That Bible study, led by Barbara Boyd, would change Janet's life.

Young Life had tried and failed several times to launch high school ministries in the Summit area. Boyd was leading a Bible study for mothers, and in the absence of vibrant youth ministries, she decided to lead one for their daughters too. Janet's mother didn't attend the study. In fact, she felt threatened by Boyd's interest in her daughter. But Boyd was just trying to help spiritually nurture young women.

"She demanded a lot, and as a result, people really stepped up, because she knew we could do more than we were willing to do sometimes," Janet remembered. "When I say she was intense, it was because she gave us a sense we were entering into the presence of Almighty God, and how could we not take this seriously?"[1]

Boyd didn't want the young women to depend on her for biblical insights. She aimed to prepare them for lifelong study of God's Word for themselves, guided by the Holy Spirit.[2] She did, however, take responsibility to ensure the teens would find Christian community when they graduated from high school and started in college.

Janet enrolled at Bucknell in the fall of 1970, the year revival came to the InterVarsity chapter. Rounding up freshmen for an evangelistic Bible study, Tim Keller showed up unannounced on her doorstep. The next person Tim picked up would later become Janet's husband, Jim Essig. The first wedding Keller ever officiated was for Jim and Janet in 1975. Afterward, several friends and family commented that they wouldn't need to attend church the next day, since Keller had delivered a thirty-minute sermon. But Keller himself could not skip church. He drove home that night so he could preach the next morning back in Hopewell, Virginia.[3]

Not long after Janet arrived at Bucknell, Barbara Boyd taught Keller how to study the Bible, too. Through seminary and doctoral studies and decades of preaching and teaching, Keller would build off the foundation laid by Boyd's inductive Bible study method and the ecumenical ethos of her employer, InterVarsity Christian Fellowship.[4]

Lordship Talk

Having begun her work in 1950, Barbara Boyd worked for InterVarsity Christian Fellowship for forty years. The first female staff member for InterVarsity, Boyd never married. An early suitor, also an InterVarsity staff member, died unexpectedly shortly after proposing to her.

She began teaching students how to lead evangelistic Bible studies in 1964. That year, she held eight weekend conferences on Bible study.[5] These would later mature into InterVarsity's renowned Bible and Life Training courses. Before long, the demand grew from eight weekends to twenty-seven each year. With campuses still engulfed by protests in 1971, Boyd led fifty Bible and Life weekends across the country for students.[6]

Boyd's Bible and Life training covered the basics for college freshmen and sophomores, including new believers. She taught them how to have a quiet time, befriend non-Christians, introduce those friends to Jesus, and lead them in Bible study as they discipled younger Christians. At the high-water mark for Bible and Life, InterVarsity staff led 130 training weekenders in one year.

Boyd also taught about the lordship of Christ, a teaching of hers that Keller would acknowledge in many sermons delivered at Redeemer over the years. The details rarely deviated in the retelling. During the summer of 1971, he attended a month-long InterVarsity camp at Bear Trap Ranch in Colorado where Boyd gave the "Lordship Talk" during her three-part Bible and Life series. For decades afterward, he kept the notes, and he could recall her message in great detail:

That was the day she looked at us, and she said something like, "If you want to invite me into your house, and you say, 'Come in, Barbara. Stay out, Boyd,' I wouldn't know what to do because I'm Barbara Boyd. In fact, I couldn't even say, 'This half is Barbara and this half is Boyd, so I'll just bring this half in,' because I'm all Barbara and I'm all Boyd. I'm both, so you either get me all or you get neither of me." Then she turned around and said, "If you say, 'I would like the loving Jesus. I would like the helping Jesus. I would like the Jesus I can ask to help me through the hard times, but I don't want the holy Jesus. I don't want the powerful Jesus. I don't want the Jesus who is great,' you get no Jesus at all." She said, "Think about this for a minute." (Some of you, if you've been around, you're going to say, "Gosh, this is where he got these things from." It has echoed ever since.) She said, "If the distance between the earth and the sun was the thickness of a piece of paper, if the 96 million miles between the earth and the sun was the thickness of a piece of paper, do you realize the distance from the earth to the nearest star would be a stack of papers 70 feet high? Just the diameter of our little galaxy would be a stack of papers 310 miles high, and our little galaxy is just a speck of the universe. The Bible says in Hebrews 1, 'Jesus Christ holds the universe together with the word of his power.'" She said, "Jesus Christ holds the universe together with his pinky." Then she looked, smiled, and said, "Do you ask somebody like that into your life to be your assistant?"[7]

After her talk, Boyd invited every student at Bear Trap to spend an hour talking with God about any area of life they had not yet ceded to Christ. Keller can still recall when he sat alone to pray. It was the most serious self-examination he had done with God to that point in his life.[8]

Boyd taught that if this Jesus reveals himself in his Word, then we should give careful attention to it. Leading a Bible study, Boyd challenged students, including Keller, to observe fifty things from Mark 1:17

in thirty minutes. After ten minutes, most of the students figured they'd found everything they could from the passage: "And Jesus said to them, 'Follow me, and I will make you become fishers of men.'"

But Boyd wasn't satisfied. She demanded they dig deeper. After another twenty minutes, the students realized how such intense focus on one short verse could concentrate their powers of observation. When the time concluded, Boyd asked if anyone had discovered their most powerful takeaway during the opening five minutes of the exercise. Keller never forgot the answer. No one raised a hand.[9] After all, no one finds the deepest veins of gold at the mouth of the cave. You find the greatest treasures after thorough exploration.

Barbara Boyd didn't just leave the students to explore by themselves though. Janet Essig recalled how she also primed them with a methodology for observation, interpretation, and application:

1. Read through the passage at least twice. In the second reading, slow down and observe what is in the passage.
2. Identify who is involved and what is happening—where and when. How and why might also apply.
3. Note words that are repeated or words of contrast or words of cause and effect.
4. Paraphrase the passage.
5. Note any questions you have about the passage. See if there are answers within the passage. If this involves historical context or the meaning of words, other resources can be used.
6. Determine the overall theme.
7. Outline the passage—showing the movement of ideas and noting connectors or contrasts between sections—looking at words such as *and, but, so, therefore, then,* and so on.
8. Move to interpretation to see how the mechanics of the passage illuminate what the passage is about. Reword the theme if needed.

9. Finally, in light of all that you have seen in the passage, what does the passage mean? How does it apply to you? What thinking or actions do you need to change? What have you learned about yourself? What have you learned about God? What are the implications of this truth?[10]

For Keller this method was an epiphany. He loved the methodical approach. No matter how familiar the passage, Boyd's method always seemed to yield new insights. Reading the Bible this way would become second nature to Keller as he prepared to teach. Thanks to Boyd, he learned to grasp the structure behind each book of the Bible.

"If you get the structure, which is made up of cause and effect, repetition, contrast, all those different means of composition, if you get the structure, you get the person's meaning," Boyd said. "And if you get the meaning, that's what you're supposed to get and apply."[11]

Some may have felt Barbara Boyd's method was formulaic. But she believed that when Christians ask for the Holy Spirit's guidance and patiently allow the Bible to speak for itself, truth can be known and experienced. If you followed these steps, you'd emerge not only with intellectual knowledge of the Bible, but also with a palpable sense of God's presence.[12] That was true when Boyd led the teens in Summit as she developed her Bible and Life materials. And it was true when Tim and other Bucknell students employed the methods through InterVarsity evangelistic studies.

"It wasn't so much that she taught Tim to preach," Janet Essig said. "She taught him how to extract from Scripture amazing truth. I meet with people today in groups who listen to Tim's sermons, and they'll say, 'My goodness, how did he get all that from that passage?' That's really what Barbara Boyd's fundamental influence was."[13]

Boyd helped Keller mine the depths of Scripture. Later, when Keller got to Gordon-Conwell, Ed Clowney would open another door to help him read across the breadth of Scripture.

Let the Facts of the Gospel Speak

Through Barbara Boyd, Keller would be introduced directly and indirectly to several other key figures in mid-century InterVarsity. Boyd had been shaped in her focus on Bible study, quiet time, and the lordship of Christ by C. Stacey Woods, Jane Hollingsworth, and Charles Troutman. During her first Campus-in-the-Woods in Canada in 1945, Boyd herself had been studying Mark's gospel with Hollingsworth when Bible study came alive for her.

After a brief stint teaching elementary school, Boyd headed on a five-week tour of Europe with friends. She filled out her application for Biblical Seminary in New York while sitting in the sand and basking in the sun of the French Riviera. After she joined InterVarsity in 1950, she worked on campuses in California for nine years before switching to women's colleges in the Northeast for three years, focusing on Bryn Mawr, Vassar, Mount Holyoke, Smith, and Wellesley.

When she started out in California, she didn't see immediate results. During her first several months, she didn't lead any students to new faith in Jesus. As she lamented this failure, her staff leader handed her a pamphlet on Romans 1:16 written by Martyn Lloyd-Jones, the famed London pastor who would also shape Keller's ministry. In the pamphlet, Lloyd-Jones argued that evangelists should not appeal to experience or opinion but only to the person and work of Christ in the gospel. As a reminder and encouragement, she brought this pamphlet with her around campus at Long Beach State College.

"When I went to talk in a dorm or with a small group of girls somewhere, I'd tell the facts of the gospel, and it happened," Boyd said. "God uses the facts of the gospel to lead people to Christ."[14]

Barbara Boyd's straightforward approach would thrive on campuses across the country even as the 1950s gave way to the confusion and revolution of the late 1960s and 1970s.[15] Boyd kept alive the original InterVarsity vision to evangelize universities.[16]

When Keller led evangelistic studies for Janet Essig and other freshmen in the 1970s, they may have assumed campuses were always in upheaval.[17] But they would have also thought it was normal for evangelism and Bible study to thrive at the same time. The InterVarsity that influenced Keller focused on Bible study, quiet times, the lordship of Christ, zealous prayer for revival, and personal evangelism.[18] Mixing believers and nonbelievers to study the Bible together would become a hallmark of Redeemer Presbyterian Church, including Keller's expectation that he was always preaching to Christians and skeptics at the same time. Keller would also bring to Redeemer the InterVarsity mentality that the students do the work. Redeemer did not start as a top-down church but as more of a lay-led movement, recalling Keller's formative years at Bucknell.

Inventing Evangelicalism

The first time Tim Keller attended Urbana, the triennial InterVarsity missions conference, was 1976. Tim was married, had already graduated from Gordon-Conwell, and was pastor of a church in Hopewell, Virginia. Unbeknownst to Tim and his wife, Kathy, as they drove to Illinois, one of their elderly church members back in Hopewell had died. So the first thing they heard when they arrived at Urbana was a PA announcement asking Tim Keller to come to the administrative office on an urgent matter.[19] Of the more than 17,000 students in attendance, everyone who knew Tim was immediately alerted that he was there.

Urbana 1976 featured the who's who of transatlantic evangelical speakers of the era. It was the last Urbana directed by David Howard before he left to work with Leighton Ford and plan the 1980 Lausanne Committee for World Evangelization meetings in Pattaya, Thailand.[20] Unified around the theme "Declare His Glory Among the Nations," Helen Roseveare spoke on declaring God's glory in the midst of suffering, to which the crowd responded with a standing ovation. Billy

Graham spoke on responding to God's glory. After she had given the first major Urbana address from a woman in 1973, Elisabeth Elliot returned to speak on the glory of God's will. John Perkins spoke on declaring God's glory in the community.

Edmund Clowney addressed the 1976 conference, as he had in 1973 when he gave a memorable talk on the lostness of man.[21] The InterVarsity staff recalled that this time, "Edmund Clowney gave a stellar address on the glory of God, a subject almost too profound for words and almost too glorious for young students to grasp."[22]

John Stott delivered four expositions on the biblical basis for missions. By this time, Stott had become perhaps the leading light in the global InterVarsity movement. He was Keller's first model for expositional preaching. During the 1960s, Stott's influence gradually eclipsed that of the older Martyn Lloyd-Jones, with whom he had fallen out in 1966 over whether evangelicals should stay in the Church of England. Lloyd-Jones had resigned in 1959 as the chair of the International Fellowship of Evangelical Students—an umbrella organization that included InterVarsity Christian Fellowship in Canada and the United States, led by C. Stacey Woods.

Lloyd-Jones was a role model for Woods, the InterVarsity leader who meant so much to Barbara Boyd. Woods also led the officer retreat Keller attended as an undergraduate with Bruce Henderson. According to Woods's biographer:

> It would be hard to overestimate the influence that Martyn Lloyd-Jones had on Stacey Woods. . . . Stacey felt the Doctor had no equal as an expositor of Scripture, and Lloyd-Jones's opening of the Bible greatly influenced Stacey's own teaching and preaching, weaning it away from his earlier dispensationalism and letting the text speak for itself rather than imposing patterns on it. . . . He deplored the increasing lack of expository preaching and attributed the shallowness of contemporary evangelicalism to its disappearance.[23]

Since Keller was an American, and much younger, he didn't have to choose between Lloyd-Jones and Stott. Both men preached with utmost confidence in the authority of the Word and with careful attention to the text.[24] Keller ultimately combined much of Lloyd-Jones's theological specificity with Stott's ecumenical instincts.

Like Woods, Keller followed Lloyd-Jones's lead to study the Puritans. Keller shared Lloyd-Jones passion for revival and initially emulated him in preaching evangelistic messages during all Redeemer services. When Keller moved to New York in 1989, he listened to hundreds of sermons by Lloyd-Jones and reread his book *Preaching and Preachers*. He found a parallel in postwar London for that post-Christian setting of Manhattan. He picked up from Lloyd-Jones the same thing he loved about Barbara Boyd's Bible studies, the same thing he loved about InterVarsity in general. He didn't need to choose between edifying believers and evangelizing nonbelievers. Lloyd-Jones showed him he could—indeed, he should—do both at the same time. "Evangelize as you edify, and edify as you evangelize."[25]

In terms of his demeanor, however, Keller resembles Stott more than Lloyd-Jones. Keller doesn't display the separatist and polemic instincts of Lloyd-Jones. Rarely in his ministry has Keller emphasized his differences with other Christians, as Lloyd-Jones did. Like Stott, he emphasizes the contrast between Christians and the unbelieving world. As a college student Keller read Stott's book *Basic Christianity*. "He truly was, in some ways, the first person who spoke the word of God to me," Keller said at the US memorial service for Stott, convened by Langham Partnership. "It was through his literature."[26]

The memorial service for Stott is instructive. By selecting Keller to give the keynote eulogy for the event, Stott's legacy ministry saw something of a parallel between Stott and Keller. But the lessons Keller identified from Stott—"the most irenic man I've ever known"—tell us as much about the former as the latter.

Keller credited Stott for reinventing expository preaching through deep observation of the text, with no frills added—essentially the kind of Bible study he learned in InterVarsity from Barbara Boyd. And he also credited Stott for inventing the modern "city center church"— equally committed to evangelizing professionals and serving the poor. Such churches—including Redeemer and All Souls, Langham Place— balance word and deed in their preaching of the Bible and their pursuit of social justice.

Keller also spoke of hearing Stott in person, including Urbana in 1976. Keller went so far as to say that John Stott, more than anyone else, created evangelicalism as the middle space between fundamentalism and liberalism:

> Who was it, though, who kept coming over here in the '50s and '60s and '70s to raise up all these young troops at InterVarsity? Who was it who spoke at Urbana? Not Carl Henry. Not Harold Ockenga. Not Billy Graham, usually. It was John Stott. He epitomized absolutely rock-ribbed commitment to the authority of Scripture and at the same time being utterly abreast of scholarship, yet at the same time accessible, bringing the scholarship down to where it was accessible. He was the perfect creator of this middle space. At least for the last thirty or forty years, this has been the part of Christianity that's grown the most—not fundamentalism, not liberalism, but that space. He was prophetic from the center, and you can read it in his book *The Cross of Christ*, his masterpiece, absolutely firm on traditional substitutionary atonement, penal substitution, and yet he takes the implications of it and brings it to social justice and brings it to community. He's prophetic from the center—doesn't have to reengineer traditional evangelical doctrine, but he engages with it. We can't forget these things. It worries me that an awful lot of younger evangelical leaders barely know what John Stott stood for.[27]

For Keller, John Stott represented the best in evangelicalism and in InterVarsity. Through Redeemer City to City, the global church planting network Keller later cofounded and chaired, he would also seek to expand on Stott's commitment to serving the global church. During Urbana 1976, 50 percent from the crowd of seventeen thousand signed decision cards to serve the cause of world evangelism. That number had jumped from 6 percent of twelve thousand in 1970 and 28 percent of fifteen thousand in 1973.[28]

Keller also represented the broader growth of InterVarsity on US campuses around the time of Urbana 1976. In the years before Keller arrived for college, InterVarsity mostly attracted students who grew up in Christian families.[29] Fueled by increased campus conversions, however, the number of InterVarsity-affiliated chapters reached a peak of 882 in 1973–74 (just after Keller graduated), with 135 paid staff workers.[30]

After Bucknell, Keller completed his field work during seminary as an InterVarsity associate staff member. For two years he helped start an InterVarsity chapter at Framingham State University, which proved challenging, since it was a commuter school without much campus life.[31]

Even when Keller left InterVarsity for the local church, he brought InterVarsity's instincts with him. He learned that Christians must never compromise on their core values, which he identified as the infallibility of the Bible, the substitutionary death of Jesus on the cross, the necessity of the new birth, and the full deity of Jesus. A list of fundamentals from the early twentieth century wouldn't look much different.

At the same time InterVarsity taught him to value what Christians hold in common over the doctrines that divide them. That doesn't mean that what separates Presbyterians from Baptists or Pentecostals is unimportant. "But the core is the core," he said. "You ought to be collegial and open-minded to other Christians who differ on the secondary issues. I learned that from InterVarsity."[32]

FOUR

KATHY THE VALIANT

Kathy Kristy

When twelve-year-old Kathy Kristy wrote to C. S. Lewis, she had no idea he was famous. She considered the author her personal friend, her private discovery. She had been reading his Chronicles of Narnia since the second grade, when she came across them on the bookmobile in a mall parking lot. But when she looked in stores and libraries for other works, she couldn't find any. As far as she knew, no one else in the United States knew anything about the Oxford don who wrote children's stories.

So when Kathy wrote Lewis, she thought she was cheering up a rather obscure author by letting him know that someone had actually read his books. She wrote him about mundane matters—relationships with friends, frustrations with parents, updates on her neighborhood. She wrote about what she learned in school and how she cleaned up around the house.

Lewis first wrote back from Oxford on November 30, 1962, the

41

day after he turned sixty-four years old.[1] The next April, he mediated a dispute between Kathy and her English teacher.[2] A letter she wrote in the summer never arrived at The Kilns. But Lewis wrote back again in October as his time on earth neared its end. "How am I?" he wrote. "I'm pretty well for a man who has become a permanent invalid, and if I cannot make much use of my legs I can still use my head, and am able to continue to write."[3]

Lewis sent his last letter to Kathy less than two weeks before he died. He offered sympathy for her "maddening experience." In the previous letter, he had noted Kathy's newspaper work and frustrations about editing. But he didn't offer much comfort. "I can assure you that this is one of the occupational risks of authorship; the same sort of thing has happened to me more than once," Lewis wrote. "There is nothing to be done about it!"[4]

Lewis died on November 22, 1963, the same day as Oxford-trained Aldous Huxley, author of *Brave New World*. The same day United States president John F. Kennedy was assassinated in Dallas, Texas.

Not until the 1970s, the decade after his death, did Lewis begin to become a publishing phenomenon in the United States. Kathy eventually shared her love of Lewis with another college student, Tim Keller. She encouraged Tim to read beyond *Mere Christianity*, especially Lewis's fiction. Even before Kathy Kristy took the name Keller, she would become the most formative intellectual and spiritual influence on Tim Keller's life.

When you're writing about Tim Keller, you're really writing about Tim and Kathy, a marriage between intellectual equals who met in seminary over shared commitment to ministry and love for literature, along with serious devotion to theology. Kathy has never been ordained, but she's rightly identified as cofounder of Redeemer Presbyterian Church in New York, as she also served on the Redeemer staff at its birth.

Many know Kathy in relation to Tim. But Kathy had already distinguished herself in ministry before she ever met her husband.

Straight Shooter

Kathy Kristy was born April 15, 1950, in Pittsburgh, Pennsylvania. Her mother, Mary Louise Stephens, had gone to college, which was uncommon for the era. Her father, Henry Kristy, grew up northeast of Pittsburgh in a coal mining neighborhood of Penn Hills. A bomber pilot in Europe during World War II, he changed his name after the war. His father had immigrated from Croatia, and Henry wanted to be known as Kristy rather than Kristolich. Described as a "straight shooter," Kristy worked for Westinghouse from his college graduation all the way until he retired as controller of power systems in 1986.[5]

His firstborn child was Kathy, described more than once herself as a "straight shooter." Before they studied together in seminary, Louise (Midwood) Crocker had been a classmate of Kathy's in high school back in Monroeville, Pennsylvania, about ten miles east of Pittsburgh. Around Gateway High School Kathy was known as a brilliant student. She intimidated Louise. The childhood correspondent of C. S. Lewis had become the self-proclaimed "frumpy editor of the school newspaper."[6]

Kathy was also well-known as a Christian, but when they met, Louise had not yet professed personal faith in Jesus Christ. In the first meaningful conversation they shared, at a Young Life meeting, Kathy told Louise matter-of-factly that she planned to become a Presbyterian minister.[7] Young Life had grown rapidly during that era, with forty clubs and three thousand students involved around the Pittsburgh area.[8] The growth of this evangelistic ministry focused on teens sprouted many conversations like the one that unfolded in the Kristy household. Kathy's mother couldn't understand when her eldest daughter came home one day and told her she'd become a Christian. After all, she'd gone to church her whole life. What had changed? This evangelical awakening was a bizarre, unexpected twist for their dutiful mainline Presbyterian home.

Before Kathy found Young Life, C. S. Lewis had been her only window into a different kind of Christianity from what she experienced in church. When told that Lewis intended Aslan to represent Christ, she couldn't see it. "The Jesus I had heard about was dull and boring," Kathy said, "and Aslan was vibrant and alive."

Nevertheless, the myth of Aslan had created in Kathy a hunger for Jesus. Neither Young Life nor her church imparted any deep or comprehensive theological vision for the Christian life. She never learned much about the Bible in those teen years. But Lewis temporarily filled the gap.

So precocious was twelve-year-old Kathy that when she wrote Lewis, she had been saving up money and planning to visit him in Oxford. Later she told Lewis's stepson Douglas Gresham that if she had been older, she would have been a formidable opponent of his mother. When she turned fourteen, Kathy did travel to Oxford with friends and met Lewis's brother Warnie, then still living in The Kilns. The house was covered in dust. The ceiling was stained yellow from the nicotine in their pipes. She treasured the chance to honor the man who had shaped her entire intellectual life as a Christian during that young, formative time.[9]

Through Gateway High School and Allegheny College in northwestern Pennsylvania, Kathy continued to be involved with Young Life. Then she announced her intent to pursue seminary. Kathy's younger sister Sue remembers her parents responding, "What! Seminary? Are you insane?" Her parents already worried that she wasn't popular, that she didn't date. They figured she'd never get married or have children. But seminary was a step beyond even what they had reconciled themselves to expect.[10]

But the move wasn't surprising to others who saw Kathy in action. John Guest, one of the key leaders in Pittsburgh-area evangelical work, went so far as to describe her as the most brilliant youth organizer in Pennsylvania.[11] After reading David Wilkerson's *The Cross and the Switchblade*, she resolved to serve in the toughest aspects of urban ministry.[12]

Pearls before Swine

Kathy remembers nothing special about the first time she met Tim Keller in person. Her sister Sue was a freshman at Bucknell University. Because Kathy's junior year at Allegheny didn't start until later, she tagged along when her mother made a trip to deliver furniture in September 1970. She felt sick on the trip and didn't want to meet anyone. But that didn't stop Sue from introducing her and their mother to everyone around the Young Life house near campus. Kathy remembers a tall, gangly fellow studying Greek. They nodded at each other, said hello, and that was that.[13]

They kept in touch via Sue, which became even easier when the Keller family moved to Johnstown, Pennsylvania, less than sixty miles east of Pittsburgh. When Young Life hosted a New Year's Eve square dancing party, Sue invited friends who were also involved with InterVarsity at Bucknell to stay in the Kristy home. Still, Kathy didn't pay Tim much attention. He was just one in a crowd of Sue's friends. But she did notice that he was the only student who took the time to talk with and get to know Kathy and Sue's parents.[14]

During breaks, when Sue came home to Monroeville, she gave Kathy updates on Tim. Kathy heard that Tim was reading O. Hallesby's book on prayer, so she picked up a copy for herself. And Sue took updates about Kathy back to Tim. Since C. S. Lewis's Chronicles of Narnia had been so instrumental in her professing personal faith in Jesus, Kathy told Sue to recommend the books to Tim. He read them the summer after he graduated from Bucknell. From there he launched into a lifelong passion for Lewis that they would ultimately share.

When Tim heard from Sue that Kathy was considering Gordon-Conwell Theological Seminary in New England, he decided he should check it out. Though recently established, Gordon-Conwell dwarfed the small Evangelical Congregational Church seminary in Myerstown, Pennsylvania, in resources, size, and scholarship.[15] By this time, R. C. Sproul had launched Ligonier Valley Study Center, roughly equidistant from Monroeville and Johnstown. Tim's mother and Kathy's mother attended the same weekly Bible study and exposition that Sproul led during the week for women. Tim and his sister Sharon, along with Kathy and her sister Sue, would meet up for Sproul's weekly gabfests—what he dubbed his Q and A sessions. From the Keller home in Johnstown the study center was about thirty miles away over Laurel Mountain through Laurel Ridge State Park.

"That's what we'd do all summer long," Sharon remembered. "It was really glorious, actually."[16]

Before he started a gabfest, Sproul went around the room asking for everyone's name and what they were doing. In this summer before Tim and Kathy started seminary, Kathy declared her intent to attend Gordon-Conwell. And Tim did the same, with a little, knowing nod toward each other from across the room.[17]

Even before they became friends at seminary in 1972, their worlds were converging. Their mild acquaintance gave them a connection amid the unfamiliar, lonely setting of South Hamilton, Massachusetts. They were both intelligent and socially awkward. Before long, they could sense something of the "secret thread" described by Lewis that draws two people close as friends—or in some cases, as husband and wife.[18] J. R. R. Tolkien became another strand in their "secret thread," eventually bonding them through his Elvish language and *The Lord of the Rings* saga. Tim and Kathy were kindred spirits. They discovered other stories and books, even an outlook on life and a sense of joy in certain experiences that they shared.[19] Their family backgrounds contrasted in compatible ways. While Tim felt the pressure of his family, Kathy had been overlooked in favor of her younger siblings. Whatever her own anxieties and fears, she didn't suffer from Tim's affliction of a self-condemning conscience. She showered him with praise.

When Tim and Kathy started at Gordon-Conwell, Tim still had a girlfriend back at Bucknell. After that relationship collapsed, Tim and

Kathy could no longer be close friends without considering something more. But anything beyond friendship was slow to dawn on Tim. He only knew he didn't want to lose Kathy from his life.

Halfway through seminary, Tim and Kathy enrolled in a month-long course on counseling taught by Jay Adams through Westminster Theological Seminary in Philadelphia. During January 1974, they planned to live together with an elderly deaconess from a Presbyterian church in the Germantown neighborhood of Philadelphia, where Kathy had served the previous summer.

The month figured to be awkward. At the end of the previous semester, Kathy had cut off her friendship with Tim. She had waited long enough for him to make a romantic move. That's when she gave what would become known in the Keller family as the "pearls before swine" speech. Tim had indicated no interest beyond friendship, despite their increasing closeness. He was still hurting from the breakup. Kathy understood, but eventually her patience ran out. She told him:

> Look, I can't take this anymore. I have been expecting to be promoted from friend to girlfriend. I know you don't mean to be saying this, but every day you don't choose me to be more than a friend, it feels as if I've been weighed and found wanting—I feel it as a rejection. So I just can't keep going on the same way, hoping that someday you'll want me to be more than a friend. I'm not calling myself a pearl, and I'm not calling you a pig, but one of the reasons Jesus told his disciples not to cast pearls before swine was because a pig can't recognize the value of a pearl. It would seem like just a pebble. If you can't see me as valuable to you, then I'm not going to keep throwing myself into your company, hoping and hoping. I can't do it. The rejection that I perceive, whether you intend it or not, is just too painful.[20]

Even then, Tim didn't assume they should begin dating. He didn't know how they would even transition from best friends and kindred spirits to boyfriend and girlfriend. You can't just casually go to dinner and a movie. When you start dating after this level of intimacy, the next thing you know, you're naming future children.

Tim spent a couple weeks praying and thinking. Then he made the choice. They returned to Boston as an item.[21] At the beginning of the month, he sat with their friend David Midwood in the front seat while Kathy sat in the back with their friend Louise Crocker. Louise remembers, "Until that January I don't know if Tim knew his right shoe from his left shoe, honestly." But by the time they got back to Boston, Tim and Kathy were in the front together, and David and Louise were in the back. David and Louise married in September 1974.[22] One semester before they graduated, Tim Keller and Kathy Kristy married on January 4, 1975, in Monroeville, Pennsylvania, at Crossroads Presbyterian Church. R. C. Sproul conducted the ceremony.

In the wedding liturgy Kathy wanted to convey the biblical symbolism of marriage as pointing to Christ's redemptive love for his church, as in Ephesians 5:25–33. While Tim would represent Christ, she could represent his bride, the church. Meanwhile, the bridesmaids would each wear a different color from the liturgical year. Ultimately, Kathy's mother prevailed against this idea, which she feared would merely confuse friends and family. Instead the bridesmaids wore unflattering matching dresses, while the men wore brown tuxedos. Decades later, Kathy wrote, "I am still not convinced that mine would not have been at least as good a choice."[23] The vows included Psalm 34:1–3, which they also had engraved on the inside of their wedding bands. "O magnify the Lord with me," Psalm 34:3 reads, "and let us exalt his name together!"[24]

Wind in His Sails

When the Kellers moved to Philadelphia in order for Tim to teach at Westminster Theological Seminary, Kathy worked as a part-time editor for Great Commission Publications. That meant Tim shouldered responsibility for preparing the kids before school and caring for them over the summer.[25] All three boys had been born during his pastoral stint in Hopewell, Virginia. After a little more than three years of marriage, David came in 1978 when Tim was twenty-seven and Kathy was twenty-eight. Michael followed in 1980, and Jonathan in 1983. Tim acknowledged his three boys in his book *Counterfeit Gods*, saying, "I respect how you've grown up loving the city and have become men of integrity."[26]

Writing and parenting are both collaborative efforts for the Kellers. When staring down a strict book deadline on Tim's punishing release schedule, Tim writes his books while Kathy edits simultaneously.[27] Because Tim trusts Kathy so much, she can offer unfiltered criticism when necessary.[28]

"Her help with his writing is, I'm sure, beyond anything anybody can imagine," their friend and longtime colleague Liz Kaufmann said. "It's like having an editor in your head. They're intertwined so much that probably all the books should have her name on them."[29]

When Tim hit *The New York Times* bestseller list for the first time, the book, *The Reason for God*, was dedicated to "Kathy, the Valiant." No one else heard his sermons on Jonah in 1981 in Hopewell, 1991 in New York during Redeemer's early days, and again in 2001 in the frightening days following the 9/11 attacks. When Tim wrote *The Prodigal Prophet*, she gave unmatched editorial attention through every stage. If she didn't like what she saw, she told him to start over again.[30] In the same book in which he acknowledged their sons, Tim thanked Kathy for working on the book over the course of many months and talking with him about the ideas for years. "I must say to Kathy what John Newton wrote to his wife, Polly, namely, it is no wonder if so many years, so many endearments, so many obligations have produced such an uncommon effect, that by long habit, it is almost impossible for me to draw a breath, in which you are not involved."[31]

Their experiences began to diverge after seminary, especially as their family grew. Kathy struggled with the change. The first time Tim grabbed his briefcase and headed off to work after seminary, she stood alone in their kitchen and asked herself, *What am I supposed to do all day?* "Up until then, we had pretty much lived in a unisex world, as students taking the same classes, competing for grades on a level playing field, rarely forced into any consideration of what God's intention may have been in making us male and female. Suddenly I had to think both practically and Biblically about my role as a woman and a wife."[32]

The role would always entail looking out for Tim. She's attentive to his physical needs. Multiple friends and family observed that Kathy will get Tim water to drink, because otherwise he will forget. "Jesus is her life, but Tim is her function," Louise Midwood said. "For Tim, Kathy is the facilitator of his life."[33]

In the most important sermon of his life, the Sunday following 9/11, Tim shared his worst nightmare, which recurred at least yearly. The nightmare is that Kathy died and that he needed to make it in life without her.[34] At the time, Kathy had been struggling with Crohn's disease. She endured as many as seven surgeries in one year. He considered stepping away from ministry just to care for her and described it as the darkest time of their lives, at least through 2013.[35] When Tim was diagnosed with pancreatic cancer in 2020, he didn't allow himself to cry over any loss except one—separation from Kathy.

Kathy Armstrong often babysat for the Keller boys during early 1992. And for two years, after the boys left for school in the morning, Kathy Armstrong and Kathy Keller met to talk about life through reading. Keller asked her to read *Precious Remedies against Satan's Devices* by the seventeenth-century Puritan Thomas Brooks. Keller also recommended John Newton's collected letters. Inevitably something in the reading would connect to a current life situation, which they would discuss.[36]

Armstrong was preparing for marriage when she asked Kathy

Keller for some perspective. She wanted the unvarnished, private truth. Was Kathy really okay with being "number 2" to her husband, even though they had studied together in seminary? Was she really okay with not preaching?

"I'm not number 2," Kathy Keller responded. "We serve together, and it's a joy if I can be a wind in his sails."[37]

FIVE

TRUE MYTH

The Inklings

Makoto Fujimura always knew when Tim Keller hadn't found time to prepare his sermon for Redeemer Presbyterian Church.

That's when he'd talk about C. S. Lewis.

"And it would be absolutely magical, so we weren't complaining."[1]

Keller pleads guilty to the Lewis charge. That's what happens when someone wrote as much as Lewis did, and when Keller has read just about everything he published. But it's also about the timing of that reading. Lewis came to Keller early in college, when he was asking questions about whether there was any truth or beauty in Christianity. And shortly after he professed personal faith in Jesus, he came to know his Narnia series, recommended via Sue Kristy's sister Kathy at Allegheny College.

Aided by several biographies and intimate familiarity with Lewis's personal letters, Keller can recall dozens of Lewis quotes and stories and illustrations. If he's searching for just the right way to make his point, usually Keller will opt for Lewis, his favorite author.[2]

"When you dive that deeply into the life and works of a single figure, something interesting happens," Keller said. "You don't just get to know his writings; you get to know how his mind works. You come to know what he *would* have said in answer to a particular question or how he would have responded to a particular incident."[3]

One of C. S. Lewis's closest friends also contributed to Keller's spiritual and intellectual formation. J. R. R. Tolkien was a fellow regular in the literary discussion group dubbed the Inklings. Meeting during the 1930s and the 1940s in Oxford, England, the Inklings would help inspire some of the most beloved stories ever written in the English language. The debates between Lewis and Tolkien would produce contrasting visions for representing Christian themes in The Chronicles of Narnia and *The Lord of the Rings*.

Lewis gave Keller a model for wide reading and clear thinking. Lewis challenged Keller to deploy vivid illustrations for public apologetics in defense of Christian claims to truth and beauty. Tolkien, though, gave Keller a heart language, and not just the Elvish he occasionally recited to Kathy. Tolkien gave him ways to talk about work, to talk about hope, to talk about the stories we all hope will come true someday.

Tolkien gave Keller words of comfort amid the worst tragedy ever to befall his city.

Everything Sad Will Come Untrue

Five years after the attacks on September 11, 2001, Tim Keller was invited to speak for a service of remembrance for the victims' families. Held at St. Paul's Chapel in Lower Manhattan, only two blocks from where the Twin Towers once stood, the service was attended by President George W. Bush and his wife Laura. Keller's message recalled what he said back on September 16, 2001, on the first Sunday following the tragedy. He preached on the hope of the resurrection of Jesus, with an assist from Tolkien:

> In the last book of *The Lord of the Rings*, Sam Gamgee wakes up thinking everything is lost, and upon discovering instead that all his friends were around him, he cries out, "Gandalf! I thought you were dead! But then I thought I was dead! Is everything sad going to come untrue?" The answer is yes. And the answer of the Bible is yes. If the resurrection is true, then the answer is yes. Everything sad is going to come untrue.[4]

Quoting widely known artists helped Keller establish rapport with listeners and readers who didn't expect preachers to demonstrate broad familiarity with literature outside the Bible. When Mako Fujimura first visited Redeemer in 1992 and heard Keller preach, he remembers thinking, *This really reminds me a lot of humanities lectures I heard at Bucknell*, where he also studied as an undergraduate. For a budding artist like Fujimura, Keller's approach was intriguing. Fujimura had worked for Cru (formerly Campus Crusade for Christ) doing evangelism, but he didn't have a context for cultural engagement outside of C. S. Lewis and Francis Schaeffer. He didn't see a role in missions for a culture creator such as himself, a visual artist. He only heard culture derided as a negative, or at least suspicious, influence. When Keller showed as much fluency with the writings of Flannery O'Connor as he did with the gospel of Matthew, Fujimura decided to stick around Redeemer when only about 250 people were attending each week.[5]

O'Connor had been assigned reading for Keller in a formative Gordon-Conwell class with Richard Lovelace, professor of church history. Such was her influence that Keller quoted her short story "Wise Blood" in his first Easter sermon at Redeemer in 1990.[6] Even after Keller had read Lewis and Tolkien, O'Connor was the writer who first opened Keller's eyes to the power of Christians creating art.[7]

Voracious Reader

Keller's enthusiasm for learning, his unquenchable curiosity, would spill over with friends and family his whole life. When he discovered Tolkien, he insisted his sister read him as well. When The Gospel Coalition national conferences met in Orlando in 2013 and 2015, he'd meet with Sharon, who took care of their parents in Gainesville, Florida, and catch her up on the latest things he had been reading.

Affection for Tolkien runs so deep that Keller never stops reading him—either *The Lord of the Rings*, *The Silmarillion*, or thirteen large volumes of posthumously published works. The first time Tim faced thyroid cancer and thought he might die, he found comfort in Tolkien's works. When doctors put him under anesthesia and he didn't know where he would wake up, his mind traveled to the third and final book of *The Lord of the Rings* at a moment when it appeared darkness and evil would prevail over the besieged fellowship. Keller thought of Sam, one of Tolkien's hobbit protagonists:

> Sam saw a white star twinkle for a while. The beauty of it smote his heart, as he looked up out of the forsaken land, and hope returned to him. For like a shaft, clear and cold, the thought pierced him that in the end the Shadow was only a small and passing thing: there was light and high beauty forever beyond its reach. His song in the Tower had been defiance rather than hope; for then he was thinking of himself. Now, for a moment, his own fate . . . ceased to trouble him . . . Putting away all fear, he cast himself into a deep untroubled sleep.[8]

Keller went to sleep with firm conviction that because Jesus has died, death is a shadow. No matter what happened during his surgery, he knew he would be okay.

"There is light and high beauty forever beyond its reach because evil fell into the heart of Jesus," Keller wrote. "The only darkness that could have destroyed us forever fell into his heart."[9]

On Fairy-Stories

Never is the Inklings influence clearer than when Keller talks about the gospel as "true myth." When Keller wants to help preachers reach the heart, he takes them to Tolkien's famous essay "On Fairy-Stories." Preaching can do more than just transmit true information. Preaching can, even should, lead Christians to wonder. Keller also explains why fantasy fiction helps in ways that the realist novels cannot, even when written by the great masters Fyodor Dostoevsky and Leo Tolstoy. Fantasy and science fiction of the kind written by Lewis and Tolkien can help meet the heart's deepest hopes and desires. They can reconceive time, reverse death, imagine fellowship with nonhuman beings, defeat evil for good, and celebrate love that will never end. Even when readers know the story isn't real, they still connect with real emotions. And that's why Tolkien and Lewis remain just as relevant today as they were between the 1930s and the 1950s—or in some ways even more relevant and widely beloved today, by Christians and non-Christians alike.

Thanks to fantasy stories, readers can find existential satisfaction before they discover intellectual credibility. They can want something to be true even if they can't yet bring themselves to believe it's true. The writer can show the world as it ought to be, as it once was, and how it will be again someday. The writer can usher us into a world even better than what we can now imagine. For Tolkien, as for Keller, that's the seed of Christian belief.

"We are so deeply interested in these stories because we have intuitions of the creation/fall/redemption/restoration plotline of the Bible," Keller wrote. "Even if we repress the knowledge of that plotline intellectually, we *can't not* know it imaginatively, and our hearts are stirred by any stories that evoke it."[10]

As Keller told Redeemer in 1997, the good news of Jesus is the story behind all the other stories. "The gospel story is the story of wonder from which all other fairy tales and stories of wonder take their cues."[11] How, exactly, did Tolkien see the gospel as the mold for fantasy stories? It's in the moment when you think all hope has been lost, as when the disciples huddled together, hidden away in a house after Jesus' death on the cross. It's when victory seems to emerge from nowhere in the least likely way, as when the risen Jesus walked through walls into that house and greeted his old friends and followers. It's when someone's greatest weakness becomes the source of greatest strength. It's what Tolkien called *eucatastrophe*, or the "joyful catastrophe, the tragedy that turns out to be a triumph, the sacrifice that turns out to bring joy, the weakness that ends up being strength, the defeat that ends up being victory."[12]

Tolkien's own stories include no shortage of *dyscatastrophe*, the point when all hope seems lost, as in the Battle of the Black Gate when the Host of the West dwindle against the orcs of Mordor, who outnumber them more than ten to one. As the heroes battle on, hoping to distract Sauron from Frodo and Sam's quest to destroy the One Ring in the fires of Mount Doom, they look for *euangelium*, good news that they will not die in vain. The *eucatastrophe* commences when Gollum bites off Frodo's finger and unwittingly destroys the Ring, ending Sauron's malevolent hold on Middle-earth. For Tolkien, the incarnation of Jesus is a *eucatastrophe* after generations of men died without hope. And the resurrection is a *eucatastrophe* of the incarnation, which had appeared to fail when they laid Jesus' lifeless body in the freshly cut tomb owned by Joseph of Arimathea.[13]

When you know the Story behind the stories, then you see it everywhere, "from the ugly duckling who turns out to be a swan, to Beauty and the Beast, the Beauty who gives up all of her happiness to throw herself in the arms of this Beast and, because of her incredible sacrifice, gets a love and frees this person beyond anything she ever understood."

When you pluck the string of the gospel, it never stops reverberating in your heart.

"There really is a Beauty who kisses the beast," Keller told Redeemer in 1998. "There really is a Hercules who defeats the villain. There really is a hero. There really is Jesus."[14]

SIX

DOUBTERS WELCOME

R. C. Sproul and Ligonier Valley Study Center

B y the spring of 1971, Francis Schaeffer was no longer an obscure American missionary for beatniks in the Swiss Alps. He had become an evangelical celebrity through such bestselling books such as *The God Who Is There*, published in 1968. He could command the attention of aspiring young imitators at the first United States conference for L'Abri, held at Covenant College on Lookout Mountain in Tennessee.

One of those imitators hoped to bring a version of L'Abri to the mountains of western Pennsylvania, near the Keller and Kristy family homes. He had studied at Abraham Kuyper's Free University in Amsterdam, and after serving as a Presbyterian minister in Cincinnati, he hoped to start a Christian study center in the Ligonier Valley outside Pittsburgh. After R. C. Sproul met Francis Schaeffer on Lookout Mountain, they corresponded about how Ligonier Valley Study Center could learn from the best practices of L'Abri.[1]

That whole vision was still fresh for Sproul. Only a year earlier, a visitor had approached him with a remarkable offer while he was serving as associate pastor of teaching and evangelism at College Hill Presbyterian Church in Cincinnati. Dora Hillman, widow of a wealthy businessman, planned to launch a study and conference center near Pittsburgh to train Christian leaders who would evangelize and disciple the city. Toward this effort she would donate fifty-two acres near Stahlstown, Pennsylvania, which could be reached from Pittsburgh in less than an hour. This vision became Ligonier Valley Study Center, and R. C. and Vesta Sproul settled in Stahlstown the summer after R. C. met Schaeffer.

Schaeffer made it clear to Sproul that this work in the study center would drain him and his family. He could expect no breaks. But this kind of ministry to college students and young adults, combining education and hospitality, wasn't new to the Sprouls. R. C. was an unusually engaged professor when he taught at his alma mater, Westminster College in New Wilmington, Pennsylvania, less than sixty miles north of Pittsburgh. Almost every night, sometimes stretching into the morning hours, he and Vesta hosted students to pray and study the Bible.[2]

Therefore, it wasn't a big surprise when Pittsburgh-area leaders like John Guest recommended Sproul as the teacher who could lead the study center they envisioned with Hillman.[3] Through Ligonier Valley Study Center, R. C. Sproul would help set a theological trajectory for Tim Keller and Kathy (Kristy) Keller. And he imprinted on them the L'Abri model for evangelism that they would eventually bring inside the church through Redeemer in New York.

Edwards in Knickers

Many more students wanted to hear John Gerstner teach about Jonathan Edwards than wanted Gerstner to mark their papers about Jonathan Edwards. But Sproul risked the grading gauntlet with the outspoken conservative professor at Pittsburgh Theological Seminary.[4] Sproul enrolled at Pittsburgh in 1961 after becoming acquainted with the president, Addison Leitch, another conservative. Together Gerstner and Sproul would contribute to a citywide religious renaissance during the 1970s. Beyond Ligonier, ministries such as the Coalition for Christian Outreach and Trinity School of Ministry emerged in these memorable years for Pittsburgh, when Christian leaders decided they wanted the city to be as well-known for God as for steel.[5]

Presbyterians led the way, as they'd done in helping to found Pittsburgh in 1758 and to shape its Christian outlook well into the nineteenth century.[6] But this coalescing of evangelical institutions marked a shift for religious life in western Pennsylvania, which had been preoccupied with the same kinds of theological deconstruction that Tim and Kathy had encountered in college. When Kathy enrolled in Allegheny College, a United Methodist school in northwestern Pennsylvania, she didn't discover anything more about the Bible than she had learned in her mainline Presbyterian church.

"I thought I would sign up for every religion course to learn about this Christian thing," Kathy said. "That was naive because religion classes were to convince you you've been brainwashed. Most of my religion classes were taught by defrocked ministers who would help you lose your faith as soon as possible."[7]

Kathy wasn't daunted, in part because she could look to thoughtful alternatives such as Sproul. His own conversion as a freshman at Westminster in 1957 presaged a larger spiritual movement among college students a decade later. It was the baby boom, when student enrollment jumped 139 percent between 1960 and 1970. To win the Cold War, the federal government shifted nearly 3 percent of gross national product toward research and development. When Sproul began planning Ligonier Valley Study Center, 8.6 million students pursued undergraduate degrees.[8] Churches struggled to accommodate and adjust to a record-breaking generation that demanded changes in education and the workplace amid the challenges of the civil rights movement and the Vietnam War.[9] So when counterculture youth found Jesus, whether through street evangelism or makeshift communes or rock concerts, they didn't want to put on a suit or pantyhose and wait for Sunday morning. Many found their way to Sproul in Ligonier Valley instead.[10]

The same movement sent young adults to the Swiss Alps in search of truth with Francis and Edith Schaeffer at L'Abri. They weren't pining for the 1950s. They wanted a vibrant relationship with God, along with the music and dress and art of the bohemian avant-garde. The Schaeffers gave them cutting-edge culture, but not for its own sake. They got Jonathan Edwards and Abraham Kuyper—an entire Reformed worldview—in the vernacular of Andy Warhol and Paul McCartney, from Francis Schaeffer, dressed in Swiss lederhosen and knickers.[11] Historian Charles Cotherman observes:

> Like American artists, writers, and jazz musicians who flocked to Paris decades earlier, Europe seemed to offer Schaeffer a freedom to develop his taste for art, philosophy, and even good conversations in a context that reverberated with the newest currents in thought while simultaneously distanced from the internecine struggles that dominated American fundamentalism.[12]

As they gazed outward on the Alps, visitors to L'Abri got more than Schaeffer's wide-ranging cultural and theological analysis. They met fellow travelers from around the world, a community affirming of faith and yet somehow also unafraid of doubt. They found a community willing to discuss art in search of beauty as they weeded the vegetable garden together. They learned the hidden art of homemaking from Edith Schaeffer as they listened to the skeptical questions of a cradle Presbyterian who could never imagine returning to church.[13]

R. C. and Vesta Sproul set up Ligonier Valley Study Center like L'Abri, with programs that played to their considerable strengths. Sproul leaned into Christian education, especially Bible and theology. But the study center also trained Christians in ethics, counseling, philosophy, and even physical education. Visitors could come for two weeks or two years. Weekly Bible studies appealed beyond the Ligonier Valley, including to both Tim's and Kathy's mothers. Nothing made more memories than the gabfest on Monday night.[14] Sproul excelled speaking on his feet while thinking and talking about objections to Christianity. Between 1971 and 1981, he also served as a visiting professor of apologetics at Gordon-Conwell.

The Sprouls opened their lives to the young adults of Pittsburgh, who came from flourishing ministries across the region, including Young Life, Coalition for Christian Outreach, First Presbyterian Church of Pittsburgh, the Pittsburgh Experiment, and even the nascent charismatic movement of the Episcopal Church. Sproul gave them an open door, as he had done since his Gordon College class on contemporary theology in 1967, when his syllabus read, "Also, the Professor is always available to spend time with the student on a personal basis regarding spiritual or other problems."[15]

The Ligonier Valley Study Center may never have started if R. C. Sproul had accepted an offer from William Lane, who became Tim Keller's first New Testament professor. Lane took a train from Boston to Philadelphia to try to convince Sproul to join the faculty of the new Gordon-Conwell Theological Seminary. Sproul had been teaching for Conwell School of Theology, located on the campus of Temple University in Philadelphia. He didn't enjoy the work. He wasn't eager to do it in Boston either. "When he got to Philadelphia and met with R. C., Dr. Lane likened the occasion to William Farel asking John Calvin to stay in Geneva," Stephen Nichols wrote. "R. C. replied that Dr. Lane was not Farel, he himself was not Calvin, and Gordon was no Geneva."[16]

Sproul didn't enjoy the work at Ligonier Valley Study Center as much as he hoped either. Schaeffer's warnings proved prescient. The public nature of study center hospitality and teaching exhausted Sproul.

Neither he nor Vesta could match the extroverted hospitality of Francis and Edith Schaeffer, and even the Schaeffers had to withdraw from L'Abri's early openness.[17]

The years of Ligonier Valley Study Center were brief. But their influence spanned generations. Guests included globe-trotting author and evangelist Rebecca Manley Pippert and theologian Richard Lints, who would later give Tim Keller the language for "theological vision."[18] Ligonier Ministries left Ligonier Valley in 1984 for sunnier skies outside of Orlando, Florida. And the ministry set the trend for evangelical media by shifting away from residential formation into video distribution of Sproul's lectures.

New Conditions

Nevertheless, Ligonier Valley Study Center gave Tim Keller a taste for a Christian community closely attuned to shifting culture. When he moved to Hopewell after seminary and later planted Redeemer in New York, Tim sought to replicate this kind of community inside the church—hospitable and evangelistic, intellectual and earthy. They even brought a young convert, Graham Howell, from Hopewell to hear Sproul at Ligonier Valley. Kathy grew frustrated, though, when she thought Sproul talked too much about his beloved Pittsburgh Pirates and not enough about the Bible and theology. Tim and Kathy never adopted Sproul's love for sports.

Even though the Kellers never felt like part of his loyal and vocal inner circle, Sproul met with them for premarital counseling, then officiated and preached at their wedding in 1975.[19] Tim had never even heard of the newly formed Presbyterian Church in America until Sproul recommended it to him a week before their wedding. The Kellers stopped to see Sproul on their way to tell the bishops of the Evangelical Congregational Church that Tim could no longer sign their Wesleyan statement of faith, which included the possibility of sinless perfection on earth before Christ's return. Their relationship continued when Sproul came to Gordon-Conwell later that year to debate Gordon Fee on the topic of women's ordination. Sproul ate and prepared for the debate in the Kellers' newlywed apartment in Ipswich, Massachusetts.[20]

Though Sproul rejected full-time offers, he still visited Gordon-Conwell to teach a one-month course on apologetics. As Tim Keller developed as a Reformed apologist, he departed from Sproul's methodology. Like his mentor John Gerstner, Sproul used traditional evidence and proofs of God. Keller gravitated instead toward the neo-Calvinist approach typified by Cornelius Van Til of Westminster Theological Seminary. Keller also departed from Van Til, however, by emphasizing the doctrine of common grace.

Sproul remained a role model for Tim in other ways, even as they diverged. Sproul gave Keller a vision for how to speak persuasively to non-Christians, with intelligent command of the issues. One of Sproul's early books, *The Psychology of Atheism* (1974), took a similar approach to Francis Schaeffer in building a case for faith through appeals to modern art, literature, and philosophy. Through Schaeffer's works, which Keller began reading at Bucknell, he learned the concept of a "worldview." During these undergraduate years, Keller also came across Hans Rookmaaker's *Modern Art and the Death of a Culture*, published in 1970. Keller had assumed theology had to do with how we please God and relate to him. Now he could see that different worldviews produced different art, and that theology changed the way we do and see everything in life. Rookmaaker's neo-Calvinism rubbed off on Francis Schaeffer when they met in 1948. Rookmaaker began his own branch of L'Abri in the Netherlands to go along with Schaeffer's ministry to the disaffected and doubting in Switzerland.

The logos and pathos of neo-Calvinism, as he read it in these writers and saw it in their evangelistic communities, animated Keller's entire ministry. He advocated for a Christianity that is orthodox and modern at the same time. Believers cannot withdraw from the modern world but must engage every aspect, from art to business to politics to family to education, with a distinct worldview built on historic, orthodox doctrine.

When Keller looks back on Ligonier Valley Study Center, however, he doesn't primarily recall ideas or debates. Rather, he remembers most fondly many dinners shared with the Sprouls in their Stahlstown home.[21] Tim Keller saw in L'Abri and Ligonier Valley Study Center models for evangelism and discipleship under the new conditions of modern belief. No longer would generations simply accept the faith of their forefathers. Everyone would need to choose for themselves, among countless voices challenging their beliefs and behaviors. Faith would need to be conscious and intentional, and no rites of passage from baptism to confirmation would guarantee continued observance.

Keller didn't believe the church could afford merely to administer stage-of-life programs under such conditions. The church would need to adopt the parachurch mentality and go to the doubters and skeptics, find the wounded and wandering. The church must become a place where doubters would be welcome, where questions would be honored, where critics would be answered alongside mature believers. Keller bucked the seeker trend of his boomer ministry peers. He cast a vision for teaching Christian communities that engaged, embraced, and expected non-Christians. It's what Keller found among the InterVarsity students at Bucknell before he finally professed faith in his junior year. And it's what excited him about L'Abri and its offspring, especially Ligonier Valley Study Center. The church would always need to resist the pernicious influences of culture. But through the lives of Francis Schaeffer and R. C. Sproul, he also saw how to connect the gospel to every square inch of common grace in God's creation.

"We are relentlessly aware of and glad for the presence of doubters in our midst," Keller wrote early in his tenure at Redeemer. "We are very relentless yet extremely noncombative as we present the reasonable beauty of the Christian faith in every aspect of our ministry."[22]

PART TWO

PROFESSORS
AND PEERS

1972 to 1975

SEVEN

THEOLOGICAL SMORGASBORD

Gordon-Conwell Theological Seminary

When Tim Keller enrolled at Gordon-Conwell Theological Seminary in 1972, the school was undergoing significant changes—which must have startled the administration, since the school had only just begun in 1969.

Gordon-Conwell merged two schools, Conwell School of Theology in Philadelphia and Gordon Divinity School in Boston, which had both been founded by Baptists in the 1880s. Evangelist Billy Graham played the key role in securing financing and selecting leaders. Oil magnate J. Howard Pew, a longtime Graham backer, contributed two million dollars for the new school, which purchased a former Carmelite seminary north of Boston in South Hamilton, Massachusetts.

Gordon-Conwell conveyed a compelling sense of destiny to students in its early years. Seminary leaders invited global leaders such as

John Stott to lecture students and project confidence in their vision for an evangelical movement distinct from fundamentalism and liberalism. The mission to fill New England pulpits with evangelicals recalled the First Great Awakening heyday of Jonathan Edwards and also the new frontier of encroaching secularism in the Northeast.

Graham selected another longtime ally as president—Harold John Ockenga, then the pastor of historic Park Street Church on the northeast corner of Boston Common. Graham, Ockenga, and Pew had worked on several ventures together, notably *Christianity Today* magazine, which they founded in 1956. That experience offered a clue for the kind of challenges they would face with Gordon-Conwell. Only one year before they launched Gordon-Conwell, *Christianity Today* founding editor Carl F. H. Henry resigned under duress after a long conflict with Pew over politics. Henry's replacement, Harold Lindsell, visited Gordon-Conwell in 1972 to lecture in favor of biblical inerrancy, the view that no error can be found in the original Scriptures.

Gordon-Conwell had been launched as a kind of northeastern counterpart to Fuller Theological Seminary in Pasadena, California, where Ockenga previously served as founding president, even while he continued to pastor Park Street in Boston. Ockenga stepped down in 1963 after what became known as Black Saturday—December 1, 1962. The school's incoming dean, Daniel Fuller, son of school founder Charles Fuller, collided with Ockenga by insisting that the school's new doctrinal statement move beyond the Old Princeton articulation of inerrancy to offer a more general position on the Bible's "infallibility." While he didn't want to come out and say the Bible had "errors," that's what his position amounted to, and conservatives like Ockenga said so. But Daniel Fuller, with the support of his parents, ultimately won the day.[1] In 1976, Ockenga wrote the foreword for Lindsell's explosive book *The Battle for the Bible*, which criticized Fuller.

Inerrancy was just one of the many issues debated among faculty and students at Gordon-Conwell in the early 1970s.[2] The nondenominational seminary's professors hailed from every evangelical point on the compass. They (mostly politely) disagreed over race relations, over social justice, over missions strategy. They disagreed over the role of women in the church. They debated the question, "What is a woman?" Sometimes they even struggled to define feminine and masculine.

After one chapel session, in which a range of views toward women in ministry were argued, Kathy's friend and fellow student Louise Midwood remembers bumping into Ockenga. He turned to her and said, "I'm certainly glad that nothing like *that* is being espoused in my seminary." Midwood thought, *If you only knew.*[3] In fact, Gordon-Conwell academic dean William Kerr had asked Midwood and a female friend to take a class on twentieth-century feminism in the Christian church. Midwood believes he wanted spies to learn what was being taught in the class, because he asked them to report back to him.

Big Teapot, Little Spout

Independent from any denomination, Gordon-Conwell has always been a kind of theological smorgasbord. Two students starting at the same time could, with careful attention (or divine intervention), graduate with entirely different views. One could find the professors and classes that taught Reformed theology, and graduate a Presbyterian, or find classes and professors that were Wesleyan, Arminian, or Pentecostal.

Several professors left a lasting impression on Tim Keller, and not always for their approval. Gwyn Walters gave Tim a C in preaching and said, "You are like a big teapot with a little spout. You need to learn how to let it out." Sometimes a professor's influence would not become clear until later. Orlando Costas, a Latin American theologian, previewed what Keller would learn more thoroughly in Philadelphia. In his one-week course on "World Mission of the Church," Costas taught liberation theology appreciatively from an evangelical perspective. To Keller, he made a compelling case for social action and justice as part of Christians' work in the world.[4]

Students arrived early to Meredith Kline's 8:00 a.m. classes on the Pentateuch just to hear him open in prayer. Tim Keller took six courses—more than with any other professor—with Kline, who originally studied and taught at Westminster Theological Seminary in Philadelphia. Through Kline's courses, Keller first learned how to read the Bible "redemptive-historically"—along the story line of the Bible—by reading Geerhardus Vos's main works, *Biblical Theology* and *The Pauline Eschatology*. Many of Keller's biblical and theological questions were answered as he learned about the "overlap of the ages," also known as the "already/not yet" of inaugurated eschatology.

More than anything else though, Keller learned covenant theology from Kline, author of *By Oath Consigned*. Such important doctrines as penal substitution and imputed righteousness didn't click until Kline explained how Christ fulfilled the covenant of works that Adam failed during his probation, or what Kline called the "covenant of creation." Believing in Christ puts us "beyond" probation. Kathy Keller would go so far as to say that she didn't really understand the gospel of salvation by *grace*—not by our good works—until she studied with Kline.

Another Gordon-Conwell professor, William Lane, contributed to the main planks of Tim Keller's atonement theology.[5] He laid the groundwork for Keller's knowledge of the English Bible by requiring students to memorize the contents of every chapter of the New Testament. Lane, who was Keller's first New Testament teacher, published his commentary on the gospel of Mark in 1974 for the New International Commentary on the New Testament (NICNT) series. After his personal encounter with Christ at Bucknell, Keller turned to British writers for cutting-edge biblical scholarship that engaged with critics. Americans just weren't doing that work at the time. Lane was the first scholar born and trained in the United States to contribute to the prestigious NICNT series. In fact, his work might be said to be the first major evangelical biblical commentary by an American since that of J. Gresham Machen, who died in 1937. Lane had studied with series editor Ned Stonehouse and knew F. F. Bruce, who took over when Stonehouse died in 1962.

"Lane's commentary was probably the most thorough effort by an American evangelical since the publication of Broadus's *Matthew* nearly a century before," historian Mark Noll wrote. "His notes took account of current scholarship; his text was a model of patient, judicious exegesis. His conclusions on critical issues were conservative, but the pathway to those judgments was marked by persuasive learning."[6]

Keller only studied with Lane for one year.[7] He overlapped even less with Andrew Lincoln—only one semester. In fact, Lincoln didn't stay around Gordon-Conwell for long, only between 1975 and 1979. But one semester studying with Lincoln was long enough to change the entire direction of Keller's life. Keller took two New Testament courses with Lincoln, who at the time taught a Reformed view similar to that held by Geerhardus Vos and Herman Ridderbos. These courses helped tip Keller off the balance beam where he'd been straddling Reformed and Arminian theology.[8]

This Calvinism gave Keller perspective on the unexpected trajectory of his life. He often cited this story as an example of God's mysterious providence at work. In fact, the experience with Lincoln had been so formative for Keller that he told the story in one of his first sermons at Redeemer Presbyterian Church on July 9, 1989.[9] At another stage, he explained how this unexpected circumstance brought him to New York. But in this message, Hopewell was still his focus, and he wanted to show why he had become a Presbyterian and broken the promise to his mother and Evangelical Congregational Church pastor that he would never become Reformed.

Against the backdrop of Romans 8:28, Keller explained in his sermon how Lincoln had been expected to miss the entire school year.

Gordon-Conwell dean William Kerr asked the students to pray that God would make a way for Lincoln to get his visa:

> At the last minute somebody cut through the red tape. He came, and I fell under his influence. Do you know why the red tape was cut? The dean of my seminary was on his knees praying about how we were going to get this guy over here when Mike Ford, Gerald Ford's son, walked in and asked him what he was praying for. Mike Ford was a student at the seminary at that time. Do you know why Mike Ford was able to cut the red tape? Because his father was the president. Do you know why his father was the president? Because Nixon had resigned. Do you know why Nixon resigned? Because of the Watergate scandal. Do you know why there was a Watergate scandal? Because one day a guard noticed in the Watergate building a particular door ajar that should have been closed.

Keller returned to this story whenever he needed an illustration of how God's sovereign power attends to the smallest details. In 2003, the story illustrated his exposition of Joseph, whose brothers intended evil, but God intended good by elevating him to the heights of political power in Egypt (Genesis 42; 45; 50).[10]

As with Joseph, Keller could only have discerned God's hand of providence in retrospect. Only God knew at the outset of seminary how these years would transform every aspect of Keller's life, from his family to his friends to his ministry.

EIGHT

TABLE TALK

Elisabeth Elliot and the Robins

After his first spring semester Tim Keller studied modern liberal theology with Addison Leitch, one of Gordon-Conwell's biggest draws as a professor. Course readings and lectures helped Keller read theologians such as Paul Tillich critically and yet also appreciatively.

But another aspect of the course made a deeper impression on Keller. On the last day of their May intensive class, Leitch learned that his cancer had returned. Leitch didn't hold back his thoughts from the students. Some of his reactions were angry, others devout, as he faced death.

Addison Leitch was only sixty-four when he died of cancer during the fall semester on September 17, 1973.

At his memorial service, students expected to hear a few tearful and heart-wrenching remarks from his widow. But until this moment, Tim and Kathy didn't know Elisabeth Leitch, who had been married to Addison since 1969. And this wasn't the first time she grieved as a widow. Known more commonly as Elisabeth Elliot, she lost her first husband in 1956 during one of the most high-profile martyrdoms of the twentieth century.

When Elisabeth rose, tall and imposing, she scolded students for depersonalizing and dehumanizing their professors. They're not immune to pain and suffering. They should be treated like fellow members of the body of Christ. They need prayerful encouragement and support.

This was no demure widow dabbing her tears with a tissue. Tim and Kathy met a woman who faced suffering without fear or self-pity. She trusted in the sovereignty of God and warned Christians not to question his judgments. Amid social upheaval, the example of her steely faith stiffened a generation, including her students Tim and Kathy Keller.

"Class on Manners"

The same year the Kellers started Gordon-Conwell, the Equal Rights Amendment (ERA) passed the United States Senate, stating that equal rights under the law cannot be denied or abridged on account of sex. Also in 1972, Phyllis Schlafly started Stop ERA, which became the Eagle Forum, a staunch advocate of conservative causes such as the traditional family. Even if they had wanted to, graduate students preparing for ministry couldn't just bury their heads in Hebrew, Greek, history, and theology. Perhaps as never before—or since—in American history, society tugged apart at the seams over war, racism, and sex. At the beginning of the Kellers' second semester at Gordon-Conwell, the Supreme Court decided *Roe v. Wade*, which struck down state restrictions on abortion.

Elisabeth Elliot taught both Kellers in her class on "Christian Expression in Speech, Writing, and Behavior," dubbed "Betty Elliot's Class on Manners" by some of her student detractors. She argued that when God prohibits women from teaching or usurping authority over men, it's not because women are incompetent or lacking in giftedness. Rather, church and home show us how God in the Old Testament relates to his covenant people, and how in the New Testament Christ relates to his bride, the church. Both relationships require subordination. "The Church has always seen such imagery as highly important, not random, accidental, or trivial, and therefore not to be tampered with," Elliot said. She saw male and female as woven into the creative fabric of the world. "It is the very magnetism of two opposite poles which not only signifies vast eternal verities but also lends interest, fascination, even a certain glamor to our earthly life which those who agitate for equality and-or interchangeability seem completely to ignore—or what is much worse, to hate."[1]

Kathy Keller recalled a class when "Betty" Elliot walked up and down the aisles, listing her qualifications to be ordained. "I am better versed in Hebrew and Greek than any of you," she said, "as well as multiple other languages. I have more communication skills than do any of you, male or female. I am comfortable speaking in front of large crowds and skillful in one-to-one conversations. I have a depth of understanding of God born of suffering that few of you will match. My giftedness is far beyond most of you. And yet God has not called me to use those gifts in an ordained capacity. Does that mean they are of less worth? I know that not to be true. Calling is different from giftedness or even desire."

Kathy credited EE (as she was quietly known) for being the first person to help her understand gender roles as a gift from God instead of as an embarrassment or curse. And she learned how to distinguish God's commands from cultural expectations. Kathy cited Elliot's experience working in Ecuador with the Auca Indians, who defied many Western gender stereotypes. Kathy learned from Elliot that the Auca saw arts such as poetry and decoration as masculine concepts, while femininity included aspects of farming.[2] In this example, you can see how the Kellers would often juxtapose the value of authority and flexibility, not just with gender roles but in everyday life and ministry. The Kellers upheld biblical teaching on male leadership in marriage and the church while defying some cultural expectations on men and women.

Every Friday in Elliot's class, students were required to submit a two-page paper. The hardest assignment of the semester was identifying masculinity and femininity. Kathy cringes a bit today at her "very purple prose."[3] But Elliot would have recognized several of her own emphases in Kathy Keller's paper. Elliot liked Kathy's paper so much that she quoted it at length in her bestselling 1976 book *Let Me Be a Woman*. Kathy wrote:

> Creation has as one of its fundamental themes the pattern of rule and submission. Power and passivity, ebb and flow, generativity and receptivity are but a few of the ways that these paired polarities have been described. The Chinese called them *yin* and *yang* and made the symbol of their religion a graphic representation of their interaction. Even the physical realm is founded on and held together by the positive and negative attraction of atomic particles. Everywhere the universe displays its division into pairs of interlocking opposites. . . .
>
> We know that this order of rule and submission is descended from the nature of God Himself. Within the Godhead there is both the just and legitimate authority of the Father and the willing and joyful submission of the Son. From the union of the Father and the Son proceed a third personality, the Holy Spirit. He proceeds from them not as a child proceeds from the union of a man and woman, but rather as the personality of a marriage proceeds from the one flesh which is established from the union of two separate personalities. Here, in the reflection of the nature of the Trinity in the institution of marriage is the key to the definition of masculinity and femininity. The image of God could not be fully reflected without the elements of rule, submission, and union.[4]

At a time when many women demanded equal rights, Elliot encouraged them to yield to men's leadership, as if dancing. At a time when many women sought liberation, she told them joyful submission would set them free. Eve's damnable sin was hubris, Elliot argued. Eve sought to usurp God, a sin that was "fatal beyond their worst imaginings." Instead, Eve should have told the Serpent: "Let me be a woman."[5]

Likewise, women should not seek ordination for any reason, whether the need of the church, their gifting to teach, or their urge to serve in this role, Elliot warned. Nor should any sociological arguments about women's liberation factor in their decision. That would be thinking on a merely human plane about ordination, which "has to do with things vastly more fundamental and permanent, and the meaning of womanhood is one of those things. . . . She is free not by disobeying the rules but by obeying them."[6]

Kathy had grown up in the United Presbyterian Church, which ordained women and eventually became part of the Presbyterian Church (USA). And that's the future Kathy had envisioned for herself after she came to faith. But Elliot showed Kathy Keller a different path of future ministry. Elliot didn't merely append to a man. Neither did she seek to assume any unbiblical role. Instead, Kathy saw how she could serve God and support her husband while upholding the absolute authority of God as revealed in his Word. Kathy considered Jesus' own view of the Scriptures. He trusted the Old Testament. He promised to inspire the New Testament. Since she trusted Jesus, why shouldn't she also view the Bible as authoritative, even inerrant? "This was a game-changing realization for me," she wrote. "And it changed a lot more."[7]

Kathy entered Gordon-Conwell under the care of the Pittsburgh Presbytery, which had once been the largest presbytery in the world.[8] She was on track for ordination. When she changed her mind, the presbytery required her to give notice. She came to the floor of the presbytery, where church leaders questioned her shift to the status of "commissioned church worker." She insisted that the Bible did not allow for women's ordination. At least half of the 350 pastors and elders booed and hissed. She was the latest fodder in a long-running war over women's ordination in the presbytery.[9]

Elliot didn't just narrowly shape how the Kellers would answer the question of women's ordination or gender roles in the home. Tim later credited Elliot for contributing to his entire view of humans' relationship to God. Few could match Elliot's credibility when it came to trusting God with what we don't understand, which Tim identified as a theme across all her writing and teaching. Only when we can see God as far surpassing us in goodness and wisdom, when we behold him in glory, can we obey what we don't necessarily comprehend in his commands.[10]

Pittsburgh Edge

Around Gordon-Conwell, they called it the "Pittsburgh edge." Of the five hundred students at the South Hamilton campus in 1973, more than 125 came from the Pittsburgh area.[11] But it wasn't just their numbers that stood out. These students showed up active and organized. And determined to become campus leaders and uphold the Reformed orthodoxy they learned back home from the likes of R. C. Sproul and John Gerstner. Many of them gravitated toward Elisabeth Elliot.

Among the Pittsburgh contingent, Kathy's friend Louise (Crocker) Midwood didn't adjust well to Gordon-Conwell. She couldn't handle its theological diversity. She had already been mentored by Sproul and Francis Schaeffer. She hadn't come to Gordon-Conwell just to learn. "When I came to seminary," she said, "I was wielding the sword of the Lord." She didn't even think Arminians could be saved.

Another reason she didn't fit in was that she chose Gordon-Conwell to study under three professors in particular—William Lane, Stuart Barton Babbage, and Elliot's late husband, Addison Leitch. None of them were still at the school when she arrived.[12] Without the mentors she had expected, Louise was feeling dislocated and lost until her old Pittsburgh acquaintance Kathy Kristy invited her to join a pseudo-campus group. It consisted of only three members: David Midwood, Tim Keller, and Louise's friend, Kathy Kristy. They had started the group in 1972 with only one tongue-in-cheek condition for entry: you had to agree that Ed Clowney was the greatest preacher of all time.

Louise didn't make a strong first impression on the group. As the trio engaged in their usual dialogue over theology and experience, she immediately found fault with their theology. David Midwood remarked that she was the angriest woman he had ever met. Tim Keller recommended a book—*Life Together* by Dietrich Bonhoeffer. "He's a rank liberal!" Louise responded with her Pittsburgh edge.

Within a year, David and Louise would be married. And she and David would be lifelong friends with the Kellers.

The Edmund P. Clowney Fan Club bonded through shared theology and shared pain. All of them loved to read. All of them had suffered strained and broken relationships—so, so many personal problems, Louise remembers. John Calvin's sermons on Job brought comfort to Tim and Kathy as they discussed the meaning and purpose of suffering. True to their name, the fan club traveled together down to Cambridge to hear Clowney speak at Harvard for an InterVarsity event. The club also shared an obsession with J. R. R. Tolkien, C. S. Lewis, and Jonathan Edwards. This was right up Louise's alley, because she had come to love Edwards back in Pittsburgh under the influence of Sproul and during visits to Gerstner's home. She and Tim discussed Edwards's treatise on the freedom of the will, and how God's love tastes sweet like honey on the tongue. This imagery would later surface in subsequent decades of Tim's preaching.

"When you light on a subject that Tim really feels inside, you get to explore it," Louise remembers, "and you get to hear him expound, not in sermons, but they might as well be."

Louise's first impression of Tim Keller was more telling than her own introduction to the club. She met him in September 1973, when Kathy and Tim had jobs in the kitchen on campus. Tim was leaning against a wall, wearing a cardigan, holding an open book as the world buzzed past. "That has not changed in fifty years," she said. "That's still Tim. He's always reading."

Kathy spoke out in class, but Tim kept to himself during class lectures. You'd have to sit down with him to recognize his notable intellect. Or attend one of his impromptu post-class lectures. Immediately after class finished, students would regather in Tim's dorm room at Pilgrim Hall, where he'd lecture on the lecture they had just heard. Louise remembers:

> He could take all the information we're getting from the fire hydrant, of the subject or the professor, and he would reinterpret it for us. He would translate it. He would do synopses of it. He would synthesize things. The way he did it, it was exactly what the professor had been teaching, except it was accessible now. He would put it into a framework.

Students like Louise scrambled to take notes from Tim's summaries. He didn't give answers to tests or cheat the system. And he wasn't trying to undermine his professors. Louise explained, "He was renegotiating the texts in a way that sounded so brilliant. It was better than what the professor was doing. He wasn't changing a jot or tittle of theology. But he was giving it to us in a format we couldn't forget."[13]

Each class, each passing year, added layers of additional influences Tim would retranslate for the students, a practice that later surfaced in his own preaching and writing. Tim had a natural knack for producing an original synthesis, all while claiming he wasn't an original thinker.

More often than not, however, Tim worked out his intellectual and spiritual formation over meals with his friends in the cafeteria. They argued and laughed so hard that sometimes milk came out of Tim's nose.[14] The Pittsburghers enjoyed a heated discussion, and it wasn't unusual for them to be gathered until 9:00 p.m. when the cafeteria staff would turn out the lights and throw them out. The conversations of these years were the heart of Tim's formative theological development, akin to Martin Luther's mealtime discussions with pastors in training, later published as *Table Talk*.

With the rise of remote learning and commuting in our day, and the 2022 decision of Gordon-Conwell to sell the South Hamilton campus, it's not an experience many seminary students can enjoy any longer. For Tim, Gordon-Conwell was an extension of the intense Christian communities he had sought at Bucknell and through Ligonier Valley Study Center. He once again found a quasi-monastic "hothouse" for spiritual growth, where he ate three meals each day with his single friends and mingled with the faculty who lived nearby.

The influence of these students on Tim and Kathy continues to this day. Kathy grew especially tight with five other women, all single Gordon-Conwell students. Among their group of six, five of them married Gordon-Conwell students who went into ministry. The Kellers dedicated their book *The Meaning of Marriage* to these five couples— Doug and Adele Calhoun, Wayne and Jane Frazier, David and Louise Midwood, Gary and Gayle Somers, and Jim and Cindy Widmer.

In addition to remaining friends for several decades, the women still circulate a "round-robin" letter. When the recipient receives a packet of six letters from the others, she reads the other five and writes a new letter to replace her own. Then she sends them all to the next person. These "Robins" have stuck close through theological changes, child rearing, and vacations together. None of the couples have divorced. For many years, David Midwood in particular shepherded the other Robins with warmth and love—and a willingness to push at times. For Tim, this accountability became even more important as he attained growing prominence as a pastor and writer.

After graduating from Gordon-Conwell, David Midwood earned

his doctorate from Fuller Theological Seminary and served as pastor of West Congregational Church in Haverhill, Massachusetts, from 1975 to 2000. He died in 2014 of colon cancer. Louise keeps a birthday card sent from Tim to David.

"We have no greater friends than the Midwoods," Tim wrote, "and I have no greater friend than you. And friends are up there with life's greatest blessings."

Table Talk

Tim Keller may not have spoken up very often in his classes at Gordon-Conwell. And unlike Elisabeth Elliot, he isn't known for a polemical edge. But Tim and his friends in the Pittsburgh contingent in seminary hatched a bold plan that thrust them into some of the hottest debates on campus about gender roles and biblical authority.

Only in seminary can you name a student newspaper *Qoheleth*. When no one else wanted to run it, Tim and his friends took over the tiny press and came up with the far more prosaic name—*Table Talk*. The designer of *Table Talk*, Stu Boehmig, had been a Young Life leader in Pittsburgh, where Kathy knew him. He was especially close to R. C. and Vesta Sproul. Boehmig would later become executive director at Ligonier, which adopted the initial design and title of the campus paper for their own long-running signature publication.

None of the articles or reviews for the seminary paper were signed. After all, students critiquing the liberal theology of some of their professors or the shabby treatment of someone with whom they disagreed was something done better anonymously.

Table Talk's lead editorial took on Nancy Hardesty, whose 1974 book, written with Letha Dawson Scanzoni, *All We're Meant to Be: A Biblical Approach to Women's Liberation*, helped launch evangelical feminism. In 2006, *Christianity Today* placed the book at number twenty-three on its list of the fifty most influential books among evangelicals. When Hardesty visited Gordon-Conwell to give a guest lecture around the time of the launch of her book, she was still in graduate school. But *Table Talk* didn't pull any punches after the Hardesty visit, criticizing her in their lead article, "Womanstand." The students chided her for reinterpreting Ephesians 5:23–24 and saying that we live in a new order of the Spirit that has replaced the order of authority. Professor Ramsey Michaels had offered the same argument in a previous edition of the student paper. Several of Keller's future themes in his writing and preaching, especially the upside-down nature of the kingdom, come through in the editorial, even though he didn't draft it. They likewise echo Elisabeth Elliot's classroom teaching:

> It is unfortunate that Miss Hardesty had to leave us with a chaotic, lawless universe and an impotent, covenant Lord simply because she could not see that human authority does not entail superiority but rather service. She chose to ignore the biblical pattern, perfected in Christ, of victory and fullness of life through submission, through lowering ourselves, through "regarding others as more important than ourselves"—not through self-assertion and denial of authority.

The *Table Talk* editors may have strongly disagreed with Hardesty's interpretation of the Bible, but they also lamented how she had been treated on campus. Students stood up in the middle of the lecture to denounce her. One of Louise Midwood's friends yelled, "Woman, sit down!" Afterward, Louise saw Hardesty weeping outside the lecture hall, crumpled against the wall.[15] That she had been invited in the first place, along with the reaction of many students, gives a sense of the tense climate around this issue on campus, which reflected the broader culture at the time. The *Table Talk* editors said Hardesty "was met with emotional abuse undeserved by even the most outspoken critic of the faith, much less by a sister in the faith."

Tim didn't sign his name to *Table Talk*'s other hard-hitting article, "Hermeneutical Nestorianism," either. But forty years later, Kathy could still recall the article and attributed it to Tim.[16] Tim's co-conspirator John Palafoutas later explained, "The publication was intended to protest the GCTS New Testament Department and shake things up a bit. The professors in that department understood what we had done."[17]

In keeping with the style of the paper, Tim wrote the article in the first-person plural. He opened with the kind of bold claim common among young seminary students. "We would like to take issue with the GCTS New Testament department on its methodological presuppositions in hermeneutics." He explained, "The GCTS NT department"—he identified Ramsey Michaels and David Scholer—"believes strongly that all theological presuppositions must be put behind us when go to the text of the Bible."

Keller rebutted. "Nonetheless, what 'put your theological presuppositions behind you' really means is 'put behind you the assumption that there is a divine author and assume that it is human.' Thus the two natures are separated and dealt with apart from each other." This led to Keller's charge of Nestorianism, the ancient heresy that teaches there are two persons, one human and one divine, in Christ. The orthodox formulation counters that Christ is one person with two natures, fully man and fully God. Keller objected to how "hermeneutical Nestorianism" likewise separates the human and divine authorship of Scripture, so that the Bible becomes culturally captive to the author's immediate context.

Keller also acknowledged the opposite temptation—any kind of Monophysite error that would underappreciate human authorship in favor of the divine. Still, he judged the Nestorian threat to be more imminent. "To separate the two natures in a Nestorian fashion tends to diminish the divine nature for the human."

In this early article you can begin to recognize Keller's habit of steering between problems on both sides of a debate, his search for a "third way." "As orthodox believers, we must not be obscurantists, yet we must not assume that the world's scholarship, performed by rebellious fallen men (as are we), is somehow neutral and without inclination to resist truth when it runs counter to modern convictions," he wrote. But he did not regard himself as above critique: "Our own hearts should show us this."

The debate Keller highlighted would not be settled by his article in *Table Talk*. After twenty-five years of teaching, both before and after the merger of Gordon-Conwell, Ramsey Michaels resigned under accusations of undermining biblical authority in 1983 after the 1981 publication of his book *Servant and Son*.[18] In 2008, Keller's former employer, Westminster Theological Seminary, suspended Peter Enns for a similar hermeneutic in his book *Inspiration and Incarnation*. Reminiscent of his writing as a seminary student, Keller warned against this teaching again in his own book, *Center Church*: "An evangelical theology of Scripture acknowledges that the Bible is a thoroughly human book, each author being embedded in human culture, but it believes that God specifically chose each author's culture and even the very life circumstances so that God's overruling providence sovereignly determined every word to be written just as it was."[19]

The other professor Keller was responding to in his *Table Talk* article, David Scholer, would end up at Fuller Theological Seminary in 1994. Before Scholer's death in 2008, he taught a class on "Women, the Bible, and the Church," the most popular elective among Fuller students.[20] Elisabeth Elliot would not have approved.

On a faculty as diverse as Gordon-Conwell, class choice often dictated theological trajectory, which varied widely from student to student. For Tim Keller, that trajectory was set with the help of his Pittsburgh friends and their role model, Elisabeth Elliot.

NINE

DISAGREE WITHOUT BEING DISAGREEABLE

Roger Nicole and Neo-Calvinism

A leading scholar of Reformed theology and biblical inerrancy, Roger Nicole excelled at teaching his own views alongside opposing views. He covered their strengths and weaknesses while keeping the truth of the gospel in mind. His methods sometimes worked a little too well, according to Mark Dever, a Baptist pastor who studied with Nicole at Gordon-Conwell between 1984 and 1986.

"In fact, so well would he describe the strengths of the positions he did not hold that it may be that there is more than one noted paedo-baptist minister today who became paedo-baptist through the Baptist Roger Nicole's lectures," Dever wrote.[1]

Nicole has been largely forgotten today, except by his students, because he focused more on classroom teaching than on writing books and journal articles. Working for Gordon Divinity School and Gordon-Conwell from 1949 to 1986, Nicole helped shore up the institution in practical ways. Along with William Kerr, Nicole drove his station wagon around the Northeast to buy theological works discarded by mainline Protestant seminaries. They assembled the seminary library on a discount budget.[2] Nicole himself built the largest private collection of theological writings—more than twenty-five thousand theological works, highlighted by rare books dating back to the Reformation era of the sixteenth and seventeenth centuries. Reformed Theological Seminary in Orlando now hosts the collection.[3]

Tim Keller didn't take any courses in systematic theology until his second year. But he had already begun to warm toward Reformed theology in conversations with his friend Kathy Kristy. At this point, she wasn't completely convinced of Reformed theology herself, but she could still explain its appeal to him as accessible and practical, even common sense. At one point she said to Tim, "If I wasn't a Calvinist, I would be afraid to get out of bed in the morning." As he observed Kathy's outlook and life, he began to move toward embracing Calvinism.[4]

Another big step toward Reformed theology came in three lecture courses Tim took with the Swiss native Roger Nicole: Systematic Theology I and II, and an elective on the doctrine of Christ. Nicole's demeanor made him a bridge builder on the eclectic Gordon-Conwell faculty of the 1970s and 1980s. He held to Reformed theology in a way that was strong and broad at the same time. His personal kindness helped draw out the best from fellow professors. He frustrated some students because he wouldn't attack other professors in class, even when he disagreed with his colleagues. Students would later see him in the cafeteria warmly embracing those same professors.[5] Since Nicole didn't take criticism personally, he could tolerate and teach students, whether immature or precocious, when they objected to his views.

In one class, a student disagreed with Nicole's view on predestination.

"That makes God the author of sin and evil!" she charged. Nicole kept his cool and acknowledged that many Christians prefer the Arminian view because then God cannot be faulted for evil and sin. But he still believed anything commendable in the Arminian view could not account for the detractions. "And he proceeded to sweetly take the Arminian position apart," Keller remembered.

Nicole's lectures followed a plain structure, which delighted notetakers. First he gave the theological topic. Next he explained the different views, whether Wesleyan or Lutheran or Catholic or Reformed or Orthodox. Then he assessed the strengths and weaknesses of each view and also described why he found the Reformed perspective most compelling. He ended by supporting his conclusion with biblical proofs.

"This was quite literally *systematic* theology," Keller wrote, "and I was just blown away by it." Keller may have entered Gordon-Conwell an Arminian with a vow to enter ministry in the Evangelical Congregational Church. But he graduated from Gordon-Conwell summa cum laude as a Calvinist, in large part because of Nicole.[6]

Under Nicole's influence, Keller continued his trajectory toward continental neo-Calvinism, rather than the British-American Reformed theology associated with Princeton Theological Seminary in the nineteenth century. Nicole assigned Louis Berkhof's *Systematic Theology*, which tracks closely with Herman Bavinck's *Reformed Dogmatics*, as the textbook for his theology courses. Nicole also assigned parts of Bavinck's *Our Reasonable Faith* and his *Doctrine of God*—at that time, no other section of his *Dogmatics* had been translated into English.

The differences in these two strains of Reformed theology illuminate Keller's apologetic approach. Princeton theology, exemplified in Charles Hodge, begins by seeking to prove the existence of God by showing nonbelievers that Christianity is built on rational arguments. The continental neo-Calvinism of Bavinck and Berkhof begins by assuming from Romans 1 that everyone already knows God and many things about him by general revelation that they suppress in sin

(Romans 1). The job of the apologist, then, is to show nonbelievers how Christianity explains what they know in their hearts but deny with their lips.

In the newly formed Presbyterian Church in America of the 1970s, several streams of Reformed theology converged. The largest of those reflected the influence of Hodge and Princeton. Keller never entirely rejected the "doctrinalist" stream from Princeton. But with this early influence from Gordon-Conwell, he became more closely associated with the "pietist" stream of English Puritans such as John Owen and the "culturalist" stream of the Dutch theologians Abraham Kuyper and Herman Bavinck. Keller advocated inside and outside his denomination for several key tenets of neo-Calvinism:

1. Faith is a matter of head and heart. Evangelism directs nonbelievers' aspirations toward their only consolation in Christ.
2. The story of Scripture across both Testaments finds fulfillment in Christ. As Keller's friend Sally Lloyd-Jones would later put it, "Every story whispers his name."[7]
3. Antithesis and common grace coexist. Some worldviews flatly contradict Christianity. But many nonbelievers know better than they realize. So even as Christians critique, they respect.
4. Grace restores nature. In this cosmic view of salvation, Christians evangelize as they also fight against social injustice.

As a true disciple of Nicole, Keller identified several flaws in neo-Calvinism. He never found a strong enough ecclesiology. And as a pietist he judged the neo-Calvinists for their lack of evangelism. As an apologist, Keller learned to recognize the weak spots in his own views.

The influence of Nicole on Keller didn't stop with his irenic spirit or neo-Calvinist readings. Nicole shaped Keller's views on substitutionary atonement and made it a lifelong priority in Keller's writing and preaching. Nicole showed him that no matter how the Bible talks about atonement, Jesus is always the substitute. Keller wrote in *Center Church*:

> Jesus fights the powers, pays the price, bears the exiles, makes the sacrifice, and bears the punishment *for* us, in our place, on our behalf. In every grammar, Jesus does for us what we cannot do for ourselves. *He* accomplishes salvation; we do nothing at all. And therefore the substitutionary sacrifice of Jesus is at the heart of everything.[8]

Memories of his time as a student under Nicole also brought some disappointment for Keller, however. Several times he applied for the Byington Fellowship, a prestigious scholarship that paid for the best students to work as teaching assistants with the top professors. Desiring a mentor, Tim had hoped to study with Nicole. But every time Tim applied, he was passed over.

Other students and faculty may have known that the Kellers were intelligent. They were broadly liked on campus. But the Kellers knew they didn't possess the social skills typically expected of ministry leaders. While dejected, Tim and Kathy weren't surprised.[9] They graduated with excellent academic reputations but middling ministry prospects.

Even though he never formally mentored Keller, Nicole still helped set his ministry path. No other professor at Gordon-Conwell so shaped Keller's insistence on bringing an irenic spirit to theological disagreement and representing opponents in ways they would view themselves.[10]

"For the four of us, other than the Edmund P. Clowney Fan Club," Louise Midwood said, "probably the best thing to happen to us at seminary was to see, in terms of our own personal development within a church and theological framework, that you can disagree without being disagreeable."[11]

TEN

PNEUMODYNAMICS

Richard Lovelace and Jonathan Edwards

It was Tim Keller's first course at Gordon-Conwell. It was the first time the professor, Richard Lovelace, had ever taught the course.

It was called Pneumodynamics. For anyone not familiar with Koine Greek, that's "Spiritual Dynamics." From this course in the fall of 1972 would come Lovelace's book *Dynamics of Spiritual Life*, which Keller recommends frequently. It's not a stretch to say the class changed his life.[1]

"To say that my time studying with Richard Lovelace was seminal to my thinking and way of doing ministry is an understatement," Keller said. More than any other book, with the exception of the Bible, *Dynamics of Spiritual Life* shaped his views of the church and directed the course of his ministry. "Anyone who knows my ministry and reads [*Dynamics of Spiritual Life*] will say, 'So that's where Keller got all this stuff!'"[2]

Studying with Lovelace was an unforgettable experience. Tall and broad, with a close-trimmed beard, Lovelace typically wore a tweed jacket, sometimes with a vest. He carried a leather attaché case and used overhead projectors as he taught large classes of students. No one struggled to hear him, but students often struggled to follow him. Easily sidetracked, occasionally frustrating, and sometimes profound, Lovelace didn't have much of a personal touch in his interactions with students. They wondered if he was ever fully present in the classroom. "He was notoriously absentminded," the Kellers' friend Louise Midwood remembered.

Keller took only one other course with Lovelace, a course on the history of revivals. But his short time with Lovelace helped Keller make sense of his past and gain a clearer vision of the future. And he picked up a new lifelong dialogue partner as he studied the works of American revivalist Jonathan Edwards.

Unconscious Conspiracy

The reading assignments from Lovelace were a perfect fit for Keller's voracious, wide-ranging tastes. Keller read Flannery O'Connor for the first time in her short story "A Good Man Is Hard to Find," which was assigned by Lovelace to teach about sin. Lovelace paired her with John Owen's *Mortification of Sin*. For Keller the effect was nothing short of electrifying. In O'Connor, who died in 1964, he gained respect for the work of Christians in the arts. In Owen, who died in 1683, Tim caught glimpses of the pastoral theology of British Puritanism following the Reformation.

Mostly, though, Keller learned from Lovelace about the dynamics of revival. Lovelace argued that the church loses its way when Christians confuse law and gospel. Lovelace taught that the church must avoid both dead orthodoxy and legalism, as well as heterodoxy and antinomianism. Conditions are ripe for revival—a powerful work of the Spirit to bless God's people—when justification and sanctification are neither separated nor conflated. In a revival, the moralists realize they don't know the gospel and get converted. And Christians stuck in their sin enjoy new freedom when they realize the liberating power of their union with Christ and justification. Even many outside the church convert during revivals, because for the first time, they hear the gospel as the power to raise the dead rather than a stump speech for moral and conservative values. As he studied these spiritual dynamics under Lovelace, Keller began to understand what had happened to him and his InterVarsity chapter back at Bucknell.

Following Lovelace, and Edwards as well, Keller advocated for revival in his own writing and preaching. He argued that revival intensifies the Spirit's normal work of convicting sinners, regenerating and sanctifying them, and assuring them of God's grace. The Spirit does so through the ordinary means of grace—namely, preaching, prayer, and sacraments.[3] Revival may be discerned when these ordinary means result in a surprising surge of converted sinners and renewed believers.[4] From Lovelace's history of revivals, Keller learned that the famous Northampton 1734 awakening followed Edwards's two sermons on Romans 4:5 ("Justification by Faith Alone"). Much the same pattern held for the British revivalists John Wesley and George Whitefield when they articulated salvation by grace alone instead of moral exertion.[5]

Lovelace taught Keller that whatever differences in place and time and manifestations exist, revivals share a common heart. Even when Christians know in their heads that God accepts them by faith through the grace of Christ's atoning sacrifice, they don't always live that way. Day to day, they believe that God loves them because they obey his law. They draw "their assurance of acceptance with God from their sincerity, their past experience of conversion, their recent religious performance or the relative infrequency of their conscious, willful disobedience."[6] That's why we need revivals, so that we can be weaned off our natural-born proclivity to works-righteousness and live in light of the gospel of grace.[7]

Christians enjoy revival when they appropriate the justifying work of Christ for their everyday lives, just as Martin Luther claimed the alien righteousness of Christ as his only defense before a holy and righteous God. Only then can true sanctification proceed as the outworking of love and thankfulness. "Much that we have interpreted as a defect of sanctification in church people is really an outgrowth of their loss of bearing with respect to justification," Lovelace wrote in *Dynamics of Spiritual Life*. He explained that when Christians don't know God accepts them on Jesus' behalf, they become insecure. "Their insecurity shows itself in pride, a fierce defensive assertion of their own righteousness and defensive criticism of others. They come naturally to hate other cultural styles and other races in order to bolster their own security and discharge their suppressed anger."[8]

This theme would recur in many of Keller's sermons and writings, including most notably *The Prodigal God*.[9] Lovelace introduced Keller to the cultural dynamics of revival and the way insecure Christians resent unfamiliar cultural styles and other races because animosity bolsters self-righteousness. Race, political party, and culture become means of superiority that stifle the inner whisper of doubt. Such Christians don't realize that self-love prevents them from enjoying freedom and joy in Christ, whose grace abounds to all who repent of their vain moral efforts.

Dividing the world between good and bad people misses the heart of what makes Christianity so revolutionary. Preferences about displays of emotion, song selection, and length of service can vary from culture to culture while still conveying the same Christian faith. But Christians often treat their preferences as absolute requirements for faithful practice.[10] Revival, however, breaks down the world's barriers, as Christians trust only in Jesus and not in their cultural preferences. Lovelace believed he saw such a revival in the Jesus Movement—a movement other Christian leaders viewed with suspicion because of the counter-culture's dress and music.

Lovelace interpreted the Jesus Movement as a welcome challenge to the status quo. Keller brought this revival dynamic into the church, first in Hopewell and then in New York. He heeded the warning from Lovelace:

> Confronted with this kind of violent reaction when they seek to mold their congregations into instruments of evangelism and social healing, pastors gradually settle down and lose interest in being change agents in the church. An unconscious conspiracy arises between their flesh and that of their congregations. It becomes tacitly understood that the laity will give pastors special honor in the exercise of their gifts, if the pastors will agree to leave their congregations' pre-Christian lifestyles undisturbed and do not call for the mobilization of lay gifts for the work of the kingdom. Pastors are permitted to become ministerial superstars. Their pride is fed as their congregations are permitted to remain herds of sheep in which each has cheerfully turned to his own way.[11]

Even when Keller became world-famous while in New York, he kept prodding his congregation away from complacency and toward revival, as Lovelace taught him.

True Virtue

Among Keller's biggest influences, only Jonathan Edwards shared his pastoral vocation. Keller never wrote fantasy novels like C. S. Lewis and J. R. R. Tolkien. He never served as a seminary president like Ed Clowney. Keller picked up his interest in Edwards from Richard Lovelace, and it later showed up in frequent Redeemer sermon quotations, especially between 1996 and 1998, when Keller cited him fifty-three times. While he was pastoring in Hopewell, Keller worked through the two-volume Banner of Truth edition of *The Works of Jonathan Edwards.*

Two aspects of Edwards's theology and practice stood out to Keller. First, Edwards gave Keller a desire for mystical experiences of God. He longed for revival, and he especially loved Edwards's *Personal Narrative.* Edwards's way of describing spiritual experience in "A Divine and Supernatural Light" changed the way Keller prayed and preached. John Owen's *Communion with God* called Keller to experience God. But Edwards gave Keller the best account of how it happens. Passages such as Romans 5:5; 8:15–16; and 1 Peter 1:8 took on new life for Keller.

Second, Keller saw how Edwards shifted his preaching, adopting the model of George Whitefield in the First Great Awakening. Edwards combined the doctrinal preaching of his Puritan upbringing with the vivid metaphors and images of the new revivalism of Whitefield. Edwards brought to preaching what Keller appreciated in the writing of C. S. Lewis. Logic, when fired with captivating illustrations, changes hearts.

Keller cited Edwards from the pulpit for a variety of purposes. Sometimes the application was direct. In his first pastoral call, Keller drew on a 1733 sermon from Edwards. Citing "The Duty of Charity to the Poor," Keller convinced the West Hopewell Presbyterian Church deacons that they should still support a single mother who had squandered their charity on bikes and eating out with her kids.[12]

Often the application of Edwards was more conceptual. Keller found Edwards's distinction between "common virtue" and "true virtue" in *The Nature of True Virtue* especially helpful. "Common virtues"—such as love for family, nation, and self—breed rivalry. We put our families ahead of others. We pit our nation against others. We choose our self-interest over the interest of others. But the kind of "true virtue" we see in revived Christians, when God becomes their *summum bonum*, or ultimate good and center, blesses everyone.[13]

"Only if our highest love is God himself can we love and serve all people, families, classes, races; and only God's saving grace can bring us to the place where we are loving and serving God for himself alone and not for what he can give us," Keller explained. "Unless we understand the gospel, we are *always* obeying God for our sake and not for his."[14]

Historian George Marsden explains that Edwards wrote *The Nature of True Virtue* at a time when philosophers believed scientific advances would end the religious wars that pitted competing moral systems against each other. Objective morality would supposedly replace ancient dogmas.[15] Unlike his *Concerning the End for Which God Created the World*, Edwards didn't even quote the Bible in *The Nature of True Virtue*. "His object was to establish an analysis in which, if one granted merely a few essential principles of Christian theology, one would be forced to reconsider the whole direction of eighteenth-century moral philosophy," Marsden wrote.[16]

Edwards could see no hope for the universal benevolence these philosophers sought apart from God, the source of all love and beauty. Because God himself is love, we cannot love anything as we should without God.[17] True love will align with others such that when they rejoice, we rejoice; when they weep, we weep.[18] You can't weep for another family when your family benefits at their expense. You can't rejoice with another nation when they defeat yours. You can celebrate your colleague's promotion, but you still feel the sting when it means you've been passed over. That's why we need a higher love, a true virtue. "True love is the widest possible affection for persons and all that is good (being) in the universe," Marsden explained. "It is doing good for its own sake—for its beauty. Merely natural 'virtue,' which superficially may look very similar, is ultimately motivated by humans' natural inclinations to love themselves and their own kind."[19]

Edwards showed Keller how Christians can work for justice in ways that will help them avoid unintentionally perpetuating injustice. Only when we work for God can we properly serve our neighbors in need. Keller wrote in *Generous Justice*:

Edwards taught that if, through an experience of God's grace, you come to find him beautiful, then you do not serve the poor because you want to think well of yourself, or in order to get a good reputation, or because you think it will be good for your business, or even because it will pay off for your family in creating a better city to live in. You do it because serving the poor honors and pleases God, and honoring and pleasing God is a delight to you in and of itself.[20]

Edwards didn't compose *The Nature of True Virtue* amid his fame in Northampton but during his wilderness years as a missionary to the Native Americans of Stockbridge. It's hard to imagine a fired pastor exiled to the backwoods of western Massachusetts capturing the attention of philosophers across the ocean. But Edwards produced another one of his most enduringly influential works, *The Freedom of the Will*, during those years in Stockbridge. Edwards didn't flatter the fashionable philosophers of his day as he upheld the Calvinism of his Puritan forebears.[21] The social critic Christopher Lasch observed that "Edwards's formulation of Calvinism flew in the face of the whole trend of enlightened thought."[22] However, Edwards still attracted Calvinist critics who complained that he focused too much on inner experience. But it's precisely because Edwards challenged contemporary philosophers, and because he didn't separate head from heart, that he still influences Tim Keller and so many others today.

Sweet as Honey

While Keller cited many different sermons and treatises by Edwards, the same themes repeated. Keller often returned to Edwards's mark of true Christianity as engaging not only the intellect but also the affections. Writing amid the First Great Awakening in *The Religious Affections*, Edwards distinguished between "understanding," which is how we judge between true and false, and "inclination," when we decide that we like or dislike what we understand. Our "will" determines what we will do, in concert with our "heart," which is drawn to beauty. From our "heart" comes "affections," known in the Bible as "fruit of the Spirit" (Galatians 5), such as love, joy, peace, patience, kindness, and self-control.[23]

Edwards's framing guided Keller's basic approach to preaching as well. A good and faithful sermon will help Christians see the excellency of Jesus and not merely his usefulness. We need more than understanding, more than a notion of God; we need a sense of pleasure and delight in him. In what Keller described as "perhaps [Edwards's] best discussion of this dynamic,"[24] Edwards argued:

> Thus there is a difference between having an *opinion*, that God is holy and gracious, and having a *sense* of the loveliness and beauty of that holiness and grace. There is a difference between having a rational judgment that honey is sweet and having a sense of its sweetness. A man may have the former, that knows not how honey tastes; but a man cannot have the latter unless he has an idea of the taste of honey in his mind.[25]

Keller wrote that as a preacher he could sense the moment when he crossed this boundary from information to impression. He didn't mind the congregation taking notes in the first part of the sermon as they were learning information. But if they stopped taking notes and looked up at him in the end, then he knew he had touched their affections.[26] They didn't need him to explain how honey is sweet. They'd tasted it themselves.[27] Then when suffering would eventually come, when life would inevitably disappoint, they would know more than the *fact* that God loves them. They would experience that love of God as palpable.[28]

Keller found a complementary illustration in the writing of nineteenth-century theologian Archibald Alexander, the first professor of Princeton Theological Seminary.[29] Knowledge is like the inscription on a seal. We only see that raised image the way it was intended when we impress it on the wax. "Thus it is found that nothing tends more to confirm and elucidate the truths contained in the Word," Alexander said, "than an inward experience of their efficacy on the heart."[30] In other words, when knowledge about God's love travels from our head into the feeling of God's love in our hearts, that's revival.

And from the head to the heart, revival then flows outward through our hands, as Keller learned from Lovelace in his class on spiritual dynamics. True religious affections will necessarily result in loving relationships. In his sermon "Heaven Is a World of Love," Edwards argued that everyone tends to love for reciprocal benefit.[31] If we don't get what we think we deserve, we grow angry or jealous. Tim Keller wrote about the implications for husbands and wives in his book *Making Sense of God*.[32] True love is a pure flame sustained by God himself for his own sake. And from God's love, our love for each other will neither dim nor die. "Having no pride or selfishness to interrupt or hinder its exercises," Edwards said, "their hearts shall be full of love."[33]

Richard Lovelace introduced Edwards to Tim Keller at a formative time in his life, his first semester of seminary. In his second semester, he took Lovelace's class on the history of revivals. Later, when he read other classical works such as John Calvin's *Institutes of the Christian Religion*, Keller observed similarities to what he'd learned from Edwards. Keller described Calvin's work as the "greatest, deepest, and most extensive treatment of the grace of God I have ever read." What stood out to Keller was Calvin describing how heart and mind must together grasp God's love as unconditional in Jesus Christ. "Over and over again [Calvin] teaches that you are not truly converted by merely understanding doctrine, but by grasping God's love so that the inner structure and motivation of the heart are changed."[34]

Keller recognized this theme as central to Edwards's work and then emphasized the continuity from Calvin. As Keller's entryway into

Reformed theology, Edwards shaped how he perceived all subsequent theological reading. Keller found pneumodynamics wherever he looked.

By his 1975 graduation from Gordon-Conwell, most of Keller's enduring theological commitments had been settled. He subscribed to the Westminster Standards and Presbyterian-Reformed theology. He advocated for penal substitution, classic covenant theology, amillennialism, and what would later come to be known as a "complementarian" view of gender roles in the home and church. He believed in a historic, specially created Adam and Eve, in an old earth, and in the reality of biological evolution. He aligned with the neo-Calvinist approach to culture that combined evangelism and social justice. He resisted tying the church to one political agenda. He wanted the church to approach homosexuality with pastoral care without compromising the biblical sexual ethic. He prayed for the kind of revival Edwards saw in his day.

The popularity of these beliefs might wax and wane, both inside and outside the church. But Keller didn't do anything more than tweak some of these views after 1975. Gordon-Conwell helped lay the foundation for his first ministry call—and his last.

PART THREE

TRIAL BY FIRE

1975 to 1989

ELEVEN

CHEMICAL CAPITAL OF THE SOUTH

Hopewell, Virginia

At a certain point on Route 10 as you drive south into Hopewell, Virginia, you can look out over the whole city. At its peak in the 1970s, and when the Kellers moved to town in 1975 after Tim accepted his first call as a pastor, Hopewell boasted a population of just over twenty-three thousand. One day, Kathy crested this road with one of their church's oldest members and saw a panorama of smokestacks belching yellow and purple emissions. The woman said to Kathy, "Don't it just make you so proud? These chemical plants put food on the table for families across the city." Kathy wasn't so sure she should be proud. *We're all gonna die here!* she thought.[1]

At some point during the 1970s, the signs that had long boasted of Hopewell as the chemical capital of the South were removed.[2] More than a decade later, in 1988, chemical factories run by the likes of AlliedSignal and Firestone discharged 59.8 million pounds of hazardous waste into outlets such as the James River, which surrounds the city's northeast corner. The same year the Kellers moved to Hopewell, the governor of Virginia prohibited all fishing on the James River from Richmond, eighteen miles northwest of Hopewell, to the Chesapeake Bay, eighty miles downriver. The state feared the effects from the manufacture and release of an insecticide called Kepone, similar to DDT, that had been dumped into the river from 1966 until 1975.[3] The scandal broke just as Tim and Kathy arrived in town.

The Kellers, however, were just happy to have a job. Having cut ties with the Evangelical Congregational Church, they had not yet established any real connection with the Presbyterian Church in America, and the Kellers were prepared for a long wait before they would find a church to serve. They preferred to stay in New England, but having decided to seek Presbyterian ordination, openings in this beautiful and spiritually needy region were uncommon. To support themselves, they both took the US Postal carrier test and received job offers from a Massachusetts post office to begin working there in June 1975.

Yet even as they made plans to stay in Massachusetts, Keller was connecting with a PCA pastor named Kennedy Smartt through a Gordon-Conwell student friend. Smartt recruited Keller to pastor at a small church, with no guarantee beyond a commitment of three months. Smartt reassured him that it could lead to something long-term: "I'm sure when they get to know you, they'll love you and call you to be their permanent pastor." The Kellers weren't so sure. What if Tim had no job and no home in four months? With no alternative beyond their jobs at the US Postal Service, the decision was simple. They left and accepted the call.

In May 1975, the Kellers packed a U-Haul and settled in for a three-month interim pastorate at West Hopewell Presbyterian Church. Just two years earlier, the congregation had joined the fledgling PCA, which had formed in December 1973 in Birmingham,

Alabama. Not until two months into the job did the search committee even begin to consider Keller for a full-time position. Many were hesitant to consider an inexperienced minister for a church with so many problems. Their previous pastor had been forced to resign after he developed an inappropriate relationship with the choir director. Church members were not interested in more drama. They just wanted a pastor who would love them.

West Hopewell didn't boast an elaborate building, and only about ninety people attended the church when Tim first stepped behind the pulpit. There was no distinguished pastoral study for him to work from. Virtually no one older than sixty, which was most of the church in the early years, had an education beyond the eighth grade. Most of the church members had begun working full-time on their family farms or in their family businesses and had never finished high school. None of the elders had a college education. In fact, only two members of the church had even graduated from college, and they both taught elementary school. Some members were old enough that their fathers had fought in the Civil War.

Tim's Bucknell friend Bruce Henderson was shocked when he heard that Tim had accepted the call. Bruce sensed desperation—not only from the Kellers, but also from West Hopewell. After his time at the lofty academic communities of Bucknell and Gordon-Conwell, Tim wasn't exactly a natural fit for blue-collar Hopewell. He would not have impressed its church leaders as relationally adept in an interview.[4] At least on the surface, Hopewell might not have looked like much of a challenge for a White, English-speaking American minister. But Keller needed to unlearn much of his academic training to succeed at this cross-cultural experience. His InterVarsity Bible studies flopped because many of the members didn't feel comfortable reading aloud. One woman simply got up and left and never returned. It didn't take long for Keller to realize he needed to adjust his preaching—to become more concrete, clear, and practical. Hopewell became his first foray into contextualization. He realized he needed to listen and learn before he spoke, so that he could persuade.[5]

Despite the cross-cultural challenges, Hopewell would always evoke affection from the Kellers as they remembered their time there. In Hopewell, Kathy gave birth to all three of their children, all boys. And Tim learned how to be a pastor.

Decades Ahead

For Keller, a curious student of his ministry context, Hopewell offered plenty of historical fodder. As a Yankee educated in Pennsylvania and Massachusetts, in Hopewell Keller learned firsthand about the predominantly Southern culture of his new PCA denomination.

The James River settlement of City Point, later absorbed into the city of Hopewell, dates back to 1613, just six years after Jamestown was settled nearly forty miles east. From Richmond, the James River flows about twenty miles south to City Point before turning east toward Norfolk and the Chesapeake Bay. This position on the water, along with railroad access for resupply, made City Point a strategic position for General Ulysses S. Grant to establish his headquarters during the siege of Petersburg between 1864 and 1865. President Abraham Lincoln arrived at City Point on March 24, 1865, to visit the troops and plan the end of the Civil War.

But Hopewell, which incorporated as a city in 1914, would be even more closely associated with later wars. DuPont saw in Hopewell's ports and railroads the same advantages that Grant identified decades earlier. The company chose Hopewell as the site of a factory to manufacture dynamite, which would be in high demand as World War I raged on multiple fronts across Europe. As the plant switched over to guncotton, a substitute for gunpowder, the town's population exploded with growth—the plant alone employed forty thousand people. A nearby Army camp—named not for the victorious Grant but for his Confederate adversary and Virginia native Robert E. Lee—trained sixty thousand soldiers. The end of World War I ended the plant. But Camp Lee returned in October 1940 for World War II and trained at least fifty thousand quartermaster officers and more than three hundred thousand quartermaster soldiers for the Army.[6]

Only eight years before the Kellers moved to Hopewell, the US Supreme Court overturned Virginia's ban on interracial marriage in the 1967 *Loving v. Virginia* decision. The plaintiff, Mildred Loving, grew up about sixty miles north of Hopewell. From her home to Hopewell you can follow Grant's march toward Richmond, which featured much of the Civil War's most ferocious fighting and finally ended the war in 1864 and 1865.

Coming from the eclectic theological environments of InterVarsity and Gordon-Conwell, Keller marveled at his little church's theological unity around the Westminster Confession of Faith. Though they were all new to the PCA denomination, most of the church members had been Presbyterian far longer than he had. That unity, however, didn't extend to their views on racism. Keller didn't anticipate some of the racist attitudes he encountered in Hopewell. But he believed that by preaching the whole counsel of God, verse by verse, he could address any lingering racist attitudes in the congregation.[7]

Given the circumstances, West Hopewell was not nearly as difficult as it might have been for a pastor from eastern Pennsylvania. Pastors who had gone before him paved the way by directly confronting racism and problematic versions of nationalism. West Hopewell Presbyterian Church had been planted by West End Presbyterian Church, one of the original congregations of the PCA, located just a mile north in Hopewell. William E. Hill Jr. began serving as the pastor of West End, originally known as Dupont Chapel, in 1929. He stepped down in 1958 but remained a key figure in the PCA through the 1970s until his death at more than one hundred years old in 1983.

Hill gained a reputation for tackling head-on many of the challenges common in that era to churches in the American South, especially in smaller towns. Even in an era where nearly an entire generation had served in World War II or fought in Korea, Hill didn't allow "God and Country" services on Memorial Day or the Fourth of July. No one would pledge allegiance to the flag of the United States of America while worshiping at West End. In fact, Hill didn't allow any display of the flag at the church. He went so far as to use his five-foot frame to physically block a flag-draped casket from entering the church during a funeral. Area newspapers in Petersburg and Richmond portrayed Hill as an unpatriotic Communist. As many as three hundred members left the church in protest. The church paid a steep price for his stand.

Even more surprising, Hill required the Christian school started by West End in the 1940s to integrate racially. By contrast, Farmville, less than seventy miles west of Hopewell in Prince Edward County, Virginia, closed its public schools for five years, starting in 1959, rather than integrate. Through the 1970s, church schools across the South would still be launched as "segregation academies." Hill was decades ahead of many problems that continue to unsettle churches today.

Keller began to see some change in racist attitudes even before he preached explicitly about the sin of racism. One of the members at West Hopewell, a well-respected and decent man, saw his faith as nothing but a moral obligation. When this man began to grasp the notion of grace as a free gift from God, he changed in palpable ways. He radiated a new happiness and confidence. But that wasn't all.

"You know," he told Keller, "I've been a racist all my life."

The comment caught Keller off guard. Tim hadn't yet taught or preached about racism. He hadn't made it a point of application for church members. But the man had connected the dots for himself. Grace meant he couldn't look down on anyone else. Grace meant he wasn't justified by anything he had done or by any racial identity he had inherited.[8]

Throughout his nine years in Hopewell, Keller followed Hill's lead and explicitly taught against the sin of racism. Laurie Howell remembers him preaching that there are only two races—the people of God and everyone outside the kingdom of God. That's the only interracial marriage banned by Scripture, he argued.

"That was pretty radical stuff in Hopewell in the 1970s and '80s," Howell said, "but he did not step down from that."[9]

PCA Takes Flight

William Hill continued to shape Tim Keller's ministry as he visited PCA churches in Hopewell to monitor their pulpits. He'd drive by West Hopewell, see Keller's car in the parking lot, and then call the church to offer unsolicited advice.

"I was amazed at how gently Tim interacted with this old man and respected him and revered him for the role he played in those early years of the PCA, even though he was nitpicking him to death," Howell said. "He is without a doubt the most patient man I've known."[10]

Even though Keller had committed to Reformed theology in seminary, he had never studied the Westminster Confessions and Catechisms until he sought ordination in the PCA. Teaching the standards in elder and deacon training gave him a deeper appreciation for the Presbyterian tradition. He began to see the difference between churches whose theologies were based on historic confessions compared to churches with a "statement of faith." He appreciated how their confession linked Presbyterians to the past. And he saw the confessions as not only medicine to protect against disqualified leaders but as food that nourishes the entire congregation.[11]

Before Hopewell, Keller had never even visited a PCA church. He had a lot to learn about his presbytery and the General Assembly of the PCA. But he was far from alone in learning what it meant to be in this brand-new denomination. Keller found help discerning his place in the PCA with the help of an outsider. In 1974, Nick Wolterstorff wrote of three subtraditions within his own denomination, the Christian Reformed Church. He called them doctrinalist, pietist, and Kuyperian.[12] George Marsden later applied this rubric to all Reformed churches in the United States.[13]

In his time with InterVarsity at Bucknell, Keller had learned the pietist tradition. At Gordon-Conwell, he had added the Kuyperian tradition of neo-Calvinism. But it wasn't until his contact with other PCA ministers and churches that he began to experience the doctrinalist element, which emphasizes the confessions for catechizing believers, guarding against theological deviation, and promoting continuity with historic Reformed churches.

At this point, Keller didn't yet know these three terms. But he began to see some tensions in the PCA even as he learned from Christians more exclusively committed to the doctrinalist view.

Thanks to William Hill's ongoing presence in Hopewell, Keller learned the exacting standards of a PCA statesman. But he was more personally influenced by one of Hill's successors at West End, Kennedy Smartt, the pastor who first invited Keller to fill the West Hopewell pulpit for three months. And it was Smartt who modeled for Keller the rhythms of pastoral ministry, especially in a smaller town. When they bumped into each other visiting church members in the hospital, Keller observed how Smartt engaged with the staff and patients. He knew the name of every person walking in and out of the hospital. He knew enough to ask specifics about their family members. And when he finished talking and praying with a member of his church, he'd move from room to room, checking in on other patients and offering to pray for them too.[14]

During his West Hopewell tenure, Keller picked up the Puritan paperback edition of *The Reformed Pastor* by Richard Baxter, in which he commends visiting every family in the church at least once each year.

But Keller had already seen this kind of pervasive pastoral care modeled by Smartt. Keller made it his own habit to pray through the church's membership list systematically. Through role models in books and other pastors in Hopewell, Keller learned what it meant to be a pastor and not just a preacher.

These personal demands of ministry in Hopewell took a toll on Keller, just as they would later during his ministry in New York. Even with fewer than one hundred members at West Hopewell, Keller worked sixty to seventy hours a week, all while having small children at home.[15] While many seminary graduates today look for a large church where they can continue to learn on the job, Keller had to do everything from the start of his time there—guide his session of elders, preach Sunday morning and evening, lead the Wednesday prayer meeting with another sermon, teach Sunday school, plan the youth group, deliver talks on men's and women's retreats, visit the sick, look in on members in their homes, conduct every wedding and funeral, and counsel couples in struggling marriages—sometimes as many as three or four couples at a time during especially busy seasons.[16]

Keller was invited to every high school graduation, and in those days the pastor was also expected to attend every girl's Sweet Sixteen party. Every family considered the pastor one of their own. When they invited him to the family picnic, he made sure to grab a helping of potato salad.[17] He got the 3:00 a.m. call about another suicide and then followed up with counseling for the family. When husbands left their family, he tracked them down and tried to convince them to go home and get help. He searched for runaway children. When parents died, he was the one to notify the children. After a man was electrocuted while working underneath his house, Keller and the widow verified the identity of the body in the morgue.

Nothing else, either before or after his time in Hopewell, taxed Keller in quite the same way as these days of pastoring and caring for people. Hopewell in the 1970s was a time and place where pastors provided the bulk of counseling for the community. In fact, there were no professional counselors working in Hopewell during these years. Keller searched for resources that would equip him to help Christians with depression, phobias, addictions and alcoholism, relational problems, sexual addictions, homosexuality, and more. He began to see how Christians disagreed with each other on the best biblical and psychological approaches to these problems. Nevertheless, he also saw encouraging evidence of change in the Christians he counseled—at the cost of nearly burning out in ministry. Hopewell taught him that pastors shouldn't do this much counseling. They need the help of professional Christian counselors for referrals.[18]

Looking back, Keller saw this time as a trial by fire—ministry in a small town that would prepare him for church planting in the nation's biggest city. Both contexts demanded generalist skills rather than specialization. And they both required a pastor to minister to people unlike him, people who weren't likely to be his friends if they weren't connected through the church. The people at West Hopewell didn't share Tim's Anglophile affinities for J. R. R. Tolkien and C. S. Lewis. And he couldn't relate to their blue-collar jobs working at the chemical plants. There was no special relational chemistry or shared affinity. They didn't need Keller to build their community, because they already loved spending time together. They needed their pastor to show he cared for them by showing up.

For his part, Tim made efforts to connect. He learned the game of football so he could better relate to the men in Hopewell. Back in Allentown, Keller didn't play many sports. And despite his time as the marching band drum major in high school and college, he hadn't picked up the nuances of football. Since Kathy had grown up near Pittsburgh, Tim adopted the Steelers, who were also the passionate fixation of R. C. Sproul. Keller picked the right time to follow the Steelers, as they won the Super Bowl in 1975, 1976, 1978, and 1979. He enjoyed gloating with the mostly Washington fans in Virginia. He even managed to shock the congregation when he untied his tie, took off his jacket, and unbuttoned his shirt in the midst of a service to reveal a Steelers T-shirt underneath. The drum major learned some new tricks as a pastor.

"That was not Tim Keller when he arrived," Laurie Howell said, "and it ceased to be Tim Keller when he left West Hopewell."[19]

If Gordon-Conwell had given Tim some lifelong friends, Hopewell taught him how to shepherd all the sheep God had entrusted to him.

Most Formative Ministry Years

The ministry years at Hopewell did yield some lifelong friends for Tim and Kathy, however. Graham Howell had grown up at West Hopewell and married young, as many others did at that time and place. And like many young couples, their marriage quickly ran into trouble. Only seven months into their marriage, Howell didn't know where to turn for help, but he hoped the church might have some answers.

He didn't know Keller when he dropped in on the church. And Keller wasn't the kind of pastor he expected. Keller did more than pray and send Howell on his way; instead he asked penetrating questions and drew diagrams to illustrate biblical points. Keller scheduled follow-up meetings and assigned homework from the Christian Counseling and Education Foundation, founded in 1968.

Howell, who was twenty-two at the time, professed new faith in Christ. He later wrote about his experience with Tim and Kathy's personal ministry:

> The pastor ended up staying at this little church for nine years, honing his preaching skills and walking with people through the ups and downs of their lives. I leaned heavily on him for counsel and asked all sorts of questions about life and faith. I was a baby Christian growing in my faith through prayer and Scripture, but what really

authenticated the faith was the way [Tim] and his wife pursued and
loved me. One expects to have family support in hard times, but this
level of care from people who had only recently been strangers was
incomprehensible to me. *Why would someone do that*, I thought? I
recall one night coming out of a bar after a particularly hard day, feeling accused and alone, to find a handwritten note from them on my
car telling me to come over when I could. They prayed for me, taught
me, shared meals with me, even took me on vacation with them when
the inevitable divorce became final. I will never forget how they
poured into my life. It is a debt I will never repay.[20]

The Kellers encouraged Howell to attend college. They let him live
with them while he attended Virginia Commonwealth University and
before he married Laurie, the girl next door. On vacations, they browsed
used bookstores together for hours. Howell ran occasional errands for
Tim. When Howell returned books for Tim at Union Theological
Seminary (now Union Presbyterian Seminary) in Richmond, he sometimes found that the old theology books Tim preferred hadn't been
checked out in more than a hundred years.[21]

Keller recalled his time in Hopewell as the most formative ministry
years of his life.[22] For Keller, Hopewell ingrained the dynamic exchange
between pastoral care and teaching. Of course, not everyone responded
the way Graham Howell did. Most members of West Hopewell didn't
take up Tim's book recommendations. He couldn't lead them the same
way he would in a college town or large city. Hopewell was Tim's first
experience outside what he called the "doctrine-driven model." Since
his conversion at Bucknell, he had never joined or served in a church
not populated by professors and students. He didn't know any approach
except to deliver biblical expositions, teach topical classes, and lead
intense small group Bible studies. Keller admitted his frustration as he
slowly realized this strategy wouldn't bring renewal to West Hopewell,
which never grew beyond 150 in attendance over the thirty years before

he arrived. So Keller learned to summarize the insights he gleaned from reading into his own teaching three times a week—Sunday morning, Sunday evening, and Wednesday evening.

In those nine years, he gained invaluable preaching reps with more than 1,500 sermons. In 2015, Keller wrote in the acknowledgments of his book *Preaching*, "I first want to thank the members of West Hopewell Presbyterian Church . . . [who] provided me with a loving, supportive community in which my very weak early efforts were received with appreciation."[23] For at least the first hundred sermons, no preacher can be any good, Keller concluded from his experience in Hopewell. Given the small, relational setting of that church, he found he could refine his teaching for next time in response to any confusion about his message.

Tim asked questions to see if the preaching addressed real problems, and he learned to listen longer than his instincts suggested. Keller found that preaching fails to connect when it's not answering questions. Pastors either become distant and abstract in their teaching, or they work out their own problems in the pulpit. Private counseling gave him perspective on how church members were changing, or not. "This combination of practice with feedback and loving support made me a far better preacher than I could have ever been had I gone to another place where I was not worked as hard or loved as well."[24]

No doubt it helped that he stayed at the church for nine years, long enough for the church to begin shifting to take on his teaching and evangelism strengths and for Tim to overcome his initial stubbornness and accept the church for its own strengths of practical service. Keller didn't learn everything he'd later write for the PCA on diaconate ministry from purely biblical and historical study. He saw it lived out in the members of West Hopewell Presbyterian Church.

At Hopewell, Keller saw the "word ministry" of preaching and teaching converge with the "deed ministry" of serving the poor. In fact, Keller enrolled in the Doctor of Ministry (DMin) program through

Westminster Theological Seminary in 1979 while serving as the senior pastor at Hopewell. It was a dream come true for Keller to get back on a campus and learn from so many renowned teachers, including Jack Miller on evangelism, Harvie Conn on missions, and Ed Clowney on preaching.

When Tim began at Westminster, he had no idea what his major project would be. George Fuller told him, "Work on deacons—no one knows how important that office is anymore." Keller investigated how the role of deacons had shifted in Presbyterian life away from serving the poor and needy into tasks like keeping books and managing facilities. At a local university, he researched contemporary secular textbooks on social work and also studied how churches in the Reformed epicenters of Geneva, Amsterdam, Edinburgh, and Glasgow had developed the first structures for public social service through their diaconates. He was compelled to study more of the Bible's teaching on the poor and models for ministry among them. Clowney shared in this journey with Keller toward the importance of doing justice and mercy for the marginalized.[25]

Keller first implemented some of his diaconate training at West Hopewell.[26] But the full program, reflected in his book *Ministries of Mercy*, would wait until his time at Redeemer in New York City to be fully implemented. Keller's DMin studies also set him up for the two jobs that pulled him away from Hopewell in 1984—as an adjunct professor of practical theology at Westminster and as director of mercy ministry for the Mission to North America Committee of the PCA.

Growing Up Together

When Tim had been ordained for twenty-five years in the PCA, and Redeemer was flourishing in New York, he and Kathy returned to Hopewell for a reception planned by their friend Laurie Howell. Church members were invited to recall what they appreciated about Keller's ministry. Not a single person mentioned anything he had preached. No one quoted a sermon. But several members recalled something he said to them privately in counseling and visitation.

"To the degree that people knew he cared, to that degree and that degree only, were they interested in what he had to say from the pulpit," Laurie Howell said.[27]

Keller recalled this experience to explain a key difference in ministry contexts. Some contexts, such as Hopewell, demand pastoring that sets up preaching. Others, such as New York City, expect preaching that establishes credibility for counseling and congregational leadership.[28]

Many have concluded that in Hopewell, Keller learned to "put the cookies on the bottom shelf." Indeed, it would be neat and tidy to say that Hopewell's blue-collar congregation forced Keller to develop his skill for distilling difficult and complicated concepts in ways that Christians and non-Christians alike can understand.[29] If he would have jumped straight from seminary to a highly educated congregation, he might never have become a widely popular writer or preacher. He might never have produced the material that challenges motivated students and still edifies the rest.

But the picture looks somewhat different in chronology than from retrospect. Keller needed to learn the basics of pastoral ministry somewhere, and Hopewell happened to be that place. When he graduated from seminary, he didn't know how to do weddings and funerals or what to say on retreats and in nursing homes and Christian school chapels. He didn't see himself as a ministry genius or as God's gift to this small Southern town. He was simply a young pastor, a young husband, and a young father, not entirely secure in any of these new roles. The Kellers grew up together in Hopewell.

Even as she gave birth to three boys, Kathy was involved in various leadership roles in the church. Naturally, Kathy led the youth group, which Laurie McCollum (later Howell) joined at age fifteen. "She was an in-your-face gal, and I had not had that kind of Sunday school teacher or youth leader," Laurie Howell recalled of Kathy.[30] The Kellers borrowed the gabfest concept from Ligonier Valley Study Center and hosted these gatherings in their home on Sunday night after the evening service at West Hopewell. They encouraged young people to bring snacks and friends from inside and outside the church and ask Tim any question. And in case they didn't know what to ask, Tim wrote up and distributed dozens of possible questions.

Gabfests could run for up to three and a half hours on a day when Keller had already led and preached two distinct services. Just his answer to the opening question could sometimes run for an hour. Gabfests gave Keller a chance to develop his theological thinking and apologetic acumen. Kathy often joined in during Tim's answer, as she would later do in the post-service Q and A sessions at Redeemer.

The questions were not only academic but also practical. And often deeply personal. Laurie Howell remembers asking how she could be happy in heaven when people she loved would be in hell. She doesn't recall the exact answer, but she remembers Tim following her afterward into the dining room to talk personally.

Tim would have kept the gabfests going longer into the night if not for Kathy's insistence. Everyone knew that the evening's gabfest was done when Kathy got up and went to their bedroom and put on her nightgown. When she returned, she would announce to everyone, "This is a hint. Go home!"[31]

Raising three young boys didn't come naturally to either Tim or Kathy. Tim's heavy teaching load, along with his visitation and counseling duties, wasn't easy on the family, which added David (1978), Michael (1980), and Jonathan (1983) in Hopewell. Marriage wasn't nearly as big a change for Tim and Kathy as parenthood. Responsibility for his sons kept Tim from some of his worst tendencies toward workaholism. As a father, Tim began to see more of his selfishness and desire to control his own life. Parenthood demanded self-sacrifice and self-control.[32] Time for hobbies such as playing the trumpet grew scarce for Tim. Down the street from the church, a video arcade featured Tim's favorite game, *Space Invaders*, which debuted in 1978. Kathy didn't necessarily appreciate it when he stopped to play after work. It was a little more acceptable when they took rolls of quarters to the arcade for Graham Howell's bachelor party.[33]

Along with time, money constrained the young Keller family. At the beginning of his tenure, Keller earned eight thousand dollars a year, in addition to free housing. By his final year, when church attendance had grown from less than one hundred to about three hundred, he made twelve thousand dollars annually, which would be equivalent to about thirty thousand dollars today. The church budget didn't include a book allowance. So he asked Kathy and other family and friends to buy him books as Christmas gifts. He would read those ten to twenty books all year long.

Working from the recommendations of Richard Lovelace, he feasted on Banner of Truth titles, mostly by authors such as Thomas Brooks, John Owen, and Charles Spurgeon. Keller incorporated elements of Spurgeon's appeals to the heart. In his later books, Tim still referred to the works he read while in Hopewell. After his diagnosis with pancreatic cancer decades later, Keller told John Piper that John Owen's work had been especially encouraging as he looked forward to heaven.[34] Owen's own suffering helped illustrate how God can use suffering to kill off our sin.[35]

No Puritan influenced Keller more than John Owen. But Owen was far from the only Puritan to inform his thinking. Keller trained pastoral interns in Hopewell by reading together through *The Bruised Reed* by Richard Sibbes. One intern, John Hanford, remembers seeing Keller drive around Hopewell with a Puritan paperback from Banner of Truth resting on his steering wheel. He read extensively from Sibbes, John Flavel, and Stephen Charnock. These works equipped him for pastoral counseling more than for preaching. Their Augustinian "heart" psychology steered him away from that era's fashionable psychology with its focus on the therapeutic self. In *Precious Remedies against Satan's Devices* by Thomas Brooks, Keller learned to use Scripture and the gospel to treat Christians struggling with accusation, temptation, and spiritual dryness and apathy.

During the Hopewell years, Keller also came across seventy sermons of the First Great Awakening evangelist George Whitefield, and that brilliant orator began to shape Keller's own preaching, and especially his evangelism. "During a three-year period, Whitefield passed into me," Keller recalled. "It brought me a new boldness. I was amazed by how undaunted he was."[36] If not for Whitefield, Keller never would have embraced the challenge of planting a church in New York. All of Keller's theoretical study of ministry found historical shape in the example of Whitefield's world-changing evangelism—his creativity, his innovation, and his seemingly tireless drive. Keller sensed thunder and lightning with the very presence of God as he read both volumes of Arnold Dallimore's biography of Whitefield in 1979 and 1980, as well as the more critical scholarly work of the historian Harry Stout.[37]

But Whitefield didn't easily translate to the 1970s, not least because later revelations showed Keller how Whitefield had promoted slavery. With this Puritan immersion in Hopewell, Keller risked turning himself into a mouthpiece from the seventeenth or eighteenth century. He resisted that assimilation for two reasons. Other than Sibbes and Owen, many of the Puritans struck Keller as heavy on guilt and light on the freedom enjoyed by justified sinners. And because Keller had already committed to the modern while orthodox outlook of neo-Calvinism, some Puritans came across to Keller as pedantic and antiquated. He found a more contemporary model for ministry in Martyn Lloyd-Jones, a twentieth-century preacher who likewise leaned on the Puritans. Keller wouldn't be tempted to parrot Lloyd-Jones, because their personalities were so obviously different. But the fiery Welshman helped Keller understand that he didn't need to choose between closely reading the text and inviting Christians and non-Christians alike to enter into the presence of the Lord. Lloyd-Jones seemed to Keller like a modern version of George Whitefield and Jonathan Edwards in combining an uncompromising Reformed theology with calls to deep spiritual experience. Like Lloyd-Jones, Keller didn't just want to tell people how to change their lives. He wanted the Holy Spirit to change them on the spot, in the moment.

Keller passed along this newfound boldness to West Hopewell through the Evangelism Explosion program first developed by D. James Kennedy at Coral Ridge Presbyterian Church in Fort Lauderdale, Florida. The program trained teams of Christians to share the gospel as they visited neighbors. Not many in Hopewell could have been considered "secular" in 1980, and Evangelism Explosion contributed to between twenty and thirty professions of faith each year. About half of these converts joined the church. Back then, it was no hindrance that Evangelism Explosion assumed belief in God, the afterlife, sin, and the authoritative Scriptures—no apologetics necessary. Ted Powers joined the West Hopewell staff and brought his personal gift for evangelism as the church grew from the original attendance of 90 to 100 in 1975 to between 250 and 300 by the time Keller left.

That growth didn't satisfy Keller, however. He longed for the spiritual power and surge of conversions he had witnessed at Bucknell and read about with Richard Lovelace in studying the history of revivals. When Keller connected with Jack Miller's New Life Presbyterian Church outside Philadelphia, Miller's church sent a team to help stimulate a spiritual awakening at West Hopewell. But revival never came.

Pac-Man

If you only knew Tim Keller as a famous New York pastor and author, you'd still recognize him at West Hopewell for his professorial style, for his tendency to cogitate over an answer to your question by gazing off into the upper corner of the room. His mannerisms and demeanor didn't change between small town and big city contexts. And you'd also recognize his refusal to settle for the spiritual and evangelistic status quo in a church. His ambition resulted in some surprising outcomes.

In his final year at West Hopewell, Keller's sermons began to circulate among various pastors in the denomination. And though he might not have been particularly well-known during his days at Gordon-Conwell, students from his alma mater started to notice his ministry down in Virginia. One such student was John Hanford, whose best friend at Gordon-Conwell had served with Keller's friend David Midwood. When Hanford, elected as Gordon-Conwell's student body president, looked for additional training after graduation, Midwood sent him to Hopewell to learn under Keller. During his one-year internship, Hanford lived with the Kellers while Kathy was pregnant with their third and final son, Jonathan. Kathy didn't appreciate Hanford roughhousing with the older two boys so close to their bedtime and making it harder for them to fall asleep.

Hanford caught a rare glimpse of life inside the hectic Keller manse. During these years, *Pac-Man* became a global sensation, and Keller enjoyed playing on the home television. On Sunday afternoons, he sometimes watched football, at least with one eye, with the other eye on three commentaries sprawled out in front of him for study. With three messages to prepare each week, Keller couldn't afford not to multitask.

Hanford's calling changed during his year in Hopewell. Keller was the first person in whom he confided about a growing burden to help churches around the world as they endured persecution.[38] Keller encouraged him to pursue this new calling, in part because Hanford's connections in Washington made him especially well-suited for the task. Hanford's aunt Elizabeth was married to the United States senator Bob Dole, who had been President Gerald Ford's running mate in 1976.

Hanford went on to lead the team that wrote the International

Religious Freedom Act, signed by President Clinton into law in 1998. Under President George W. Bush, Hanford served as the second US ambassador for international religious freedom, a position he held between 2002 and 2009.

Hopewell put John Hanford on a trajectory that would change American foreign policy, not to mention the lives of countless Christians persecuted for the faith.[39] And Hopewell likewise prepared Tim Keller for many challenges ahead—as a husband, father, and pastor. When Keller was about to leave Hopewell, a friend asked Tim if he could photocopy all of his sermons and talks. Only thirty-four years old at the time, Keller had already preached more than 1,500 sermons, covering about three-fourths of the Bible. He had preached as much in nine years as many pastors do in a lifetime. When Keller needed inspiration, he could still pull off the shelf a sermon from Charles Simeon, Alexander MacLaren, or Charles Spurgeon. When he prepared his Sunday evening sermon between two and four on Sunday afternoon, he could lean on Martyn Lloyd-Jones's detailed expositions of Romans and Ephesians.

By the time the Keller family of five was packing up to leave Hopewell, Tim could preach on most passages of the Bible without relying on outside help. He had survived the trial by fire in the chemical capital of the South. He was ready to begin his lifelong work of training the next generation of pastors.

TWELVE

UNFOLDING DRAMA

Edmund P. Clowney

Tim Keller may have received a C in his preaching class at Gordon-Conwell. But what pried him away from Hopewell and brought him to Philadelphia was the invitation to replace his only personal mentor as a preaching professor.

Other than his wife, Kathy, Ed Clowney is the only close personal influence who knew Tim Keller from his awkward Bucknell years in Lewisburg through the Redeemer megachurch years in New York. By the end of Clowney's life, he and Keller were teaching together. That partnership began with a simple trip to visit a seminary friend.

After their first year studying at Gordon-Conwell in 1973, Tim Keller and Kathy Kristy headed to the Pennsylvania Poconos to attend the Pinebrook Bible Conference. Their trip coincided with a visit from Edmund Clowney, who had driven up from Philadelphia, where he was serving as president of Westminster Theological Seminary. Tim had been acquainted with Clowney from college when Clowney led the

Camus outreach at Bucknell and subsequent InterVarsity retreat on the church. That same spring, Tim and Kathy had also heard Clowney lecture at Gordon-Conwell on preaching Christ from all of Scripture.

But they were not prepared for how this trip would change their lives. Tim returned home having just met one of his "fathers in the faith."[1]

Since Tim wasn't Reformed during his time at Bucknell, he didn't consider attending Westminster. Clowney himself had encouraged Tim to think about Gordon-Conwell as an alternative. And since he had spurned attending Clowney's school, Keller felt a bit awkward approaching Clowney at Pinebrook. But Clowney invited Keller to take a walk with him as they sipped sodas and talked about life and ministry and the future. Keller was deeply touched by the gesture.[2] He was also shocked out of his wits.[3]

From that moment, Clowney became the only mentor to go out of his way to help Keller through transitions in his life and ministry. Much of what the world knows best about Keller—especially how he preaches Christ from the Old Testament and his interpretation of the two sons in Luke 15—he first learned from Clowney.

Preaching Fathers

Clowney was born in the middle of the First World War on July 30, 1917. An only child, Clowney grew up in Philadelphia, where his father built cabinets. He studied at Wheaton College for his first bachelor's degree, then earned his second from Westminster in the middle of the Second World War in 1942. That same year he was ordained in the Orthodox Presbyterian Church, founded in 1936 by J. Gresham Machen after fundamentalists lost the battle for orthodoxy in the northern Presbyterian Church. As Clowney served a church in Connecticut, he earned his Master of Sacred Theology degree from Yale Divinity School, where he studied Søren Kierkegaard. He went on to lead churches in New Jersey and Illinois and received his honorary Doctor of Divinity back at Wheaton College in 1966 as the Vietnam War continued to escalate.

Clowney had been teaching practical theology at Westminster as far back as 1952. Then in 1966, Westminster elected him as their first president, a new position dictated by the seminary's desire to be accredited by the Association of Theological Schools.[4] Clowney held that role until his retirement in 1984, when Westminster hired a young pastor out of Hopewell, Virginia, to take over the classes he had been teaching on pastoral leadership and preaching.

Though much of what became known as Christ-centered preaching would be attributed to Clowney, he drew on the legacy of Reformed covenant theology and the work of Geerhardus Vos in particular as he found connections in God's redemptive work across the Old and New Testaments.[5] Vos had been installed in 1892 as the first professor of biblical theology at Princeton Theological Seminary. He declined to join Machen in forming Westminster and retired in 1932. Two years later, Vos published the landmark *Biblical Theology: Old and New Testaments*, and Clowney applied Vos's insights for the students and pastors he taught at Westminster.

Clowney called it the "unfolding drama" or mystery, the story line of the entire Bible. Christians can grow up learning lots of isolated Bible stories but never actually know the story of the Bible and how it all fits together.[6] We think Samson is a kind of comic book Superman. We think David is a brave little boy and example for how we can defeat the giants of our life. Yet when these stories are isolated from their place in the "unfolding drama" of redemption, we miss the character of a God who delivers his people when they cry out to him in repentance and faith.[7]

According to theologian J. I. Packer, Edmund Clowney helped rescue Old Testament preaching about Christ. If an earlier generation took liberties with the text and injected Christ where he should not be

found in the Old Testament, a subsequent generation didn't go looking for him at all.[8] Clowney wasn't alone in this rescue. Another key
influence on Keller in the study of biblical theology was Alec Motyer,
whom Keller heard in the summer between Bucknell and Gordon-
Conwell when R. C. Sproul hosted Motyer for his weekly gabfest at
Ligonier Valley Study Center. At that time, still young in his faith,
Keller didn't know what to make of the Old Testament. He knew he
didn't enjoy reading it.

At the gabfest meeting, Sproul asked Motyer a question about Old
Testament Israel and the church. Key to biblical theology is identifying
continuity and discontinuity between the Old and New Testaments.
Motyer drew out the continuity between the people of God in their
testimony of salvation, before and after Jesus. Speaking in his Irish
accent, Motyer offered what a sample Hebrew testimony might have
included and challenged the audience to draw any contrast with their
own Christian testimony.

> We were in a foreign land, in bondage, under the sentence of death.
> But our mediator—the one who stands between us and God—came
> to us with the promise of deliverance. We trusted in the promises of
> God, took shelter under the blood of the Lamb, and he led us out.
> Now we are on the way to the Promised Land. We are not there yet,
> of course, but we have the law to guide us, and through blood sacri-
> fice we also have his presence in our midst. So he will stay with us
> until we get to our true country, our everlasting home.[9]

Keller couldn't believe what he was hearing. He had always thought
Old Testament believers were saved from their sin by obeying the law,
as opposed to the New Testament's invitation to faith. He wrote, "This
little thought experiment showed me, in a stroke, not only that the
Israelites had been saved by grace and that God's salvation had been
by costly atonement and grace all along, but also that the pursuit of

holiness, pilgrimage, obedience, and deep community should characterize Christians as well."

Keller credits Motyer, along with Clowney, for these and many
other insights, calling them "the fathers of my preaching ministry."[10]

If Motyer's insight struck Keller like a lightning bolt that summer,
then Clowney's lectures would hit Keller like a thunderstorm that following spring.

Fan Club

The history of Westminster sheds some important light on why
Gordon-Conwell invited Edmund Clowney to deliver the prestigious
Staley lectures in 1973.

Like Fuller Theological Seminary in California, Gordon-Conwell
sought to train students in an interdenominational and evangelical
setting. Many graduates went on to serve mainline Protestant congregations. Charles Fuller's original vision in 1947 had been to reclaim the
mainline lost in the 1930s, the era when J. Gresham Machen started
Westminster. But before long, Fuller began to drift into some of the
same mainline views on biblical authority that had thwarted Machen
before he launched the Orthodox Presbyterian Church. Gordon-
Conwell likewise trained mainline students, such as Kathy Kristy.
When Tim Keller objected to his New Testament professors' deficient
hermeneutics, it was because Gordon-Conwell was facing some of the
same controversies as Fuller faced.

For some, Gordon-Conwell represented several of the exact
problems Machen had founded Westminster to prevent. Many Westminster faculty members preferred the school to be small—only sixty
or so students when Clowney arrived—training the future leaders of
the Orthodox Presbyterian Church. But Clowney had a bigger vision.
He saw Westminster as the successor to Princeton's glory days of the

nineteenth century, when students across denominations were attracted by the best proponents of Reformed orthodoxy. He set out to grow Westminster, and the Jesus Movement obliged. Enrollment quickly increased to between three and four hundred early in Clowney's tenure and to about six hundred by the end.[11] No doubt it helped that Clowney spoke in front of fifteen thousand young Christians at Urbana in 1973, the same year he lectured at Gordon-Conwell on preaching Christ in all of Scripture.

The lectures made a strong impression on first-year students Tim Keller and Kathy Kristy. It wasn't his dynamic delivery that they admired, however. When they heard him pull together the threads of biblical theology, they didn't know whether to shout hallelujah or weep.[12] These lectures contributed at least three or four major building blocks in Keller's emerging ministry philosophy. Millions of Christians have read and listened to Keller show how Christ-centered preaching changes the heart, as opposed to moralistic preaching that merely confronts the will. But not many know that he learned these differences from Clowney, beginning with that week in 1973.[13]

Until 2021 the Clowney lectures sat untouched in the Gordon-Conwell archives on reel-to-reel tapes. But as part of the writing of this book, Gordon-Conwell digitized them, and the Kellers heard them again for the first time since they were twenty-two years old. Many have listened to Clowney's class on preaching, the one he and Keller led for Doctor of Ministry students at Reformed Theological Seminary in the 1990s. But in the Staley lectures, he sounds more vibrant and youthful, and almost suspiciously like Don Knotts, except with an uncommon unction.

God's Oath

Clowney observed that when we look for moral heroes in the Old Testament, even the positive examples disturb us. What are we supposed to learn from Samson's suicide? Should we pray imprecatory psalms? Do we imitate Joshua's conquest of Jericho?[14] That's the problem with moralizing the Old Testament. When you look to the great heroes of faith, it seems impossible for anyone to please God. And as the Old Testament progresses, God's promises appear to be more and more impossible to fulfill. Just consider the son of the promise to Abraham. Months and years separated promise from fulfillment. But God kept his word.

"He kept it when it was ridiculously impossible!" Clowney exclaimed. Keller eventually connected this biblical theology with J. R. R. Tolkien's description of the gospel story as *eucatastrophe*. "It's that stretch, it's that tension, it's that utter incompatibility between the promise of God and the realities between how men see them that has *always* been the stretching space of faith. This *is* the span of faith—to live between the time of the giving of the promise and the completion of the promise when the promise looks utterly impossible."

God worked the same way in Judah's exile. From a pile of dry bones God's Spirit raised a mighty army. The whole structure of the history of salvation, Clowney told his students, is God working the impossible. He is the God who tells the virgin she will bear his only Son. Camus has nothing on the true absurdity of God, who keeps his promises by coming himself to save his people.

Clowney's lectures combined biblical, historical, systematic, and practical theology without clear delineation. Full of biblical and theological detail, they simmered until he approached the fulfillment of Christ, when they began to sizzle in volume and intensity.

Clowney's lecture on God's self-maledictory oath began with the story of Isaac, the chosen and beloved son of the promise. God demanded that Abraham offer his son as a sacrifice in Genesis 22. When Abraham obeyed in faith, God showed grace by providing a ram caught in the thicket as an acceptable substitute.

Clowney then returned to another passage on sacrifice, Genesis

15, to illustrate the escalation of God's promise as he took the self-maledictory oath. Abraham cut the animals to pieces and placed their parts on the ground. Then a flaming torch passed between the pieces. This was the visible appearance of God himself.

We understand the meaning when we look to Jeremiah 34:18–19. Oaths taken in this manner bind the two parties to death—cut to pieces like the animals—if they do not keep their word. "Now God, in binding himself in his covenant to Abraham," Clowney explained, "takes upon himself this oath in this particularly vivid form, committing himself as it were his own life and existence to the fulfillment of the promise he's given to Abraham."

Clowney then turned to Exodus 17 and the smiting of the rock by Moses. Clowney argued that the story deserved more attention from preachers because God promised to stand before Moses as he struck the rock in Horeb. But why was this a big deal? Because in no other passage of the Old Testament did God stand before man. Clowney argued that this meant God has been accused of breaking his covenant! "To use C. S. Lewis's phrase, this is God in the dock," Clowney said. "This is God taking the place of the accused."

Is it any wonder that Moses got into so much trouble when he struck the rock a second time after the people complained of thirst? God wasn't performing a trick by bringing water from the rock. He was illustrating perhaps the most important point of the entire Old Testament. As Clowney explained:

> In this passage, you have God identifying himself with the sin of the people. It has no other explanation. You see, how can you have justice? The people want a court case. How can you have a court case with the God of justice and go on? There has got to be justice! The rod has got to fall! The sentence has to be delivered! And here, God receives the smiting so that Israel might be delivered and spared. So you see I think there's a theme in the Old Testament, a

very profound theme, a theme that's often echoed—the theme of God's identification with his people, that in some sense, God bears their smiting.

Pointing to Isaiah 63:9, Clowney said the Old Testament gives a pattern for the affliction of Jesus Christ. We see his suffering in the images of the son, the lamb, and even God himself as the rock.[15] Inspired by these lectures, Keller would himself make the self-sacrifice of God the climax of countless sermons. In fact, he argued that the only real love that changes lives is substitutionary sacrifice:

> That's where the God of the Bible is most radically different from the primitive gods of old. The ancients understood the idea of the wrath of God, they understood the idea of justice, the idea of a debt and a necessary punishment, but *they had no idea that God would come and pay it himself.* The cross is the self-substitution of God. . . .
>
> God created the world in an instant, and it was a beautiful process. He *re*-created the world on the cross—and it was a horrible process. That's how it works. Love that really changes things and redeems things is always a substitutionary sacrifice.[16]

Clowney lamented that few preachers ever come close to glimpsing the full color spectrum in the Old Testament's witness to Christ.[17] Many just don't know the Old Testament background well enough. A Jewish scholar, Robert Alter, of the University of California, Berkeley, would appear frequently in several of Keller's sermons and later books. Keller found him helpful in unlocking some of Israel's mysteries in context. Alter helped Keller explain the immediate context of the Hebrew Bible before he progressed to salvific fulfillment in Christ.

Clowney worried that preachers would just grab anything they could somehow relate to Jesus. Instead, preachers must labor to get specific with the events and structure of salvation history and how they point to Jesus as the climax, as the fulfillment, as the unity between faith and grace. He wanted preachers, and every Christian who heard them, to see that Genesis 22 set the stage for John 3:16, so we could understand the price the Father would pay in the sacrifice of his Son.

When Keller spoke, as he often did, about the suffering of Christ in the abandonment of the Father, he echoed Clowney's teaching on Psalm 22 at Gordon-Conwell. No suffering could ever compare to what Christ had endured in that moment when the words "My God, my God, why have you forsaken me?" escaped with his dying breaths.

"In no one could there be the contrast that our Lord experienced between total trust and total knowledge of all the Lord's goodness and mercy and the total horror of abandonment by God," Clowney said. "For only Jesus Christ really trusted the Lord, you know, and only Jesus Christ really trusted in all the fullness of broken, unblemished, undeviating trust. And it's the one who only trusted who is completely abandoned."[18]

Clowney understood he could be accused of teaching difficult doctrines. But he was no stranger to theological controversy. His InterVarsity retreats often ended with him discussing the doctrine of election with students late into the night. Clowney married piety with predestination when he told the Gordon-Conwell students that we only ever understand doctrine on our knees before God. In prayer we can praise what we don't prefer. Clowney would explain:

> Oh friends, you don't come to God with offers of amendment with reference to his plan of salvation. You don't come with suggestions. God's eternal counsel has not been delegated to subcommittees. It's of the Lord! And the Lord has his purposes, he has his design, and he's fulfilling them. It's of him, and it's through him. He's the only King of salvation![19]

Clowney pleaded with the students to make preaching Christ their specialty. He warned them not to wander into fads about what's new and relevant and engaging. Look for the unfolding drama, he urged. The only limit, Clowney concluded, is Christ's fullness.[20]

Preach Christ on principle, Clowney told the Gordon-Conwell students. Look for him from Genesis to Revelation, because we know he's there. If it's in the Old Testament, it tells us something about the history of salvation. And because it tells us about salvation, it shows us Christ.

"And if you see that," Clowney said, "it changes everything."[21]

That was certainly true for Tim Keller.

True and Better

Edmund Clowney also challenged students to approach the Bible with hearts broken by their sin and humbled by a recognition of their hypocrisy. Other students would attest to his gracious spirit, owing to his love for Christ.[22] The fear of God produces wisdom, and Jesus is the true Solomon, Clowney said, because he never succumbed to lust for this world.[23] Clowney encouraged Gordon-Conwell students to look and see what message stands out from Genesis to Revelation. The story of the Bible is not about how we can be wise like Solomon. It's about God! Only the power of God can save.[24]

As Keller would later put it, crediting Clowney, the Bible is either about what we're supposed to do or what Jesus has done.[25] In 2007, when Keller gave his first public address for The Gospel Coalition (TGC), he was still expanding on what he had learned at age twenty-two from Clowney.

"Do you believe the Bible is basically about you or basically about him?" he asked five hundred church leaders in the chapel at Trinity Evangelical Divinity School, north of Chicago.

Is David and Goliath basically about you and how you can be like David? Or is the story basically about Jesus, the one who really took on the only giants that can really kill us and whose victory is imputed to us? Who's it really about? That's the fundamental question. And when that happens, then you start to read the Bible anew.[26]

Keller cofounded TGC with New Testament scholar D. A. Carson and served for more than a decade as vice president. His TGC talk on gospel-centered ministry popularized a riff that inspired a whole new generation to preach the way he had been taught by Clowney. Keller first spoke in 2001 at Redeemer Presbyterian Church about Jesus as the "true and better" fulfillment of God's redemptive plan when compared to everyone from Adam to Abel to Isaac to Joseph to David to Esther to Job. "Everything points to Jesus," he said.[27] He repeated this original riff again in 2004 at Redeemer before bringing it to an audience of church leaders at TGC in 2007.

The difference between a lecture and a sermon, Keller explained, is the instinct to see everything pointing to Christ, who produces praise. His lines on Moses explicitly recall Clowney's Gordon-Conwell talks:

Jesus is the true and better Adam who passed the test in the garden, a much tougher garden, and whose obedience is imputed to us.

Jesus is the true and better Abel who, though innocently slain, has blood that cries out, not for our condemnation, but for our acquittal.

Jesus is the true and better Abraham who answered the call of God to leave all the comfortable and familiar and go into the void, not knowing whither he went.

Jesus is the true and better Isaac who was not just offered up by his father on the mount but was truly sacrificed for us all. What God said to Abraham, "Now I know you love me because you did not withhold your son—your only son whom you love—from me," now we, at the foot of the cross, can say to God, "Now we know that you love me because you did not withhold your Son—your only Son whom you love—from me."

Jesus is the true and better Jacob who wrestled and took the blow of justice we deserve so we, like Jacob, only receive the wounds of grace that wake us up and discipline us.

Jesus is the true and better Joseph who sits at the right hand of the King and forgives those who betrayed and sold him and uses his power to save them.

Jesus is the true and better Moses who stands in the gap between the people and the Lord and who mediates a new covenant.

Jesus is the true and better rock of Moses who, when struck with a rod of God's justice, now gives us water in the desert.

Jesus is the true and better Job who became a truly innocent sufferer and now intercedes for and saves his stupid friends.

Jesus is the true and better David whose victory becomes his people's victory, though they never lifted a stone to accomplish it themselves.

Jesus is the true and better Esther who didn't just risk losing an earthly palace but lost the ultimate heavenly one, who didn't just risk his life but gave his life, who didn't just say, "If I perish, I perish," but also, "When I perish, I'll perish to save my people."

Jesus is the true and better Jonah who was cast out into the storm so we could be brought in.

Jesus is the real Passover lamb.

Jesus is the true temple, the true prophet, the true priest, the true king, the true sacrifice, the true lamb, the true light, the true bread.[28]

Once Keller saw Jesus through Clowney's eyes, he found his Savior everywhere. According to Keller's friend Tremper Longman, reading the Bible is like watching *The Sixth Sense*. The ending of the film sends you back to look at everything afresh, seeing with different eyes as you begin again.

Prodigal God

It's not difficult to trace the origin of Tim Keller's ideas. But Tim does far more than repeat what others have said. When these ideas come out in his own preaching and writing, they've been expanded and tweaked in ways that make them original. Nowhere is this pattern more evident than in perhaps his most beloved message, which appears in his 2008 bestselling book *The Prodigal God*, dedicated to Edmund Clowney. Keller never pretended the interpretation of the parable from Luke 15 was original to him. He admitted that he first heard it from Clowney at Gordon-Conwell in the Staley lectures in 1973.

Clowney taught that preachers should look for Jesus in his parables, and when we do, we see that what's commonly known as the parable of the prodigal son in Luke 15 is not about the younger brother; it's about the older brother. The Pharisees and the teachers of the law are the true target of Jesus' story, because like the older brother, they don't understand the Father's mercy. The older brother doesn't go looking for the younger brother when he leaves home. Even worse, the older brother won't even join the celebration when his brother returns. Grace and mercy offend his sense of justice.

So why does Jesus tell the story? Clowney explained that Jesus revealed himself as the true older brother. He ate with tax collectors and sinners. He searched for the lost among the unclean pigs. "Because he came to seek and save that which is lost, because he's the good shepherd looking for the sheep, because he's the elder brother that brings home the younger brother."[29]

In other words, the parable isn't about how people get saved, Clowney argued. It's about the right and wrong kind of elder brother. "Because it just so happens that nobody ever comes home from the pigpen who hasn't had the arm of the elder brother around his shoulder."

When Keller heard this message, he felt like he had "discovered the secret heart of Christianity." And as he preached this parable from Luke

15 over the years, he saw "more people encouraged, enlightened, and helped by this passage, when I explained the true meaning of it, than by any other text."[30]

Clowney himself heard Keller preach this parable in Luke 15 in 1998 while visiting New York.[31] In keeping with his pattern, Keller fused Clowney's basic insights with elements he had adopted from other teachers. The semester before Clowney visited Gordon-Conwell, Tim developed his theology of revival in Richard Lovelace's Pneumodynamics class. Keller observed that whenever the church recovers the gospel and enjoys revival, the so-called good people who take pride in their morality leave the church in outrage. Meanwhile, the outcasts flock in to hear the message of grace. Jesus was always harder on the Pharisees than on the pimps and prostitutes. And he was harder on the older brother than the younger brother in Luke 15.

"It doesn't just say the elder brother is as lost as the younger brother," Keller preached. "This story is actually telling us the elder brother is *more* lost than the younger brother." He then quoted his friend John Gerstner, the Jonathan Edwards scholar from Pittsburgh, as saying, "The thing that really separates us from God is not so much our sin, but our damnable good works."

You're not a Christian because you obey the will of God, Keller explained. You're a Christian because you obey the will of God for the right reasons. You love God because he loved you first. The influence of Jonathan Edwards helped Keller escape a mode of preaching that simply explained the text, gave an application, and exhorted Christians to live a certain way with God's help. The influence of Edwards, combined with Clowney, taught Keller to hold up Jesus as faithful where we have failed. By faith in Christ, we see the beauty of Christ and find motivation from the heart to obey his law. We don't obey primarily because we fear the consequences of sin; we obey because we do not want to grieve our beloved Savior.

"It's your goodness that makes you miserable," Keller said. "It's your goodness that's at the heart of all the problems. It's your self-righteousness. Self-righteousness is the cause of racism. It's the cause of classism. It's the cause of so much of the family breakdown."[32]

And it's the cause, according to Keller, of spiritually stagnant churches. While Jesus attracted outsiders and offended insiders, churches today tend to do the opposite. The moralistic, self-righteous people know they need to be in church. But the broken and marginalized don't feel welcome. That can mean only one thing, Keller concludes in *The Prodigal God*. We must not be preaching the same message Jesus did in Luke 15. We have become like the elder brother Jesus warned us against.[33] Preaching this message to his Presbyterian congregation in New York, Keller encouraged them to find their joy in Christ.

> There is no more perfect and no more wonderful story that gives us the whole meaning of the gospel than this. . . . If there is no dance, if there is no music, if there is no joy in your life it's because, either like the prodigal you're letting your badness get in the way of God, or like the Pharisee you're letting your goodness get in the way. You're trying to control him one way or the other. I don't care how religious you are. If there's no joy and there's no dance, you still don't get it.[34]

When Keller later taught a Doctor of Ministry course on preaching with Clowney, he explained how the Staley lectures had unlocked Luke 15 for him. Keller didn't just crib his mentor though. Clowney credited Keller with several applications that hadn't occurred to him. When discerning the difference between Keller and Clowney, it's the application that stands out. Clowney tended to leave the listener with a generic sense of need for God as he contrasted man's sin with God's grace.[35] Keller, however, influenced by Lovelace, saw the spiritual dynamics of revival at work.

Later, Keller added another dimension to his application of Clowney's biblical theology. When he moved to Philadelphia to replace

Clowney in the practical ministry department, Keller became better acquainted with biblical counseling, and in particular the work of David Powlison through the Christian Counseling and Education Foundation (CCEF).[36] CCEF, founded by Jay Adams, worked across the street from Westminster, and eventually Keller joined Powlison and his CCEF colleague Ed Welch on the session at New Life Presbyterian Church in Glenside, which had been founded by Jack and Rose Marie Miller in the early 1970s.[37]

While Clowney gave Keller his instincts to search the text for Christ, Powlison gave Keller the tools he needed to apply the gospel as a spiritual surgeon. Powlison's seminal article "Idols of the Heart and 'Vanity Fair'" crystallized much of what Keller read in the Puritans about pastoral counseling.[38] And this counseling worked its way into his preaching as he aimed to expose the idols of the culture and of the heart.

Rare Combination

Edmund Clowney died on March 20, 2005. Writing three years later, Keller remembered his only personal mentor for teaching him that "it was possible to be theologically sound and completely orthodox and yet unfailingly gracious—a rare and precious combination."[39]

In Redeemer's early years Keller saw revival along the lines of what he had hoped for when Clowney had taught him from Luke 15. His sermons reached spiritual seekers and recovering Pharisees alike. They challenged the younger and older brothers at the same time.

"Redeemer became a church for recovering Christians, for people who realized their dreams didn't deliver. We were searching for authentic religion," said Steve Arcieri, an early Redeemer member. "Tim re-explained Christianity in every sermon."[40]

Keller added many layers to his preaching as well as additional influences in the decades after Clowney visited South Hamilton.

Martyn Lloyd-Jones helped him by reaffirming the need to edify and evangelize in the same sermon. Jonathan Edwards helped him reach the heart, not just the mind, with vivid illustrations. John Stott modeled how to apply the text to contemporary culture. Keller listened to so many Dick Lucas sermons that Kathy told him to be careful, because Tim was going to sound like a parrot.[41] Keller's reading tended to follow a pattern. When he found sermons or books from a new preacher (like Lucas), he jumped all in, so much so that he adopted too much of their themes and cadences. This happened with Lucas, Whitefield, Lloyd-Jones, and Sproul. When he moved on to new obsessions, he kept some of their best insights as permanent additions to his teaching repertoire, as he did with Lucas's style of biblical exposition. By the time he got to New York he had so many layers of great preachers' influences that new ones didn't have the same all-shaping effect. In New York the various influences integrated into his distinctive preaching voice.

Starting in 1961, Dick Lucas served as the pastor of St Helen's Bishopsgate in London for thirty-seven years. He started Proclamation Trust in 1986 to encourage expositional preaching. For Keller, an admitted Anglophile, there was nothing better than a British preacher expounding God's Word from a church that dated to the thirteenth century, with arches that could be traced to 1480—all more than half a century before the Reformation dawned in England.

In Lucas, as well as John Stott at All Souls, Langham Place, Keller found models for fruitful city-center ministries that had remained faithful to historic Christian orthodoxy. St Helen's is less than one mile from the Tower of London, and only about five blocks from London Bridge on the Thames. Lucas, Stott, and even Lloyd-Jones faced more secular audiences than anything American preachers had yet seen, so Keller preferred their sermons to other Americans in preparation for addressing secular New Yorkers.

Keller also adopted the type of *lectio continua* practiced by Lucas and Stott—preaching every verse from shorter books or select chapters from longer books.[42] These influences combined to guide Keller as he preached Christ from every text, applying the gospel in specific ways to meet personal needs within every unique cultural context and seeking spiritual transformation more than information transfer. Common to all great preachers, Keller found, is gentle love practiced with humility and combined with great courage that comes from spiritual authority rooted in the power of God.

Despite a wealth of diverse preaching influences, however, no other preacher reached Tim Keller like Edmund Clowney. No other preacher took personal interest in him in quite the same way, giving Keller confidence he could lead a church. And no one better modeled for Keller how to train future generations to find Jesus in the Scriptures, looking from Genesis to Revelation and seeing him as the true and better fulfillment of our most absurd hopes.

THIRTEEN

"MOULDED BY THE GOSPEL"

Westminster Theological Seminary

1984 to 1989

E ven working two half-time jobs, which in reality were more like two nearly full-time jobs, felt like a sabbatical for Tim Keller when his family moved from Hopewell to Philadelphia in the summer of 1984. During the week, Keller taught Edmund Clowney's old preaching and pastoral leadership courses at Westminster Theological Seminary. On the weekends, he traveled to provide training for PCA churches in how to do mercy ministry through their diaconates. Though it was a heavy load, it felt light compared to his former task of preaching three sermons and visiting or counseling between ten and twenty people per week.

Not even two jobs could pay the mortgage, however, on the first and only home Tim and Kathy ever purchased. So Kathy had to take a part-time job editing Sunday school curriculum for Great Commission Publications in a building shared with the headquarters of the Orthodox Presbyterian Church. Kathy's work meant Tim was responsible for feeding, dressing, and taking the boys to school. In Hopewell, Tim didn't have time for this level of practical help with the boys, who were six, four, and one when the Kellers made the move to Philadelphia.

But seminary teaching didn't just allow Tim more time with his boys. It brought huge relief, releasing him from the pressure he felt every Sunday to deliver life-changing sermons. Even mentoring and counseling students felt light compared to the heavy load of evangelism and crisis intervention he had carried in Hopewell. Teaching the same courses year after year afforded him time and mental space to read deeply in church leadership, pastoral counseling, evangelism, and preaching. The seminary even demanded that he take time off from his teaching duties to read. Tim didn't need to be told twice.

Despite the relief Keller felt in stepping away from ministry, Westminster was an unlikely place for him to find respite. Something in the school's culture, ever since its founding by J. Gresham Machen in the ominous year of 1929, seemed to breed controversy, especially among the faculty. When Keller arrived on campus, the school had only recently emerged from acute infighting over Norman Shepherd's controversial views on justification. But the years 1984 to 1989, and even extending to 1992 while Keller served on the school's board and continued to teach, were some of the most peaceful the school has ever enjoyed. Tremper Longman and Bruce Waltke in Old Testament, Sinclair Ferguson and Dick Gaffin in theology, Moisés Silva and Vern Poythress in New Testament—Keller grew close with many of the seminary's esteemed faculty.

The trajectory leading him to this season of his life had been set nearly twenty years earlier—when Keller was still a student at Bucknell—by his mentor Ed Clowney.

The Keller family moved into their new Allentown, Pennsylvania, house in 1967, the year before Tim (far left) started college at Bucknell. Tim's mother, Louise, stands next to him, holding the family cat. Billy (center) died in 1998. Sharon stands next to their father, Bill (far right).

Bucknell students went on strike in May 1970 to protest the National Guard killing of four Kent State students after President Nixon expanded the Vietnam War. Tim and other InterVarsity members engaged the striking students in evangelistic conversations.

Barbara Boyd delivered her "Lordship Talk" at Bear Trap Ranch in Colorado, the InterVarsity camp Tim attended for a month in the summer of 1971. Boyd's "Bible and Life" series provided him with his foundation for studying God's Word.

Ed Clowney is the only close personal influence who knew Tim from his awkward Bucknell years in Lewisburg, Pennsylvania, through the Redeemer megachurch years in New York City. By the end of Clowney's life, he and Keller were teaching together at Reformed Theological Seminary.

23 April 6?

Dear Kathy
Congratulations on keeping house!
By the way I also ned. say "I got a book." But
your teacher and I are not "English teachers" in
the same sense. She has to put across an idea
of what the English language ought to be: I'm
concerned entirely with what it is and how it
came to be what it is. In fact she is a
gardener distinguishing "flowers" from "weeds";
I am a botanist and am interested in both
as vegetable organisms.
     — use your ruler.
          yours
          C. S. Lewis

C. S. Lewis mediated a dispute between twelve-year-old Kathy Keller and her English teacher in this letter from April 1963. His last letter to her was sent less than two weeks before he died on November 22, 1963. Kathy shared her love for Lewis's Narnia series with Tim.

Francis Schaeffer advised R. C. Sproul on plans for Ligonier Valley Study Center based on the fruitful but exhausting experience of L'Abri in Switzerland.

Classes offered by Ligonier Valley Study Center the summer before Tim and Kathy began seminary illustrate the broader Reformed revival underway in the Pittsburgh area during the early 1970s.

L I G O N I E R   V A L L E Y   S T U D Y   C E N T E R
SUMMER SCHEDULE - 1972

May 30-June 9 BASIC OLD TESTAMENT THEMES
An introduction to basic Old Testament Theology with focus on themes of creation, fall, covenant, law, prophetic criticism, wisdom literature etc. This course is designed to encourage and facilitate study of the Old Testament.

June 12 - June 23 PERSON AND WORK OF THE HOLY SPIRIT
A study of the person of the Holy Spirit as revealed in Old and New Testament. Special attention will be given to the work of the Spirit in Creation and Redemption. The controversial matter of the "Baptism" and "Gifts" of the Spirit will also be studied.

June 26 - June 30 CHURCH AND SACRAMENTS (one week - $30)
An investigation of the Biblical view of the Church and Sacraments as well as a survey of the development of these themes in Church History. Special attention will be given to the controversial issue of infant baptism.

July 10 - July 21 CHRISTIAN ETHICS
An introduction to principles of Christian personal and social ethics with particular attention given to controversial issues of the present. Questions of war, abortion, sexual behaviour, capital punishment, etc. will be dealt with.

July 24 - Aug. 4 PERSON AND WORK OF CHRIST
An investiagtion into the New Testament portrait of Jesus with special attention given to the titles of Jesus such as "Messiah", "Son of Man", "Lord", etc. and a survey of the critical events in the life of Jesus such as his birth, baptism, crucifixion, resurrection, ascension, etc.

Aug. 7 - Aug. 18 CHRISTIANITY AND EXISTENTIALISM
A survey of existential thought dealing with the works of Nietzche, Kierkegaard, Heidegger, Sartre, Camus, Jaspers, et al with a special view to their influence upon, and conflict with, classical Christianity.

Aug. 28 - Sept. 8 BASIC NEW TESTAMENT THEMES
An introduction into the theology of the New Testament with a special view to the concept of the Kingdom of God. The distinctives of Pauline and Johannine theology will be studied.

Sept. 11 - Sept. 22 BASIC REFORMED THEOLOGY
An introduction into the distinctive theological issues of the reformation including the question of authority, justification, predestination, etc. - the thought of Luther and Calvin will be given special attention.

COST: $60, includes room and board. Some work scholarships available.

TO REGISTER: send $10 non-refundable deposit to

Jim Thompson
Ligonier Valley Study Center
Stahlstown, Pa. 15687

R. C. Sproul's ask-anything "gabfests" became a Monday night highlight at Ligonier Valley Study Center. Tim did the same on Sunday nights for his Hopewell church.

The faculty of Gordon-Conwell Theological Seminary offered students like the Kellers a theological smorgasbord that continued to nourish them over decades of ministry.

Gordon-Conwell students sensed they were part of something new and exciting at the school led by the architects of American evangelicalism.

Roger Nicole (left) and J. I. Packer (center) gave Tim models of theological conviction with an irenic spirit. Sometimes Nicole presented opposing views so effectively that students couldn't help but conclude that Nicole's own view was wrong.

The "notoriously absentminded" Richard Lovelace (right) introduced Tim to the pneumodynamics in writers as diverse as Flannery O'Connor and John Owen.

Elisabeth Elliot taught both Kellers in her Gordon-Conwell class on "Christian Expression in Speech, Writing, and Behavior." The tall, imposing, and deeply convictional Elliot shaped both Tim and Kathy in what came to be known as the complementary roles of men and women in the church and home.

The Kellers dedicated their book *The Meaning of Marriage* to "the Robins," a group of friends from the Gordon-Conwell days who have stuck close through theological changes, child-rearing, and vacations together. Left to right, the couples are (women in foreground) Gayle and Gary Somers, Cindy and Jim Widmer, Kathy and Tim Keller, Louise and David Midwood, and Jane and Wendy Frazier. Not pictured: Adele and Doug Calhoun.

TABLE TALK

HERMENEUTICAL NESTORIANISM

Honest Christians can differ on very basic issues. We would like to take issue with the GCTS New Testament department on its methodological presuppositions in hermeneutics. To throw the real problem into sharp relief, we will call attention to an analogy traditionally used to characterize the Scriptures and recently endorsed by men such as P. Hughes and G. Bromiley.

What is the relationship of the human element of scripture to the divine? We know the Scripture is a fully human book, with a normal grammatical, historical, psychological context. At the same time, the Bible is considered (by itself in general and Christ in particular) to be not just inspired men's words about God but God's inspired words, historically written. Thus the entire Bible can be said to be the result of one author and intent.

The only parallel example we have of such perfect divine revelation in history is Christ Himself. The analogy is obvious: just as Jesus was fully and truly divine and human yet one Person, so the Bible is fully divine message, written by men, yet one book. "To ignore either the divine or human authorship is to miss the reality of the Bible and the full profit of its teaching" (Bromiley, New Bible Commentary).

During the Reformation, two basic principles of Biblical interpretation emerged in reaction to Rome. First, the "simple, original" sense of Scripture was alone considered binding and valid (as opposed to allegorical senses, etc.). Secondly, the unity of Scripture was asserted in that Scripture was to be interpreted by Scripture (**Scriptura Scriturae interpres**), and any particular verse was to be interpreted in light of the unified sense of Scripture (the **analogia fiedei**). It is interesting to note that each of these principles serves to anchor hermeneutics firmly in each of the two natures of Scripture.

The GCTS N.T. department believes strongly that all theological presuppositions must be put behind us when we go to the text of the

Bible, **Scriptura Scripturae interpres** is a theological presupposition, says Prof. Scholer. Dr. Michaels believes we must treat the Bible as any other historical document, and thus our initial stance toward the Bible we hold in common with any unbiased neo-orthodox, liberal, Jewish or atheist historical-literary critic. We can work side by side with them to ascertain the original intent and meaning of the text, and only **subsequently** to exegesis do we look on the text, bringing now our religious tradition to bear on it to discover the "theological" application.

This is a noble try at scientific objectivity. Nonetheless, what "put your theological presuppositions behind you" really means is "put behind you the assumption that there is a divine author, and assume that it is human". Thus the two natures are separated and dealt with apart from each other. This approach, when applied to the examination of Christ's Person was branded Nestorianism. It was judged to be singularly inadequate, for the natures cannot be somehow abstracted from each other. Christ's work cannot be understood in such an artificial manner. Is this approach, then, also inadequate in examining the Bible? We believe it is, and we would note several results of this approach which attest to this.

First of all, from this point of view an unhealthy gap between Biblical and theological studies develops. Many doctrines would not be considered "Biblical" but rather "theological". A fear of systematizing Biblical content is really the result of under-crediting the unity of divine authorship; the result is a kind of "cafeteria theology" of unrelated themes. If one consciousness underlies all of Scripture, what violence is done in relating and reconciling the texts?

Not only does this Nestorian hermeneutic undermine the unity of the Bible, but ultimately even the "simple" sense of Scripture is hurt. By setting aside the "presupposition" of divine authorship and intent, the meaning of the

human author becomes culturally bound, and an actual second "theological" or "mystical" sense (**sensus plenior**) must be posited to relate the text to the 20th century. Rather than two meanings, historical and theological, we should have two hermeneutic steps. These steps should be done distinctly, yet neither without reference to both natures of Scripture. (This parallels good Christological method.)

It is important to note that to assume the unity of scripture is not a theological presupposition as such; it is an evaluation of the kind of literature to be interpreted. Any hermeneutic must adapt itself to the genre of literature to which it is being applied. If the Bible is to any degree unique literature, then to that same degree it deserves a unique hermeneutic.

We cannot fault Dr. Michaels and Scholer's scholarship of intentions. There certainly is a danger of evangelicals being monophysites or downright docetists in over-spiritualized Biblical interpretation. If the human nature of Scripture is not distinguished, there is a tendency for the divine to submerge it. Yet to separate the two natures in a Nestorian fashion tends to diminish the divine nature for the human.

We would end sounding three warnings. 1) This interpretation is impractical since it ultimately puts the "simple meaning" of the text beyond the average person's grasp, since Ignatius or Josephus throws better light on a passage from Paul than does Psalms or Peter. 2) This hermeneutic does not prepare students to move on into theological studies. By the time they take a Systematics course many find it artificial and "biased". 3) As orthodox believers, we must not be obscurantists, yet we must not assume that the world's scholarship, performed by rebellious fallen men (as are we), is somehow neutral and without inclination to resist truth when it runs counter to modern convictions. Our own hearts should show us this.

mouthing of empty cliches. If we hope to change our culture, we will have to change our lives, and take the gospel seriously. Clark H. Pinnock in *Set Forth Your Case*

The first issue of *Table Talk*, edited by Tim and several other Gordon-Conwell students, featured his article "Hermeneutical Nestorianism," which sharply criticized two professors of New Testament.

David Midwood (left) joined Tim in founding the Edmund P. Clowney Fan Club at Gordon-Conwell. Among Tim's closest friends, David died of colon cancer in 2014.

Tim returned to his alma mater of Gordon-Conwell to deliver the 2016 spring convocation address. By this time, he had become a world-renowned church leader, in contrast to his days as an intelligent but overlooked student.

Tim and Kathy joined more than seventeen thousand young Christians at Urbana '76, which featured speakers Billy Graham, John Perkins, Edmund Clowney, Elisabeth Elliot, and Helen Roseveare. John Stott delivered four expositions on the biblical basis for missions.

John Stott gave Tim his first model for expositional preaching. To Keller, Stott did more than anyone else in creating evangelicalism as the middle space between fundamentalism and liberalism.

Hopewell, Virginia, became the focus of an environmental scandal just before the Kellers arrived in this former home of a DuPont dynamite factory. All three Keller sons were born in Hopewell.

Tim's meager salary in Hopewell didn't include a book budget. But friends and family gave him Banner of Truth titles for Christmas, and he read them throughout the following year. His favorite authors included Thomas Brooks, John Owen, and Charles Spurgeon.

Tim (back row, third from left) joined the faculty of Westminster Theological Seminary in 1984 and took over his mentor Edmund Clowney's courses on preaching and pastoral leadership.

Harvie Conn served as Tim's department chair in practical theology at Westminster Theological Seminary. Conn's emphasis on contextualization paved the way for his colleague Keller to plant a city center church in New York.

Jack Miller was Tim and Kathy's pastor for five years, from 1984 to 1989, at New Life Presbyterian Church in Glenside, Pennsylvania. Before the Kellers planted Redeemer in New York, New Life showed them how a culture of gospel renewal applied to social justice, worship, evangelism, and missions.

New York in the 1970s and 1980s earned a reputation for high crime levels, which discouraged many Christians from moving there to evangelize and start churches. Early Redeemer members prayed for the renewal of the city and believed those prayers were answered as the city prospered in the 1990s.

In June 1989, the Kellers moved to Roosevelt Island in the East River and have never changed apartments. They found on the island a relatively quiet place in the city to raise their family.

Silence descended over New York after the initial cacophony of planes crashing, towers collapsing, and ambulances racing. Not long after the Tuesday attacks, Tim's mind turned to his Sunday message, which was heard by nearly double Redeemer's normal attendance.

Overseen by Kathy Keller, the fundraising brochure for what would become Redeemer Presbyterian Church touted the opportunity for ministry in this capital of finance, education, politics, and art.

New York City
A ministry strategy for the future

The leader of the PCA's church planting project in New York is Timothy Keller. A graduate of Bucknell University (B.A., 1972), Gordon-Conwell Theological Seminary (M.Div., 1975), and Westminster Theological Seminary (D.Min., 1983), Dr. Keller has had a creative and productive ministry. He began his ministry career while still in seminary as an associate staff member of Inter-Varsity Christian Fellowship. During a nine-year pastorate in Virginia, Dr. Keller saw his own church triple in size, and supervised the successful planting of 24 churches in the middle Atlantic states.

For the past five years Tim Keller has been a professor at Westminster Seminary, teaching communication, ministry and leadership. While in Philadelphia, he was involved in ministries to the business, homosexual and Muslim communities; to urban singles; and to college, graduate and foreign students. He has also been involved with several other church planting projects in the Philadelphia and New York areas. Dr. Keller has served as the Director of Mercy Ministries for Mission to North America. He also chaired the steering committee of Tenth Presbyterian Church's ministry to AIDS victims in Philadelphia.

Dr. Keller's latest book, *The Ministries of Mercy*, calls churches to obey Jesus' command to minister to the needy in their communities. Tim, his wife Kathy, and their three sons will live in Manhattan.

What can you do? You may live in New York City within reach of one of our congregations. In that case, we invite you to join us if you are not committed now to an evangelical church. Contact us discuss the details of the vision we have outlined

You may be able to contribute financial resources personally, or to encourage your congregation to do so. Financial cost is an unavoidable ministry issue in New York. The expense of working and living in the city has discouraged many churches and ministers from laboring here. We need a great deal of financial support, but the spiritual return of this project will dwarf the expenses.

You can pray for us and with us. On September 1857, a lay minister on Fulton Street in downtow Manhattan started a noontime prayer meeting f spiritual revival. Though only six people came t day—and all of them half an hour late!— by the following year, more than 10,000 businessmen i New York were praying together daily, the churches were overflowing, and the New York press was flabbergasted. In the next two years, over one million people were converted across United States as a direct result of that prayer meeting. What more could we accomplish if yo remember to pray for God's work in New York City? We invite you to join us.

Yvonne Sawyer (bride in white) served as the first leader of Hope for New York, Redeemer's mercy ministry. In the only wedding ceremony Tim ever included in a regular worship service, he preached his famous message "The Girl Nobody Wanted."

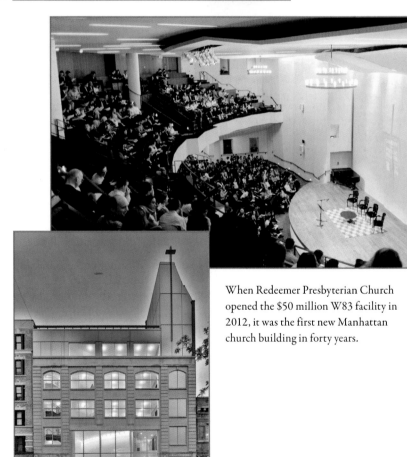

When Redeemer Presbyterian Church opened the $50 million W83 facility in 2012, it was the first new Manhattan church building in forty years.

As cofounder and vice president of The Gospel Coalition, Tim drafted its theological vision for ministry, which was debated and adopted by the full council of pastors at a 2007 meeting on the campus of Trinity Evangelical Divinity School north of Chicago.

Tim and Kathy share a lighthearted moment as they participate in a panel about the roles and gifts of men and women during The Gospel Coalition's 2014 women's conference in Orlando, Florida.

During The Gospel Coalition's inaugural 2007 national conference, Tim delivered a message on "gospel-centered ministry" in which he extolled Jesus Christ as the "true and better" fulfillment of God's redemptive plan.

Charles Taylor became a staple influence on Tim's thinking, writing, and teaching after 2013. Keller read Taylor's monumental book *A Secular Age* twice, line by line, in two years.

Tim's diagnosis of pancreatic cancer in 2020, along with the COVID-19 pandemic, kept him largely confined to his Roosevelt Island home with Kathy. Not since seminary had the Kellers spent so much time together, and Tim continued to recommend his favorite books, new and old.

Tim (left) joined author Collin Hansen at Samford University in Birmingham, Alabama, after lectures on pastoral ministry and faith and work on Election Day, November 8, 2016.

Every Head Bowed

From a clenched fist to a bowed head.

That's how Clowney described the shift from early Westminster Theological Seminary under its founder, J. Gresham Machen, to its succeeding generation in May 1969, during the school's fortieth commencement ceremony. Martyn Lloyd-Jones marked the milestone anniversary by delivering the commencement address, and he remained on campus to lecture for six weeks on preaching.

Clowney, who became president of Westminster in 1966, didn't concede any change in Westminster's theological convictions. But he captured the spirit of 1969 when he exhorted students to preach a gospel that challenged old reactionaries as much as young revolutionaries:

> Westminster in years to come must be increasingly moulded by the gospel of Christ. No other course is wise or safe.
>
> That means active, renewed subjection to the gospel. Westminster must avoid the calcifying effects of the traditions of men that do not express the gospel. There is an ever-present danger that we will take ourselves seriously instead of taking the gospel seriously. An academic community is particularly vulnerable to traditionalism and pride.[1]

Top priority for Clowney, then, was revising the seminary curriculum to prioritize biblical theology, which "takes its form as well as its content from the structure of the Bible. Biblical theology is shaped by the periods of the history of redemption as they center upon Christ. This approach provides a richer Biblical background for both systematic theology and preaching."[2] Clowney traced biblical theology back to Princeton Theological Seminary and Geerhardus Vos, who taught several of Westminster's founding faculty members.

The next step in the renewal of Westminster by the gospel, according to Clowney, involved linking piety to learning. But he didn't believe any program could deliver what the seminary needed most—revival through the Holy Spirit. "Deeper penitence, more urgent trust, more faithful obedience to Christ's commands: these mark the path of power in service to our age."[3]

Clowney also called for "fresh and immediate application of the gospel to our times." He explained: "Our task is to present the message of the gospel, to prepare the messenger of the gospel, and to do so in the contemporary world."[4] He affirmed D. Clair Davis for explaining the social backgrounds to secular German theology. He commended Jack Miller for his evening classes on American and English literature and how they helped evangelists engage the modern mind.[5]

Clowney pursued this three-step agenda for renewal by the gospel as Westminster president until 1984. When Clowney retired, the school decided to save money by splitting his teaching between two professors. Harvie Conn, who had joined the Westminster faculty in 1972, took over Clowney's course on the church. Clowney's courses on ministry, leadership, and preaching fell to Keller. Later in his pastoral ministry, Keller adapted Clowney's vision for gospel renewal at Westminster and applied it to the two church networks he helped to build. Through Redeemer City to City and The Gospel Coalition, Clowney's priorities extended to generations who would never remember his years at Westminster. Clowney saw the future without betraying the past:

> We look to the Lord to meet our needs through faithful stewards. . . . Westminster has stood for the infallible Word, and as we look to the future we seek a much stronger curriculum in the Word. Westminster has stood for the Reformed Faith, the precious doctrines of grace. As we look to the future we seek to be formed more completely by the gospel of sovereign grace, manifesting that piety that is the fruit of the Spirit of God. (We need your prayers!) Westminster has stood for the kingdom of Christ against the

tyranny of ecclesiastical modernism and demonic secularism. As we look to the future we seek to make ever clearer the truth of Christ as over against the delusions of our time.[6]

Clowney wanted the fists clenched for fighting theological liberals joined together in praying for revival. Whether or not that vision ever succeeded at Westminster, it never departed from Tim Keller's heart and mind.

Blind Spots

D. Clair Davis didn't mind when the fifteen students assigned to his Westminster small group dwindled to only five or six. After all, the same thing was happening to several other faculty members. Tim Keller's group, meanwhile, had swelled to more than sixty students. Embarrassed by the attention, Keller apologized to Davis. He didn't need to bother. "I could handle that," Davis said, "because everyone else was in the same boat."[7]

Davis, who taught on the theology of the successors to Jonathan Edwards, regularly met with Keller and fellow faculty member Tremper Longman in an accountability group. Keller and Davis were also members together at New Life Presbyterian Church in Glenside, Pennsylvania, a church founded by Jack and Rose Marie Miller in 1974. In addition to Longman and Davis, New Life Glenside between 1984 and 1987 also included among its members David Powlison and Ed Welch of CCEF.[8]

Miller's influence on the pietist wing of Reformed thought expanded Westminster's traditional reach, which had previously ranged between the doctrinalist and culturalist camps. Original faculty member John Murray represented the doctrinalist stream, while another original faculty member, Cornelius Van Til, represented the culturalist stream. When Keller arrived, Sinclair Ferguson in theology and Richard Gamble in church history anchored the British and Scottish doctrinalist position. Pulling in the continental, neo-Calvinist direction were Richard Gaffin, Vern Poythress, Harvie Conn, David Clowney, and later Bill Edgar in apologetics.

Keller saw these tensions among the Westminster faculty. True to form, Keller appropriated insights from every group, because he believed all of them contributed to a mature, biblical church. And he observed how ministry context, spiritual gifting, and emotional temperament incline Christians to some views more than others. Keller identified more closely with the pietist and culturalist traditions. But he intentionally grew closer to doctrinalist colleagues at Westminster.[9]

Keller had already met several of these Westminster colleagues during his DMin studies, when he completed one of the school's longest dissertations. He learned from Miller on evangelism, Conn on missions and culture, and Powlison on counseling as he wrote about Thomas Chalmers and the Presbyterian diaconate of Edinburgh and Glasgow, Scotland, during the nineteenth century, along with similar Reformed works in Amsterdam and Geneva.

When he joined the Westminster faculty, Keller's department chair in practical theology was Harvie Conn. Keller's experience in Hopewell could have scarcely been more different from Conn's. After twelve years as a missionary in Korea, Conn returned to the United States convinced by the same urgency that drove his contemporary Lesslie Newbigin to plead for a new missionary encounter in the West. While most Westminster faculty lived in the Philadelphia suburbs, Conn settled in the city, where he saw firsthand America's emerging post-Christian future. Keller regularly showed up fifteen minutes early to department meetings so he could ask Conn questions about urban ministry and contextualization. Conn's 1982 book *Evangelism: Doing Justice and Preaching Grace* significantly formed Keller as a professor and preacher in its critique of standard Western seminary education.[10]

"The schooling model reinforces a pattern for communication where effectiveness is largely measured in terms of the digestion of prepackaged packets of information—information aimed largely at a White Anglo-Saxon receptor," Conn wrote. "Then, ten years later at an alumni gathering, we wonder why our churches look white and Anglo-Saxon and suburban."[11]

Drawing from his experience as a missionary, Conn prioritized connecting the gospel message to different cultures' values and idols. Missionaries shouldn't export Western thinking with the same priorities and categories.[12] In his Westminster course on "contextual theology," Conn argued that the gospel changes far more than mind and spirit. The good news of Jesus changes entire societies and civilizations, with implications for everything from power to economics to art.[13]

Conn didn't argue that the Westminster Confession was wrong. Neither did he treat it as timeless or transcendent. Illustrating the point from his work in a Korean context, Conn pointed out that this seventeenth-century British confession doesn't say much about how Christians should treat their parents, ancestors, and grandparents. Yet discipleship among Koreans *must* address such topics as ancestor worship. The Westminster Confession may not be wrong, but it's not sufficient for every time and place.[14] Defending and demanding strict adherence to the Westminster Confession can't be a missionary-minded teacher's only priority.

Critics and supporters alike have often noted Keller's emphasis on contextualization. For critics he gave away too much in translation. For supporters he showed the way to be faithful to the past without getting stuck in it. Keller himself saw dangers in both too much and also too little contextualization. He wrote in *Center Church*, "The great missionary task is to express the gospel message to a new culture in a way that avoids making the message unnecessarily alien to that culture, yet without removing or obscuring the scandal and offense of biblical truth."[15]

When viewed from this missionary perspective, Western culture loses its privileged position. Every culture gets some things rights and some things wrong. Every culture succumbs to idols, and every culture tells us something about God.[16] No culture, including the West, can introduce us to the saving gospel without explicit divine revelation of Christ. Keller wrote, "No culture has the full set of prerequisite mental furniture necessary to receive the gospel, which tells us that while God is holy and must punish sin, at the same time he is loving and doesn't want to punish us for our sin, and so Christ died in our place, making him both just and the justifier of those who believe."[17]

The primary hindrance to contextualization is our own blind spots. We can't see our own culture with sufficient perspective on its strengths and weaknesses.[18] Overzealous pastors eager to reach their city will often overcontextualize and lose their theological grounding. Others, trying to survive in this pluralistic environment, will under-contextualize, and they will be content to attract only those who already agree with them.[19]

Harvie Conn didn't solve these problems for Keller, but he helped him find the tools to do this work first as an urban practitioner and then as a trainer for church planters in cities around the world.

City Growth

Harvie Conn fulfilled one aspect of Edmund Clowney's vision for Westminster by introducing Keller to cutting-edge missions' emphases on contextual teaching. He fulfilled another when he applied biblical theology to cities. From the 1990s through the 2000s, Keller's ministry became virtually synonymous with urban ministry and especially church planting. He learned much of this from Conn, who launched *Urban Mission*, the only academic journal dedicated to urban ministry. Conn also started DMin and ThM degrees in urban ministry and an MA through the Center for Urban Theological Studies (CUTS), led by Bill Krispin. CUTS trained urban ministers in several of the poorer neighborhoods of Philadelphia.

Krispin and Keller traveled together quarterly to Atlanta for Mission to North America committee meetings, and Keller was shocked when Krispin shared with him the minority perspective on racism, injustice, and urban ministry held by African American board members and CUTS students. Keller's other colleagues in practical theology included Roger and Edna Greenway, who had served as missionaries with the Christian Reformed Church (CRC) and returned after Westminster to lead the CRC's world missions agency. They were replaced by Manuel Ortiz, who was a close collaborator with Conn.

Conn influenced Keller's outlook on more than urban ministry, however. In his book *Eternal Word and Changing Worlds: Theology, Anthropology, and Mission in Trialogue*, Conn provided Keller with a vision for contextualization without compromise. Through the neo-Calvinist, presuppositional approach to knowledge, Conn showed him how to respect non-Christian thought.

Conn's theological reflections on the city set some of the most obvious trajectories for Keller's later ministry. Conn sought to overturn assumptions that Christ would return the world to its rural origins in Eden. As Christians look forward to the new Jerusalem, they do more than evangelize and disciple in the private realm; they also fulfill the cultural mandate of Genesis 1:28 by building entire civilizations, or cities, that glorify God.[20] Conn sometimes called this the "urban mandate," due to the expanding scope of human work from farming and husbandry to include city planning (Genesis 4:17).[21] While some biblical interpreters see cities as a sign of the fall after fratricidal Cain, Conn saw evidence of redemption. Writing with Manuel Ortiz in his posthumously published *Urban Ministry*, Conn argued:

> So the city to which Cain turns becomes a symbol of safety and stability from divine curse for himself and his posterity (Gen. 4:17).

But it becomes also the place of human achievement, the center of cultural innovation. Art and technology—the invention of harp and flute, the forging of bronze and iron tools—begin their developments within the city's walls (Gen. 4:20–22). The image of the city shifts from stability to mobility, new methods, new ideas, new lifestyles. Life changes, and it changes more rapidly in the city.[22]

When Keller helped launch a campus of Reformed Theological Seminary in New York in 2015, he wasn't just responding to his twenty-five years of difficulties training urban church leaders. He was fulfilling the vision for urban leadership that Conn and Ortiz laid out in their 2001 book. Cities demand a different kind of training from what traditional seminaries had been offering. Theory and practice must merge under the supervision of qualified, experienced leaders. Leadership development must account for contextual specifics of the city but also train teachers how to read the Bible with cultural intelligence.[23]

For Keller, this meant training leaders not to see church as an escape from the hated city but a place to learn how to meet the city's needs, both spiritual and physical.[24] It meant forsaking "church growth" models that *use* the city and instead deploying the church in a "city growth" model that helps everyone flourish.[25]

Aided by Harvie Conn's biblical theology of cities and his contextual missions approach, Keller sought to avoid the twin dangers that thwarted previous generations of churches in New York. The "liberal evangelicals" of the early twentieth century feared that New York's professional and artistic classes would fall into unbelief if they were expected to believe everything in the Bible. They sought communion with Christ through social reform.[26] In contrast, conservative evangelicals and fundamentalists of the early twentieth century saw Gotham as a modern Babylon, pulsating with temptations for the faithful. Keller wanted to shape a congregation that would stand apart from the city, from within the city, while loving the city—a congregation that could meet the city's physical needs without losing focus on their spiritual plight.

Through his historical study of mercy ministry, Keller came to see diaconal work as a key to breakthrough for evangelicals in urban ministry. Through the PCA in 1985, he released his first published book, *Resources for Deacons*.[27] Four years later when he moved to New York, Keller published *Ministries of Mercy: The Call of the Jericho Road* and dedicated it to Kathy. Years earlier, the first book Kathy had read after finishing everything from C. S. Lewis that was then available was *The Cross and the Switchblade* by David Wilkerson. Afterward, she set a plan for her life: she would become a pastor and move to New York and work with gangs.

During the summer of 1973, while in seminary, Kathy worked for the Philadelphia Presbytery through a church in Germantown where she walked door-to-door through twelve neighborhoods setting up block parties so people could meet their neighbors and church members and an evangelistic movie could be shown. "That very intimate experience of the city and being the only White person I saw all day long did have a profound effect on me," she recalled. "I had never known any Black people before or seen people living in dangerous conditions." Tim got one of his first tastes of urban life when he visited Kathy in Germantown.[28]

Tim Keller supplemented his meager urban ministry experience by watching and reading and talking with Harvie Conn, who understood that urban growth, especially in the largest cities, would far outpace areas where evangelicals had already built strong church networks.[29] Conn knew evangelicals would not plant churches if they feared cities, and that even if they did plant churches, they would need to do more than evangelize.[30] Michael Green, one of the era's most courageous evangelists and a role model for Keller, saw that churches could not separate evangelism from mercy ministry as previous generations of evangelicals and liberals had done. "Churches that put themselves out to meet social needs grow," Green wrote in *Evangelism through the Local Church*, a book Keller studied en route to New York. "Churches that live for themselves die by themselves. . . . If our evangelism is to be effective, the church must be concerned to meet the surrounding need."[31]

Within three years of its first informal meeting, Redeemer Presbyterian Church launched Hope for New York in 1992 to mobilize funding and volunteers for organizations meeting physical needs of the city. If the church didn't do this work, Keller warned, they would deserve the city's scorn.[32] The world isn't accustomed to a church that cares just as much about expositional preaching as it does about justice for the poor. But at Redeemer, these goals would be theologically inseparable.[33]

Just as Clowney and Conn had taught him, Keller insisted that genuine Christian faith should affect every aspect of life or it's not the best of biblical and historical Christianity.[34] To stay faithful to the gospel, churches must break stereotypes. Keller argued in *Center Church*:

> A missional church will be more deeply and practically committed to deeds of compassion and social justice than traditional fundamentalist churches and more deeply and practically committed to evangelism and conversion than traditional liberal churches. This kind of church is profoundly counterintuitive to American observers, who are no longer able to categorize (and dismiss) it as liberal or conservative. Only this kind of church has any chance in the non-Christian West.[35]

It was a bold statement, but probably one that Harvie Conn could have also made before his death in 1999. To Keller, doing justice is not a distraction from evangelism. This work helps neighbors outside the church see the good news of Jesus as plausible. Conversion growth looks like accruing power, unless those converts sacrifice to meet the needs of their neighbors, regardless of whether they share faith in Jesus. Then non-Christians can see that God's judgment and grace is the basis for justice in our world.[36]

Clowney and Conn made some long-standing Westminster supporters nervous, because they didn't just train pastors to fill traditional Reformed pulpits in the United States. For their protégé Keller, this was exactly the point. He wanted both/and churches to sprout up in cities around the world, with the biblical balance "of word *and* deed ministries; of challenging *and* affirming human culture; of cultural engagement *and* countercultural distinctiveness; of commitment to truth *and* generosity to others who don't share the same beliefs; of tradition *and* innovation in practice."[37] This "center church" vision demanded *both/and* where many conservative Presbyterians wanted *either/or*. Edmund Clowney would have recognized such churches as "moulded by the gospel" in biblical theology, personal piety, and contextual application. Keller wrote in *Center Church*:

> Because of the inside-out, substitutionary atonement aspect, the church will place great emphasis on personal conversion, experiential grace renewal, evangelism, outreach, and church planting. This makes it look like an evangelical-charismatic church. Because of the upside-down, kingdom/incarnation aspect, the church will place great emphasis on deep community, cell groups or house churches, radical giving and sharing of resources, spiritual disciplines, racial reconciliation, and living with the poor. This makes it look like an Anabaptist "peace" church. Because of the forward-back, kingdom/restoration aspect, the church will place great emphasis on seeking the welfare of the city, neighborhood and civic involvement, cultural engagement, and training people to work in "secular" vocations out of a Christian worldview. This makes it look like a mainline church or, perhaps, a Kuyperian Reformed church. Very few churches, denominations, or movements integrate all of these ministries and emphases. Yet I believe that a comprehensive view of the biblical gospel—one that grasps the

gospel's inside-out, upside-down, and forward-back aspects—will champion and cultivate them all. This is what we mean by a Center Church.[38]

Even in seeking this balance, Keller kept the priority on evangelism. Non-Christians can care for the homeless, but only Christians can invite them to eternal life. One of Keller's biggest influences helped him see how churches could stay focused on evangelism even as they do justice.[39]

Ministry Strategy for the Future

Westminster Theological Seminary, birthed from the split between fundamentalists and modernists of the early twentieth century, had no problem shaking its clenched fist at the likes of Walter Rauschenbusch, a German Baptist minister who served near Hell's Kitchen in New York City in the 1880s. Often credited as the founder of the social gospel, Rauschenbusch criticized Christians who saved souls but didn't feed stomachs. Eventually, he also argued against biblical inerrancy and substitutionary atonement and instead described Jesus as a mere example for how we should love the poor and marginalized. J. Gresham Machen excoriated this liberalism in contrast to Christianity.

But Keller looked back even further, narrating the story back beyond liberalism, all the way to colonial America and Jonathan Edwards. And there he found a different model for faithful churches. He cited Edwards's sermon "Christian Charity: The Duty of Charity to the Poor," which argued, "Where have we any command in the Bible laid down in stronger terms, and in a more peremptory urgent manner, than the command of giving to the poor?"[40]

Biblical theology doesn't work against justice. To the contrary, Keller argued, Edwards "saw involvement with the poor and classic

Biblical doctrine as indissolubly intertwined."[41] Maybe that's rare to see today, Keller admitted. But he wrote his book *Generous Justice* "for people who don't see yet what Edwards saw, namely, that when the Spirit enables us to understand what Christ has done for us, the result is a life poured out in deeds of justice and compassion for the poor."[42] In true Edwardsean fashion, reminiscent of the *Religious Affections*, Keller went so far as to argue, "A life poured out in doing justice for the poor is the inevitable sign of any real, true gospel faith."[43]

When Keller moved to New York, early Redeemer members saw this emphasis in Keller's preaching. "Tim had a unique ability to speak to young professional New Yorkers," said Steve Preston. Steve and his wife, Molly, were one of the first couples to meet and marry through Redeemer as those young professionals matched up and then started their families. "He was incisive. It felt like he was preaching to me. He used the gospel to connect theology with service and spiritual formation. It wasn't evangelism *or* service. He brought them together. He tackled every issue, including sex and singleness."[44] Preston would go on to become secretary of Housing and Urban Development under President George W. Bush and later CEO of Goodwill Industries.

The brochure introducing Keller's New York church plant bore the obvious influence of Westminster, even if it didn't have the names of Edmund Clowney and Harvie Conn on it. Kathy Keller oversaw the production of "New York City: A Ministry Strategy for the Future." The art director at Great Commission Publications offered to help and opted for brown and celery tones, which would save money in mass production. But Kathy had a different idea. She showed him a bank advertisement she had received in the mail and noted the glossy finish with green and gray colors. He balked at the cost. Kathy insisted. They decided they would pay the higher cost because that's what the New York context demanded.

The brochure introduced Tim Keller as a former associate staff member of InterVarsity Christian Fellowship and touted his nine-year ministry at Hopewell, during which he supervised twenty-four church plants in middle Atlantic states and his church tripled in size. His Philadelphia ministries ranged all the way from evangelizing business leaders, homosexuals, and Muslims to discipling urban singles as well as college, graduate, and foreign students. Keller also chaired the steering committee of Tenth Presbyterian Church's ministry to AIDS patients in Philadelphia.[45]

The brochure included two photos featuring the Twin Towers— one with the Statue of Liberty in the foreground and the other with the Brooklyn Bridge draped across them. The brochures offered an introduction to church visitors, but they were also distributed for fundraising. The second sentence could have been written by Harvie Conn to convince target donors of the need for this church and even hundreds more in New York: "Tell a Southerner that the entire metropolitan populations of Atlanta, Miami, Houston, Nashville, Richmond, New Orleans, Orlando, and Washington, D.C. could fit comfortably into New York's metropolitan area and still have room to squeeze in the citizens of Roanoke, Montgomery, and Greenville, and his eyes will glaze over." New York is a financial capital exceeding Tokyo, the brochure explained. It's an education and political powerhouse on par with Boston and Washington, D.C. And the more than one hundred thousand artists in New York objected to Paris's claim as the cultural center of civilization. "No other single city in the world excels in all these areas together!" the brochure exclaimed.

Before Redeemer even had its name, the vision for the church had been set—and it looked remarkably like the vision Edmund Clowney and Harvie Conn taught at Westminster. Already in the 1980s, the Kellers were looking ahead to the next century:

> If the Christian church hopes to have an impact on the twenty-first century, it must address the city of New York. The rapid spread of early Christianity and its transforming effect on Roman culture was due in large part to its character as an urban faith. Paul took his

missionary message to strategic cities, from which the gospel spread along routes of commerce and emigration. City dwellers were more open to change and more mobile than their rural counterparts. Because the cities were centers of trade and craft, whole professions were won to Christ with only word-of-mouth evangelism.

The brochure envisioned a church not just for White Presbyterians but also for New York's Asian population, which was estimated to double from four hundred thousand to eight hundred thousand by 1995. And the vision extended far beyond just one church. This new work would become a hub to help reach immigrants from the West Indies and Central and South America in their own languages and styles. "What if all those people had an opportunity to hear the gospel of Jesus Christ in their own languages, in churches pastored by members of their own cultures?" The nations had come to the city and broken down the traditional divides between foreign and domestic missions, as Conn and Newbigin had observed. The needs were at least as great inside the United States as in many overseas destinations.

The vision for Redeemer City to City was already in motion. And the Kellers foresaw the PCA as a church planting engine through which Christians in the South could help evangelize the rest of the country. Clowney wasn't mentioned in the church brochure, but it was his dream come true from Westminster in 1969:

> The Presbyterian Church in America, the second largest Presbyterian denomination in the country, is committed to both creative ministry and connectional support. The PCA is neither a mainline denomination nor a fundamentalist church. Rather we are committed both to the historic Christian faith and to addressing contemporary life and the issues of our day. Our aim in New York City is to join with other evangelical and Reformed churches and ministries in order to minister to the needs of people and witness to the grace found in Christ.

It's not clear whether the brochure was trying to sell New Yorkers on the PCA or selling the PCA on a new vision for church planting, one that would look quite different from Roanoke, Montgomery, and Tupelo. Either way it accomplished both of these aims. Redeemer would remain authentically PCA but with a distinctive New York sensibility—and a global vision. As Keller wrote in *Center Church*, "We believe ministry in the center of global cities is the highest priority for the church in the twenty-first century."[46] By 2021, Redeemer City to City under Keller's leadership as chairman and cofounder had started 748 churches in more than seventy-five cities around the world.

Before he stepped down as pastor of Redeemer Presbyterian Church, Keller laid out the traits of churches he believed would thrive in the coming secular city:

> In New York City, Redeemer has been a path-breaking ministry, and, if God will continue to bless and use us, there still is much more such work to do. We must find ways to preach the ancient message of the gospel in ways that both defy the illusions of the age yet resonate with the good aspirations and hopes of our neighbors.
>
> That means several things. It means to contest the self-narratives of secularity, especially its claim to inclusivity. It means to appeal to people's deepest intuitions which do not fit the secular view of the world—intuitions about moral truth, human value, and the reality of both love and beauty. It means to expose the secular culture's idolatry of prosperity and power, even as we humbly admit the church's own failure to operate on the basis of love and generosity. It means to admit the church's historic failures to execute on its own Biblical principles—the *imago Dei* dignity of every human being, love for opponents, universal care for the suffering, and justice for the oppressed—even as it argues that the source of this warranted critique is Christian truth itself. It means to neither dominate nor withdraw from society but to provoke and yet serve. It means learning

how to set forth gospel truths in an uncompromising way but also in a manner that directly answers people's most poignant questions in a disarming and compelling way. It means to offer people a meaning in life that suffering can't take away, an identity so rooted in God's love that the world's pressure is off, and a hope beyond the walls of this world. It means to be doctrinally solid but not sectarian, civically active but not partisan, committed to the arts but not subjectivistic about truth.[47]

Harvie Conn never lived to see this movement for global church planting take off. But if he had, he would have recognized the fulfilment of a vision he helped Keller develop in their years together at Westminster.

Street Preaching

Keller's road to New York passed through Philadelphia, where he learned to love urban ministry with Conn's help. But without another of Clowney's key hires at Westminster, Redeemer Presbyterian Church would likely never have existed.

Jack Miller was Tim and Kathy Keller's pastor for only five years, from 1984 to 1989, at New Life Presbyterian Church in Glenside. But in these five years, after nine years of around-the-clock ministry in Hopewell, the Kellers learned together another vision for how the church could run. On the verge of burnout when he arrived, Tim Keller needed a church where he could simply feed on the preaching of God's Word.[48] Richard Lovelace taught them about revival back at Gordon-Conwell. But at New Life, they experienced firsthand a culture of gospel renewal applied to social justice, worship, evangelism, and missions.

Like many other converts from the Jesus Movement, Tim Keller associated revival with breaking out of the church walls and bringing the gospel into the dorm room. Formal settings were seen as inhibiting the progress of the gospel. But under Miller's influence, Keller saw how the church needs revival, and revival needs the church. Without revival, the church loses spiritual vitality and evangelistic urgency. But without the church, revival undermines doctrinal precision and personal holiness.[49] As an elder at New Life, Keller got a front-row seat to a pastor who didn't think twice about canceling Sunday school so everyone could pray together for an hour over an urgent need. After Keller preached one Sunday, an elder asked to speak to the congregation. The elder repented publicly for sin and asked the entire congregation to hold him accountable. No wonder, then, that Kathy Keller's sister said after a visit, "I'm not sure I can attend this church. The Christianity is too real!"

Above all, Jack Miller taught Tim Keller how to preach grace from every text of Scripture.[50] Keller assigned every original Redeemer core group member Miller's book *Outgrowing the Ingrown Church*. In April 1991, Keller invited Miller to preach at Redeemer and then lead a church retreat along with his wife, Rose Marie. After the retreat, Keller preached from Ephesians 5:1–2 about God's dearly beloved children, which he described as the Millers' main theme.

> It's the thing God has given them to say to people, and that is that you have to think of yourself as a dearly loved child of God or you're really not able to live the Christian life at all. Unless you are governed by the idea that you are a dearly loved child, you can't live. You were built for family love. You were built for it. You were built to have a loving father, a loving parent. You were built for it, and until you see that's true of you, you can't live a life of imitation of God.[51]

This message became known as "sonship," which "emphasized the historically neglected Reformed doctrines of justification, adoption, and the fatherhood of God, as well as how partnership with the

Holy Spirit enables Christians to maintain access to the spiritual freedom and power that is theirs in Christ," according to Jack Miller's biographer.[52]

Liz Kaufmann and her husband, Dick, first met Tim and Kathy Keller when they traveled with Jack Miller to help start a revival at West Hopewell Presbyterian Church. Through their years together in Philadelphia and New York, Liz Kaufmann saw in Tim a contrast to the pride and self-assuredness of some academic circles. Keller tried to foster church cultures where people could criticize him without fear of reprisal. She traces this influence to Ed Clowney and especially Jack Miller. "Jack Miller was always trying to deal with his own pride, and he always tried to help all of us who worked with him and under him to address those underlying sins and not just focus on other people's outward sins."[53]

Jack Miller also drew out of Keller a boldness in evangelism he didn't know he could muster. Miller set an example for leading people to faith, no matter what it took. If that meant letting a hitchhiker move into his home, that's what Miller did.

"Putting personal concerns aside for the sake of the gospel—that's how Jack mentored all of us," Kaufmann said. "Sometimes it got hairy. We were crazy back then. It was the '70s!"

It was during Communion at New Life's church plant in Dresher, Pennsylvania, that Kathy Keller overcame her concerns about moving her family to New York. Around the Millers, she began to understand that the gospel is more important than safety and comfort.

Miller and Keller were different in several ways. Tim Keller wasn't nearly as daring as Jack Miller. Originally an English teacher, Miller looked the part—fuzzy hair, rumpled clothes. His faith made him impervious to criticism and fear. Longtime friends remember him standing on the street corner in Jenkintown talking to the motorcycle gangs and drug dealers. Many of them came to Christ. One of them married his daughter, went to seminary, and became his successor.

Tim's style, by contrast, is more academic and reserved, like that of his mentor Ed Clowney. But the influence of both of these men on Tim is obvious to his longtime friends from Philadelphia. "It's like a merger of those two personalities in the way he approached ministry in New York," Kaufmann said.[54]

According to Miller's biographer, no one better fulfilled Clowney's vision for Westminster than Jack. He combined the prayerful piety of the bowed head with the evangelistic boldness of the clenched fist. He bridged between the founding and successor generations of Westminster by joining Cornelius Van Til for street preaching in the 1960s and 1970s.[55] As a student and professor at Westminster, Keller saw multiple models for taking the highest level of intellectual sophistication to the urban streets.

Gospel-Centered Ministry

Jack Miller's influence runs so deep in Keller that readers have sometimes struggled to differentiate between the two in attributing their most beloved quotes. Keller often gets the credit, but Miller is the one who originally said, "Cheer up! You're a worse sinner than you ever dared imagine, and you're more loved than you ever dared hope."

Keller recognized in Miller the same dynamics of revival he first learned from Lovelace. Miller's "sonship" program treated spiritually moribund churches and Christians who had lost their grasp of the gospel of grace and begun to slide down into either legalism or antinomianism. Both of these kill spiritual vitality.

Miller wasn't the first to help Keller distinguish between law and gospel. Keller had already seen this dynamic in Martin Luther's preface to his commentary on Galatians. Within the Presbyterian tradition, the "Marrow Men" of eighteenth-century Scotland took on this issue of "properly relating works and grace, law and gospel, not merely in our systematic theology but in our preaching and pastoral ministry and, ultimately, within our own hearts."[56] But Miller rounded out Keller's zeal for revival that began with the Bucknell student strike of 1970. Keller saw in Miller a revivalist for the twentieth century in the tradition of Wesley and Whitefield and Edwards of the eighteenth century. If not for the influence of Miller and New Life, Keller's "prodigal God" message never would have come to fruition.[57]

Thanks largely to Keller and his later influence on a generation of pastors, references to "gospel-centered" ministry exploded between 2005 and 2010.[58] But as early as 1988, Jack Miller spoke about grace- and gospel-centered living in his sermons at New Life Glenside and the associated ministry of World Harvest Mission, later renamed Serge.[59]

Typical for Keller, he borrowed the concepts but also added his own spin. Miller used "gospel-centered" in psychological terms, referring to the experience of God's love despite our sin. Miller especially resonated with Christians who grew up with religious guilt. Keller deployed the term more theologically, using it in his apologetics for secular crowds to differentiate his teaching from legalism on the one hand and antinomianism on the other. It became Keller's way of saying that Redeemer wouldn't be like New York's fundamentalist or liberal churches.[60] Such gospel-centered ministry in Keller's hands included social justice, pastoral counseling, faith and vocation, diaconal work, and leadership and power in the church.

Much of the later interest in "gospel-centered" ministry in the early decades of the twenty-first century can be attributed to Keller cofounding The Gospel Coalition (TGC) with D. A. Carson. Their initial idea to invite evangelical pastors across denominations for a meeting began just before the September 11 attacks in 2001. In May 2005, Keller and Carson hosted several dozen pastors from across North America, representing Anglican, Southern Baptist, Presbyterian, Episcopal, Evangelical Free, and independent churches. This group would eventually become The Gospel Coalition, and its goals included a clear emphasis on centering ministry on the gospel so that Jesus would never be assumed or ignored in favor of other agendas. "We wanted to build a community of churches and pastors in which the gospel was the central thing, the exciting thing, what we got out of bed for in the morning," Carson said.

Carson and Keller explicitly interpreted the gospel in light of the broad Reformed heritage they shared, with emphases on justification by faith alone and penal substitutionary atonement. And they wanted the gospel to dictate emphases in biblical teaching. "There are hermeneutical and Christological implications to this understanding of gospel-centeredness—implications that affect how we preach, how we put the Bible together, the ways in which, say, the concerns for social justice are properly tied to the cross and resurrection," Carson explained.[61]

It's not difficult to see this agenda overlapping with Ed Clowney's 1969 vision for gospel renewal at Westminster. At the time of TGC's founding, Keller had not yet become a household name among evangelicals. Carson introduced him to the other pastors in 2005 as relatively unknown, largely because of his intense focus on Redeemer. When he was profiled by *The New York Times* in 2006, as Redeemer attendance topped 4,400, Keller had not yet attracted widespread attention outside the city. He hadn't yet published any bestselling books, and TGC's first national conference didn't convene until a year later in May 2007. Keller was primarily known among fellow church planters and the PCA.[62] Carson credited Keller as especially good at communicating sin to postmoderns, an allusion to his teaching on idolatry.

By the time he started TGC, Keller had been collaborating across denominations for decades. Reared by InterVarsity and educated by Gordon-Conwell, he felt comfortable in interdenominational settings. When he started Redeemer, he didn't try to compete with other evangelical pastors. As Keller would teach church planters through Redeemer City to City, God uses many types of churches to reach a whole city. For the sake of mission in a post-Christian context, Keller wrote in *Center Church*, Christians should emphasize their unity:

> In Christendom, when "everyone was a Christian," it was perhaps useful for a church to define itself primarily in contrast with other churches. Today, however, it is much more illuminating and helpful for a church to define itself in relationship to the values of the secular culture. If we spend our time bashing and criticizing other kinds of churches, we simply play into the common defeater that all Christians are intolerant. While it is right to align ourselves with denominations that share many of our distinctives, at the local level we should co-operate with, reach out to, and support the other congregations and ministries in our local area.[63]

Nevertheless, Keller started TGC with a critique of the drift away from the gospel he saw in many evangelical churches. Teaching on Luke 5:12–13 on the afternoon of May 17, 2005, Keller lamented the decline of evangelicalism compared to the previous generation, represented by John Stott and Francis Schaeffer. He wanted TGC to recover Stott and Schaeffer's desire to engage the world but not be like the world and to cooperate across denominations in mission. "Why don't we have a body of leaders/teachers/preachers who weave these things together into one whole cloth?" Keller asked his fellow pastors. "Why don't we have a body of people doing this?"

The way he answered these questions tells us much about Keller and the influence of Jonathan Edwards on his understanding of effective pastoral ministry. Citing historian Mark Noll, Keller lauded Edwards as theologically orthodox, pious, and culturally engaged at the same time. After the death of Edwards, however, his followers broke into three groups. The Princeton theologians and their Westminster successors emphasized the closed fist of theological orthodoxy. Jonathan Edwards Jr. kept the cultural apologetics. And Charles Finney promoted "new measures" for revival. TGC became Keller's vehicle for drawing these elements together again in local churches, as Jonathan Edwards had done in the First Great Awakening. Again, we can see the Clowney vision for Westminster channeled through Keller.

But Keller had yet another model in mind for what he hoped TGC could accomplish in the twenty-first century. When Keller became a Christian through InterVarsity at Bucknell, British evangelicals showed him how to be orthodox, pious, and culturally astute. Authors such as I. Howard Marshall, John Stott, J. I. Packer, Martyn Lloyd-Jones, and C. S. Lewis plugged the gap that widened as Americans split between fundamentalists and modernists. TGC also became Keller's homage to these mid-century British evangelicals. By convening pastors around the need for gospel-centered ministry, Keller hoped to give future generations of Christian leaders a place to stand between liberalism and fundamentalism.

Clowney's call for a ministry "moulded by the gospel" can be seen in Keller's explanation of how the good news of Jesus guides everything for Christians:

> The gospel is not just the ABCs but the A to Z of the Christian life. It is inaccurate to think the gospel is what saves non-Christians, and then Christians mature by trying hard to live according to biblical principles. It is more accurate to say that we are saved by believing the gospel, and then we are transformed in every part of our minds, hearts, and lives by believing the gospel more and more deeply as life goes on.[64]

Invoking Jack Miller, Keller then explained in *Center Church* how the power of the gospel progresses in two movements: "It first says, 'I am more sinful and flawed than I ever dared believe,' but then quickly follows with, 'I am more accepted and loved than I ever dared hope.' The former outflanks antinomianism, while the latter staves off legalism. One of the greatest challenges is to be vigilant in both directions *at once*."[65]

And to meet that challenge, Christians need theological vision.

Fabric of Theology

Alongside its priority on gospel-centered ministry, TGC became a platform for Keller to popularize the concept of *theological vision*. Keller didn't read *The Fabric of Theology* by Richard Lints until his fourth year in New York. Inspired by the book, Keller wrote an entire theological vision of ministry for the North American church as part of TGC's foundation documents a decade later.[66]

The concept of theological vision taught by Lints resembles Harvie Conn's insistence on contextual theology. Lints wrote, "It is . . . [critical that] the people of God [come] to an awareness of their historical, cultural, and rational filters so that they will not be ruled by them."[67] Keller explained in *Center Church* that confessional statements don't analyze our culture or dictate our approach to history and human reason, even though our position on these topics will determine the shape of our ministry. And Christians judge other churches for their different decisions as straying from their confession. Sometimes what Christians identify as doctrinal downgrade is merely a different theological vision.[68] When churches adopt theological vision, they can do more than react to culture. They can challenge culture and communicate the gospel in transformative ways. They can work together.[69]

Inspired by Lints, Keller explains theological vision as the "middleware" between the "hardware" of confessional theology and "software" of ministry programs. Churches tend to know their theology and defend their programs. But they can't connect the two in a way that suits their place and time.

"This is something more practical than just doctrinal beliefs but much more theological than 'how-to steps' for carrying out a particular ministry," Keller explained. "Once this vision is in place, with its emphases and values, it leads church leaders to make good decisions on how to worship, disciple, evangelize, serve, and engage culture in their field of ministry—whether in a city, suburb, or small town."[70]

To develop theological vision, Keller commends four steps from *The Fabric of Theology*. The first step is the same for Lints as for Clowney: listen to the Bible to develop doctrinal beliefs. The next step is the same as for Conn: reflect on culture to determine from the Bible what Christians must reject and what they must accept. Then Lints says Christians must decide what level of rational understanding of the gospel they expect from non-Christians, in how they will present the gospel—in short, whether they will follow the continental or British Reformed traditions. Finally, conclusions will depend on theological tradition—on how much deference Christians will show to previous generations' beliefs and practices.

Keller could see that theological vision would be necessary to hold together interdenominational ministries such as TGC. Anglican, Baptist, and Presbyterian pastors might agree on 99 percent of their theological confessions, but if they don't employ theological vision, they'll struggle to understand why they can't get along. They won't see the different views of culture, reason, and tradition that supersede confessional commonality.[71]

Theological vision offers a useful perspective for evaluating Westminster, even decades after Clowney and Keller had both departed. Along with D. Clair Davis, Jack Miller, Harvie Conn, and others, Clowney and Keller tolerated the volatility of evangelicals. So closely adapted to culture, evangelicals could share the gospel in accessible ways for the masses, regardless of education or ethnicity. But this same adaptability makes evangelicals susceptible to doctrinal downgrade. They can't resist culture with a clenched fist when it's necessary to preserve the integrity of the gospel message. On the other hand, some of Clowney's critics wanted a Reformed ministry that prioritized doctrinal precision, with cultural forms unchanged from previous decades or even centuries. They wouldn't turn away someone who showed interest in the gospel, but neither would they go out of their way to accommodate them until the Holy Spirit opened their eyes to the truth of Jesus. Clowney and Keller would never be content while preaching to the Reformed choir.

Over the years, critics have faulted Keller for partnering across denominations with pastors who succumbed to the pressures to accommodate. But he never gave up hope that a movement of churches would emerge and combine innovative evangelism with doctrinal preaching, personal holiness with artistic excellence, radical sharing of resources with robust integration of faith and work.

He never gave up on Ed Clowney's vision of the bowed head.

"What could lead to a growing movement of gospel-centered churches?" Keller wrote in TGC's theological vision for ministry in 2007. "The ultimate answer is that God must, for his own glory, send revival in response to the fervent, extraordinary, prevailing prayer of his people."[72]

PART FOUR

FROM GOTHAM TO GLOBE

1989 to Present

FOURTEEN

MASTERS OF
THE UNIVERSE

New York City

Kitty Genovese.

The name conjures up a clear and frightening warning for a generation of Americans who knew her story from 1964.

Or thought they did at least.

The story goes that more than twenty New Yorkers watched an assailant stab Genovese for more than twenty minutes without even bothering to report the crime, let alone intervene to help. No one assisted, even when she yelled and ran wildly across the street and back again.

"This episode thoroughly shocked Americans, and studies were launched into this urban indifference to the plight of a neighbor," Ray Bakke wrote in 1987, two years before Tim Keller planted Redeemer Presbyterian Church. "How can people stand around watching someone get killed and not get involved?"[1]

Not until 2016 did *The New York Times* finally acknowledge that their original reporting, which suggested thirty-eight people had watched Genovese die in Queens, might not bear up under scrutiny. In fact, one courageous neighbor did run to help Genovese, screamed for neighbors to call police, and then held her brutalized body until the ambulance showed up.[2]

But by then the damage had been done. *Urban* had become synonymous with *violent crime.*

After he graduated from Purdue University in Indiana, Glen Kleinknecht moved to New York in 1976, during one of the city's lowest moments. The name David Berkowitz (better known as Son of Sam) became a national obsession when he killed six people in New York City between 1976 and 1977. Kleinknecht moved to New York after reading David Wilkerson's *The Cross and the Switchblade*, published in 1963. The book inspired many zealous young evangelicals to follow Wilkerson's lead in preaching Jesus among the gangs in Brooklyn and other battered neighborhoods. Kleinknecht remembers that in the 1970s and 1980s, when you mentioned New York, you became a celebrity at parties among Christians. A hush would descend on the room. Someone would inevitably ask about crime. Kleinknecht learned a lesson about boasting of the dangers when he unwittingly talked a friend out of moving to the city.

Seemingly, everyone in New York from those years has a crime story, or several, to share. Between 1971 and 1988, the New York metro area's population declined from a peak of nearly 18.4 million residents to less than 17.9 million. Violent crimes in the city almost quadrupled between 1965 and 1990. New York reported 836 murders in 1965 and 2,605 in 1990. Over the same time period, rapes doubled and robberies quadrupled.[3]

Back then, New York University couldn't hide its geographic location. But Columbia University tried. For much of the 1970s and on into the 1980s, you couldn't be sure that even a New York resident would *heart* New York. In 1989, a poll grabbed headlines when it showed that most New Yorkers would leave the city—if that were an option.[4]

If you were a Christian, you also had to worry about the challenges of connecting with other followers of Jesus. Lora Gaston moved to New York for a job on Wall Street in the mid-1980s. But she didn't find any obvious Christian community. "I felt like the only Christian in New York City under eighty-five!"[5]

She wasn't. But Protestant, Catholic, and Jewish leaders had been reporting since at least 1975 that they felt out of favor with mainstream society in New York. They could no longer claim to speak for American values. They could perhaps offer marginal contributions to the real social influencers in entertainment and politics. *The New York Times* identified a survival mentality in New York's White Protestant churches, which struggled to collaborate with their far more numerous Black counterparts.

"The city has largely abandoned religion," the Rev. Dr. Bryant Kirkland of the Fifth Avenue Presbyterian Church, one block from the Museum of Modern Art, told the *Times*. With notable exceptions, the mainline White Protestants of previous generations had almost entirely disappeared from New York's elite society by 1975.[6] One notable exception was a mainline Protestant elite who began construction on Trump Tower across the street from Fifth Avenue Presbyterian in 1979.

Few envisioned that this developer would one day become president of the United States. It was almost as unlikely a scenario as the new evangelical wave coming ashore on Manhattan in the late-1980s.

Yuppie Evangelism

In the mid-nineteenth century, New York had been the evangelical capital of the United States. No place better illustrated what could happen when pulpits ring out with the preaching of God's Word.[7] The city's staid Anglican and Dutch Reformed history gave way to evangelical fervor. First Presbyterian Church welcomed English evangelist George Whitefield in 1739 when Anglican churches shut him out. By 1857, even North Dutch Church got in on revival when lay evangelist Jeremiah Lanphier began leading prayer meetings on Fulton Street in Lower Manhattan, mere months before financial panic descended on the city.

No awakening in American history so far has matched the scope of the Prayer Meeting Revival of 1857 and 1858. Afterward, New York became the target destination for every generation's leading evangelist, as with Dwight Moody in 1876. From the city's evangelical ferment would come such influential parachurch ministries as the Mission and Tract Society and the American Bible Society. Historian Matthew Bowman recounts:

> By the 1880s, evangelicalism was well entrenched among the governing classes of New York City. The middle class of northern European descent drove the expansion of Baptist, Presbyterian, Methodist, and evangelical Episcopal churches in mid-nineteenth-century New York. In certain neighborhoods of Manhattan, particularly the fashionable areas around Central Park, evangelical Protestantism clearly established itself as the dominant faith; affiliation with an evangelical church hovered at around a third of the population in the upper-class residential areas of Fifth Avenue in midtown.[8]

The ensuing influx of immigrants, both ethnic minorities as well as Catholics, disestablished the Protestant elite of New York. Protestant churches divided over the relationship between evangelism and mercy ministry, as well as over biblical authority and accuracy. Churches in the outer boroughs never fell as hard or as fast as those in Manhattan, which suffered severe White flight in the 1950s and 1960s. Evangelicals across the city, including the working classes that never decamped for

Connecticut and New Jersey, gathered in ethnic-specific storefront churches. Brooklyn Tabernacle had been growing since the early 1980s. But not much was happening in Manhattan south of 95th Street, at least until three evangelical churches showed signs of life as they welcomed new pastors—Jim Rose at Calvary Baptist, Gordon MacDonald at Trinity Baptist, and Martyn Minns at All Angels.

Transience remained a problem for evangelicals in a city undergoing wholesale changes. Tom Wolfe captured the mood with his 1987 number one bestseller *The Bonfire of the Vanities*, one of the books Tim Keller read before he moved from Philadelphia to New York. As the book begins, we meet Sherman McCoy in his Park Avenue co-op apartment on the Upper East Side with twelve-foot ceilings and two wings—one for the help, the other for the White Anglo-Saxon Protestant owners.[9] Racked with guilt, McCoy justifies an affair and the damage he caused his wife and daughter. After all, he's a "Master of the Universe," one of the three to five hundred men on Wall Street who could command fifty thousand dollars in commission on a single trade.[10]

McCoy shows little empathy for the "social X-rays"—his terms for his wife and her friends. They're so thin you can see the lamplight through their bones as they exchange tips about landscaping and interior design.[11] McCoy also resents the other Masters of the Universe, like his fellow prep school alumnus, who is "only forty but had looked fifty for the past twenty years."[12] All of them share a "deep worry that lives in the base of the skull of every resident of Park Avenue south of Ninety-sixth Street," the "black youth, tall, rangy, wearing white sneakers."[13]

Writing twenty years after Wolfe's work of fiction became a sensation, Jordan Belfort set his self-described memoir in the same year of 1987. Belfort borrows Wolfe's appellation, Masters of the Universe, and it's hard to tell if he's writing history or living the same Icarus fantasy as *The Bonfire of the Vanities*. Describing New York in 1987, Belfort wrote:

Wall Street was in the midst of a raging bull market, and freshly mint-
ed millionaires were being spit out a dime a dozen. Money was cheap,
and a guy named Michael Milken had invented something called
"junk bonds," which had changed the way corporate America went
about its business. It was a time of unbridled greed, a time of wanton
excess. It was the era of the yuppie.[14]

Which meant it was time for a ministry that could evangelize the yuppies. Who would introduce these Masters of the Universe to *the* Master
of the Universe?

Low-Key Fundamentalist

Art DeMoss made his millions through mail-order insurance before he
died of a heart attack on the tennis court in 1979. Six years later his
widow, Nancy DeMoss, began hosting high-class dinners for these
Masters of the Universe and their upper-class compatriots. If this crowd
would no longer go to church, she would go to them with the message
of Jesus.

In May 1988, she invited born-again former Nixon politico Chuck
Colson to a dinner with a crowd of seven hundred people. Henry
Luce III, president of the Luce Foundation and elder at Madison Avenue
Presbyterian Church, attended a DeMoss dinner in 1987.

"It's a new approach to religion, promoting it on a large scale with
sophisticated metropolitan people," he told *New York* magazine. "I'm
certain it's fundamentalist, but there was very little specific biblical quotations or theological commentary."[15] It's interesting to note that this
same model had also helped propel the Prayer Meeting Revival of 1857
and 1858.

DeMoss herself, mother to seven children, gave a simple evangelistic
appeal, recounted in the *New York* article:

My husband, Art, was one of the worst reprobates New York ever knew, but what a giant of Christianity he became.... Nine years ago, I lost Art, and that was the real beginning of my learning. Then my son died in an automobile crash, and I lost a sister and my mother too. But I consider myself one of the most fortunate people in the world. I have a perfect peace that surpasses understanding, and, you know, nothing can rob you of the peace of God. This is not my own presumptuous philosophy. This is God's plan. Do you feel a tug at your heart?[16]

Ministry didn't stop with the dinners. DeMoss House was a century-old mansion purchased in 1986 on the Upper East Side on East 73rd Street. Staff hosted Bible studies and follow-up dinners. But the DeMoss House was more eclectic than the upper-crust dinners. The setting wasn't nearly so formal. The crowd pulled more broadly from finance and fashion, Wall Street and Madison Avenue, broadcasting and law. Up to 150 attended Bible studies on Tuesday or Wednesday night. Sample topics included, "Why Bother with Jesus?" and "Can I Really Trust the Bible?" Media described the nondenominational ministry as "soft-sell, low-key fundamentalist."[17] But DeMoss House staff preferred "historical Christianity, or biblical Christianity."[18] Talks warned of eternal judgment but also answered questions about anxiety and purpose.

DeMoss House hosted Executive Ministries, part of Campus Crusade for Christ (now Cru), one of the primary beneficiaries of the DeMoss family wealth. Ron Fraser, the Executive Ministries leader, explained that even the most successful and wealthiest New Yorkers still have spiritual need. And when they come to know Christ, they can share that faith with their many influential friends.[19]

DeMoss and Executive Ministries found a way for the rising class of New York yuppies to explore Christianity among familiar social settings. There was just one thing missing.

They didn't know where to take these yuppies to church.

Garden to City

Diane Balch—who helped run the house with her husband, Dave—prayed that Tim Keller would realize he should become their pastor.[20] They needed him. And they couldn't wait.

The yuppies at DeMoss House had tried other evangelical churches. But they wanted something that felt more authentically like the New York they loved in the 1980s. They wanted it to be culturally engaged, contemporary yet classic, devoted to deep theology and evangelical outreach and spiritual renewal all at once. They wanted somewhere they could bring their friends. They didn't want a church that could have been transplanted to Milwaukee or Chattanooga. They didn't feel comfortable in those places they had left behind. New York was where they came alive. From the first time he traveled up from Philadelphia to speak for Executive Ministries at the DeMoss House, Keller captivated these young adults with the story of Scripture that starts in a garden and ends in a city, which means God loves the city. And so should they.

When Redeemer was born, these forty or so Christians from DeMoss House formed the backbone. Seven served on staff with Cru, which commissioned them for full-time personal evangelism and for training new converts to do likewise. They invited their friends to visit the church in droves. Compared to longtime New Yorkers, as well as new residents, the group from DeMoss House had far more close non-Christian friends. That's one major reason that within two or three years of Redeemer's start, 50 percent of attenders had not previously been connected to a church.

A pastor who grew up in Pennsylvania and spent most of his ministry career in Virginia should not have been the preferred pastor for DeMoss House. It's not like Keller had an innate cultural gift for reaching New York. His Bucknell friend Bruce Henderson remembers the first time he saw Keller in New York. It was a ninety-five-degree August 1969 day in Spanish Harlem when their friend Bob Pazmiño, who was from the Bronx, was getting married to a woman he had met on an InterVarsity retreat. The wedding had been delayed by several hours because the top of the bride's cake had been stolen. As they milled around outside waiting for the wedding to resume, Henderson noticed something out of the corner of his eye down the block to the west. Keller, six foot four and dressed in a green suit, was carrying a large gift box. He'd taken the wrong train and ended up on the west side of Harlem. When he realized his mistake, he walked all the way across some of the toughest streets in Harlem, conspicuous because of his ethnicity, dress, size, and of course the huge wedding gift he carried.

Even if he wanted to start a new church in New York, which he didn't, Keller faced an uphill climb, given his background. How would he relate to a Manhattan culture that disdains courtesy, modesty, and niceness? How could he start a church for people who live to work, to prove their professional worth on the world stage? In the first month after he moved to New York, he spoke with more people who experienced same-sex attraction than he'd met in the previous five years in Philadelphia. He could hardly fathom the kind of money earned on Wall Street, even by people in their first jobs. In New York, the feedback on his sermons would come fast and furious—not in response to his gentle questions, but unprompted, with no filter to protect his feelings. That criticism quickened his adjustments.

He had been warned through his time studying with Harvie Conn to expect a rough transition. Conn described the challenge facing leaders who relocate to cities:

> The urban scene is unfamiliar and foreign to these leaders' way of living and doing ministry. They come from homogenous communities that usually represent a different socioeconomic stratum. They have become aware of the needs in the city and have been drawn into the city due to what they sense is a call from the Lord. They need time and training to orient themselves to the new context.[21]

Moving from Philadelphia to New York would require the mind-set of a cross-cultural missionary. Such missionaries must not grow complacent just because they share some aspects of culture, such as language. For them the gulf of understanding might be wider than if they moved overseas.[22] Maybe Tim Keller could start a church that reached the people passing through New York from the South and Midwest for school and work. But how could he reach the born-and-bred New Yorkers who could never imagine living anywhere else?

After Terry Gyger, coordinator for Mission to North America, first approached him about the idea in March 1987, Keller mustered several objections. He couldn't generate more than 10 percent enthusiasm himself, and Kathy was surprised he thought that highly of the suggestion. He still had a year left on his contract with Westminster Seminary. He had no strong connections in the city. He didn't have an endowment to support him. One pastor warned him the church couldn't survive more than fifteen years—and that long only if the denomination propped them up financially.[23]

Besides Gyger and a few of his peers, Keller didn't find many people who thought it was a good idea for him to plant a church in New York City. He was told churches couldn't thrive in this liberal, edgy city. Churches depend on middle-class families, the exact demographic that had been fleeing New York for decades, leading to the racial and economic stratification described by Tom Wolfe. New York had become a city for the wealthy and the poor, the critics and the cynics. Yuppies enjoyed the trappings of single life too much to bother with church. New York's existing churches could barely even keep their lights on through the 1970s and '80s.[24]

Gyger had the right idea that churches inside the city could reach the suburbs, and not vice versa. He just couldn't find anyone to do it, even when the DeMoss House's success revealed a unique opportunity. Skip Ryan, who grew up in Connecticut, couldn't do it. His wife had just given birth to a daughter with special needs. Joe Novenson, who had already been recruited for the opening at Trinity Baptist, opted to stay in the South.

But by far the biggest objection to the idea of moving to New York didn't come from friends or colleagues. Tim and Kathy themselves didn't want to go. They liked their livable Philadelphia suburb. Tim had just been promoted to full-time professor at Westminster. They loved their church and the supportive seminary community. Tim enjoyed the restful retreat from pastoral ministry. If Gyger wanted a new church that could reach across the entire city, someone else would need to go. And Tim was intent on helping Gyger find that *other* pastor, even as he continued to compose epistles on prayer and waiting for Dave and Diane Balch and Ron and Patsy Fraser and the rest of the Executive Ministries team at the DeMoss House.

As the northernmost staff member for Mission to North America (MNA), Keller agreed to research New York for future church planting. Sam Ling, a PCA pastor in Flushing, New York, connected Keller to several key leaders, including Glen Kleinknecht with Here's Life and Diane Balch and Ron Fraser with Executive Ministries. At dinner on October 13, 1987, Ling and Keller, along with MNA colleague Jim Hatch, agreed to formally recommend a new PCA plant for New York.

Keller tried again without success to recruit Skip Ryan. Dick Kaufmann seemed like an ideal candidate for the plant. He had grown up in New Jersey and earned his MBA from Harvard Business School, in addition to being a CPA with Arthur Andersen. As an experienced business manager, he could match wits and ambition with the Masters of the Universe. At Harvard, he and his wife, Liz, planned their lives through age eighty.

Kaufmann went so far as to put an offer on an apartment and test their son for placement in middle school. Confident he'd found the right fit, Keller left for England on a trip where he preached nineteen times in twenty-one days. When he returned from England, he saw a message from Kaufmann on his answering machine. After three days of prayer and fasting, Kaufmann had sensed no final release from God or his church's elders to leave his current post. That door had closed.

Keller began to sense he was the only remaining option. What held him back more than anything else was the realization that his prayer and spiritual life couldn't handle the scope of this project. Keller could see the need. He could sense the opportunity. While still working at WTS, Keller had been driving between two and a half and three hours every other week, then every week, to assess the situation in New York. The city's diversity and arrogance didn't intimidate him. He wasn't scared away by the stubborn secularism and spiritual barrenness.[25] In fact, Keller sensed the same favorable conditions for revival that he had enjoyed twenty years earlier as a college student during the Jesus Movement.

God's presence was palpable. The progress of his kingdom felt inevitable. And now, Keller's vision for church had been focused through experience and study—the gospel-renewal emphasis of New Life, the city-center urban presence of Tenth Presbyterian, the neo-Calvinist cosmopolitan community outreach of L'Abri, and a love for the whole city from the Center for Urban Theological Studies.

In trying to convince others to go, Keller convinced himself.

Keller's change of mind and heart didn't come from movies, books, and music about New York; it came through a spiritual self-assessment as darkness descended on Keller, who knew he had no good reasons to turn down Dave Balch's direct invitation to take the job. Keller knew he couldn't get by on talent alone in New York. And he feared that his spiritual failings would be exposed. In the end, it was a Puritan who gave Keller the decisive nudge he needed to accept the call. In William Gurnall's *The Christian in Complete Armour*, Keller read, "It requires more prowess and greatness of spirit to obey God faithfully, than to command an army of men; to be a Christian, than to be a captain."[26] To Keller, this meant he needed to stop being a coward. No matter his decision, he needed to live more bravely. *Might as well go to New York*, he concluded. Immediately, Keller observed a breakthrough in his prayer life.

Praying Up a Storm

As he approached the final decision to move to New York City, Keller faced what felt like one last insurmountable obstacle. He waited as long as he did to commit to the Balch group because Kathy didn't want to raise their boys—then aged ten, eight, and four—in the city. Years ago, David Wilkerson's *The Cross and the Switchblade* was the first Christian book she had read by someone other than C. S. Lewis. She had resolved to move to New York and minister to gang members. But marriage and family intervened in the meantime and led to several reservations about that original plan.

She heard horror stories about marriages crumbling as an underfunded pastor's family tried to cram three kids in a New York studio apartment. What was she supposed to tell her boys to do for fun—go play in traffic? She figured her boys needed space and safety, neither of which New York could provide. And that's even after accounting for her hands-off parenting approach. Her philosophy was that you should raise your first child like your last child, and if no one died and no one went to jail, it's been a good day of parenting.[27] Already the "victims of poor parenting" in Kathy's words, she feared her boys would end up a cautionary tale in New York.

Sensitive to her reluctance, Tim insisted he wouldn't take the family there if she didn't approve. Kathy erupted. "You're not pushing this decision on me! You're the head of this household. If God calls you to New York, I'll wrestle it out with God." And so she did, over Communion at New Life Church in Philadelphia. After all God had done for her, she realized, *Was it too much for him to ask her to raise a family in New York?* "I guess we're going!" she concluded.[28]

Even then, Tim felt some reluctance about his decision. He called his Bucknell friend Bruce Henderson to talk about the move. "He was not happy about it," Henderson recalls. "He felt under pressure to take the job." Keller wanted to know if he'd ruin his kids by taking them to New York. "Will they pay you enough to live in a good place?" Henderson asked. "If yes, then go."[29]

Keller's friends back in Philadelphia had been praying for Tim for months as he first searched for a different pastor for this calling and then slowly realized he would need to go. Finally, he came to the group and said, "I have to do this myself."[30]

Kathy considers that decision "one of the most truly 'manly' things" her husband ever did.[31] The move scared him. But he felt God's call. He had no way of knowing the result would be a dynamic, growing megachurch. He just knew it was the next step of faith, even if the church were to end in failure.

The Kellers didn't move to New York City until June 1989, after they'd already launched the church. They got the best of both worlds living on Roosevelt Island, where Glen and Carole Kleinknecht were already raising two children. Roosevelt Island isn't a suburb. The Kellers were still part of the city—something that Keller knew from Harvie Conn would be vital for his pastoral leadership. But they settled in a part of the city that was separate and distinct from the busiest districts. The Kellers got approval to adjoin two apartments. The family lived in one apartment, while Tim used the other for office space, as well as for small group meetings. They could fit fifty people when necessary, which helped them in launching a church plant with no dedicated meeting space.

The Kellers have never moved since their arrival in New York in 1989. Books are scattered in every room in both apartments. Even when Redeemer rented space, Keller kept his study at home and wrote his sermons there. Marlene Hucks helped the Kellers move boxes into the apartment on the first day, and she remembers Roosevelt Island as just four big residential high-rises in 1989 shrouded in an otherworldly quiet, a much slower pace than the rest of the city. It took her ninety minutes to get from the Upper West Side to Roosevelt Island via tram and train and bus and sidewalk.[32] The Kellers were *in* the city if not entirely *of* the city.

Previous church plants had foundered between New York City's resistance and insufficient resources. Starting a church in New York wasn't like spinning off another congregation in Greenville, South Carolina. And the PCA was determined to provide for Redeemer and the Kellers. It helped that Tim developed a fundraising network in the PCA through his work on mercy ministry. Every year, Women in the Church of the PCA organized a special offering for one of the denomination's outreach ministries. In Redeemer's first year, that beneficiary was Mission to North America, Keller's former employer and the group that commissioned him for New York via Terry Gyger. Redeemer received almost ninety thousand dollars from these Presbyterian women, about one-third of the total raised for the plant.

But their support didn't stop with this gift. Kathy wrote these women what she admits were "the whiniest, most self-pitying prayer letters anyone has ever written or received."[33] From Kathy's perspective, these women were just so thankful they weren't in her position, trying to raise three boys in the big, violent city! She even received small family collections of twelve dollars earmarked for her family to eat out at McDonald's. She would never stop thanking God for these women.

"They prayed up a storm," Kathy Keller said. "It's like we couldn't make a bad decision in those early years. I'm convinced there was never a church plant, even going back to the apostle Paul and the first-century church, that had so many people, especially women, praying for it."[34]

Seemingly, every one of those women knew a young adult in New York City, some family member or friend who needed Jesus. So what do you do on day one of a New York church plant? "Tim was patient and faithful to contact each and every one," said Jackie Arthur, Tim's volunteer secretary in New York. It was just like he was a junior at Bucknell. "He emptied his pockets of little scraps of paper with names and numbers scribbled on them and started calling—a pretty remarkable beginning."[35]

Another one-third of Redeemer's initial funding came from Spanish

River Church, one of the most aggressive planting congregations in the PCA. Its pastor, David Nicholas, cofounded the Acts 29 church planting network. Nicholas was concerned when he heard that three other evangelical churches in Manhattan had just hired new pastors. But Keller assured him that plenty of people still needed a new church in Manhattan.

Keller wasn't focused on recruiting evangelicals already in the city.[36] He wanted to re-create L'Abri as a local church for a strikingly secular city. At Redeemer, Christians were encouraged to bring their non-Christian friends. He met with these friends during the week to learn their objections, and then he incorporated those objections into his sermons the next week. He added counseling insights to discern the issues beneath the questions.[37] "He had a knack for understanding or digging until he found what they were really asking," Jim Pichert said.[38] One common conversation starter was, "Is all well with your soul?"[39] Keller met so many people in the Tramway Diner at the 59th Street Bridge and 2nd Avenue that Kathy often called the kitchen phone as if it were Tim's office. The diner didn't mind, since Tim provided them with steady business, as three or four people per day visited with him.[40]

Meeting a wide variety of people helped Keller avoid the vicious cycle of preaching, where focusing on the same people leads to narrowly appealing sermons. To Redeemer member Jackie Arthur, Keller came across as a great listener.[41] Long before he wrote any bestselling books, he heard what felt like every possible objection to Jesus. And when he returned home, he'd check his books to see if he could better answer those questions. Answering questions also helped enhance his memory through repetition.[42]

New Yorkers couldn't understand how he seemed to know just what they were thinking. "His preaching was like the most extraordinary litigator you'll ever hear," Glen Kleinknecht said.[43] They didn't know how much time he spent, not speaking, but listening to improve his own culturally situated understanding of the gospel.[44]

After five years, this virtuous cycle of listening and learning led Redeemer to outgrow the Church of the Advent Hope, a Seventh-day Adventist congregation at East 87th Street between Park and Lexington. A move to Hunter College Auditorium in 1994 brought additional meeting and child care space, though its auditorium was shabby and scarred. Thousands would eventually flock to the auditorium at Hunter College, which sits at 68th Street on the Upper East Side, one block east of Park Avenue. The largest venue for Redeemer Presbyterian Church settled in among the Masters of the Universe.

Twenty years after *The Bonfire of the Vanities*, the Bronx no longer burned. The story of Kitty Genevose no longer scared away tourists or young professionals determined to make it on the nation's biggest stage. Even the Masters of the Universe now heard the gospel preached in terms they could understand, in ways that Nancy DeMoss had modeled. Sherman McCoy and Jordan Belfort would have made perfect illustrations for Nancy's post-dinner appeals.

Look for a hope no fifty-thousand-dollar commission can satisfy. Find a peace no Upper East Side co-op can deliver.

FIFTEEN

LAND OF YES

Redeemer Presbyterian Church

Redeemer's earliest leaders remember the church as "the Land of Yes."
"Redeemer had an entrepreneurial mindset that was so unusual for churches," said Yvonne Sawyer, the first leader of Hope for New York, Redeemer's mercy ministry.[1]

She traveled to several cities to learn how other churches implemented mercy ministry. From her brainstorming sessions afterward with Tim Keller and other Redeemer leaders, almost everything on the list came to fruition. "Tim set other people's gifts free."[2]

Keller cast a vision for the whole city, for a church that would not reinforce the moral superiority of Christians against their neighbors. And he erected guardrails to maintain the church's focus on the gospel. He left the details of implementation to others. He didn't need to control everything the church did. "He was always willing to listen to other people," said Tim Lemmer, an early Redeemer member and decades-long veteran of *The Wall Street Journal*, where he edits the letters section.[3]

"It felt like student ministry, the priesthood of all believers," said Katherine Leary Alsdorf, who started Redeemer's Center for Faith and Work.

It felt that way by design. A perceptive visitor once called the church "Young Life for grown-ups." And the visitor wasn't just referring to the high concentration of young adults. Keller followed the Young Life calendar in his preaching. In the fall, he focused on apologetics, especially through sermons from the Old Testament on the nature of God. In the winter, he shifted to the life of Jesus, culminating in the cross and resurrection for Good Friday and Easter. Spring and summer worked out salvation with application on how to live as a Christian.[4]

Keller also adopted the Young Life evangelistic strategy. Redeemer sought to foster a loving and hospitable Christian community that welcomed nonbelievers. Worship and discipleship wouldn't happen separately from evangelism. Redeemer wouldn't code-switch its vocabulary between Christians and non-Christians. The Christian community itself would be the evangelistic program of the church.[5] Keller believed that only this approach, which he saw in Young Life but also in L'Abri, would reach younger generations. Every other strategy would run into problems. The "seeker church" model divided evangelism from community. Personal evangelism of the Four Spiritual Laws or Evangelism Explosion variety didn't help unless the church itself became outreach oriented. And few will show up to hear a famous preacher unless they first know a Christian who will invite them.

Keller sought to translate for the local church the best parachurch insights he had seen and experienced himself. Redeemer challenged both legalism and relativism, confronted personal idols as well as cultural idols as dead ends to self-salvation, and evangelized non-Christians while edifying Christians at the same time.

Happy and exhausting, the early years of Redeemer exceeded the intensity of any other period in Tim Keller's life. He might not have been the obvious candidate to plant the kind of church New York needed. But he understood contextualization from his studies with Harvie Conn, and he learned from New Yorkers that he couldn't employ the same strategies that worked for evangelicals in suburban sprawl. Keller planned services in the vernacular of his city, with music for people who spent their Saturday nights at the symphony hall or theater.[6] New York City boasted ten full-time professional opera companies at a time when no other US city claimed more than one. Classical in the morning, with jazz and folk in the evening, Redeemer's music opened doors to the city's large community of artists, who had shunned other evangelical churches. While other evangelical pastors around the country began to dress down, like many of the young converts from the Jesus Movement, Keller dressed up in a suit for his morning service. The city's secular elite skewed older and more formal. His decisions were an effort to prioritize native New Yorkers over transient young residents.

More than anything else, Keller contextualized his preaching and teaching. He talked about sin in a way that many of these longtime Manhattan residents could understand from their experience with work and money. He talked about salvation in ways that reflected their hopes and aspirations for a better city to come. He preached the Bible in the vein of Paul at the Areopagus in Athens (Acts 17:16–34). He quoted the artists and thinkers his audience respected to support biblical conclusions.

But all the neo-Calvinist focus on renewing the city and applying the gospel to all of life would have amounted to nothing without real spiritual power. What made Redeemer unique was the combination of Harvie Conn's vision for social concern—living out faith in vocations and loving neighbors by doing justice and mercy—with what Tim Keller had learned from Richard Lovelace and Jack Miller on spiritual renewal. Keller's sermons highlighted the law/gospel distinction to help non-Christians and Christians alike discover salvation by grace alone. By studying revival, he sensed the opportune moment of those exhausting early years of Redeemer. Through reading sermons by John Flavel and Jonathan Edwards, Keller had been prepared for heightened spiritual sensitivity.

After nearly twenty years as a Christian, Keller discovered his spiritual gift for evangelism amid this revival.

When preachers have evangelistic gifts, their churches often grow. And when churches grow, they test their preacher's leadership gifts. Keller knew his leadership would be tested as he tried to hold together a growing church that leaned heavily on inviting non-Christian friends into a L'Abri-inspired community.[7] What he had seen and experienced in the Jesus Movement, as a student hanging around InterVarsity before he personally encountered Christ, was easier to foster in small numbers. This insight helped propel his urgent support for church plants that could replicate such vibrant communities.

When Redeemer's early leaders look back on the church, they remember Keller's heart-penetrating preaching. But they remember the community just as much. They saw Keller as one of them, and they shared in the burden of launching the church. If they thought the church should be praying more, they could grab one or two friends and go ahead and lead it.[8] Writing in *Center Church*, Keller contrasts movements and institutions:

> A church with movement dynamics, however, generates ideas, leaders, and initiatives from the grassroots. Ideas come less from formal strategic meetings and more from off-line conversations among friends. Since the motivation for the work is not so much about compensation and self-interest as about a shared willingness to sacrifice for the infectious vision, such churches naturally create friendships among members and staff.[9]

He's telling the story of Redeemer's growth in the 1990s. And he's telling the story of the leadership crisis that eventually exposed his weaknesses.

Leaving Narnia

New York is the city that never sleeps. Except at seven in the morning.

Even with the best bagels in the city, 7:00 a.m. prayer meetings are a tough ask for professionals working long days that usually don't start until after nine.

But the young Christians who prayed while wiping schmear from their mouths would never forget those mornings around Redeemer at the close of the 1980s.

"There was a strong sense that God was getting ready to do something, a very strong sense of the Holy Spirit moving among us," said Lorraine Zechmann, who helped lead outreach in Redeemer's early years. She likened the prayer meetings to the heartwarming experience of conversion.[10] Another Redeemer leader, Lane Arthur, credits these prayers, which focused on the peace and prosperity of the city, for the downturn in crime in New York during the 1990s.[11]

In just one generation, between 1989 and 2019, the number of Manhattan residents attending evangelical churches grew from nine thousand to more than eighty thousand.[12] That kind of church growth doesn't usually happen without the "extraordinary prayer" advocated by Jonathan Edwards in the First Great Awakening. Keller commended this bold prayer, which pleads for God to unite the church in advancing his kingdom on earth.[13]

Writing in *Outgrowing the Ingrown Church*, one of the most popular books in Redeemer's early history, Jack Miller contrasted "frontline" prayer with "maintenance" prayer. Most people only know prayer meetings as maintenance. Christians share concerns for the physical well-being of known members. But frontline prayer confesses sin, seeks humility, pursues the lost, and yearns to know God face-to-face, to encounter his glory.[14]

That's the kind of prayer that compelled Redeemer members during the first Iraq War to begin all-night intercession based on the model of the Korean revivals in the early twentieth century. For several months, starting at 9:00 on Friday evenings, a group of Redeemer members prayed together until 6:00 on Saturday morning.

No Redeemer members mentioned Keller's presence at those meetings. They knew he was a gifted pastor, but they saw God doing the work.[15] And that's how the Kellers saw Redeemer too.

"You want to know how to plant a successful church?" Kathy Keller said. "Find out where God is beginning a revival, and move there the month before."[16]

The Kellers and other early Redeemer leaders say they backed into most of the things God blessed at the church. Sometimes this talk obscures the intentional strategy Tim Keller deployed. But it also reflects Keller's approach to leadership, his willingness to ask questions and share responsibility. Not even the name Redeemer Presbyterian Church belongs to the Kellers. The church needed a name before Kathy could open a postal box. The Kellers recommended Christ the King. Years later, Tim published a book with the title *Jesus the King*.

The reaction to their proposed name was swift and overwhelmingly negative. Members who had lived in the city for longer thought the name was too triumphant, almost martial. They needed an alternative, and the winning suggestion came from Marlene Hucks. She had only moved to New York in December 1988 when she heard about plans for the church plant. She had recently returned from Ireland, where she served with World Harvest Mission, founded by Jack Miller. When Tim Keller drove up from Philadelphia before moving to Roosevelt Island, he met with her for coffee every week from January to June 1989. He asked questions about missions, about the city, about the church. For Hucks, then in her twenties, Keller's eagerness to learn from her came as a surprise.

"You meet men who don't know that they view women with suspicion as opposed to partnership," said Hucks, who later became the area director for InterVarsity in New York. "I never felt like I had to, because I was female, lay aside my gifting or influence."

After the Kellers moved to New York, she shared dinner with the Kellers every Monday for eighteen months. She saw in the Kellers a model of marriage in which both parties respected the other.[17]

Back in Winston-Salem, North Carolina, Hucks had been involved with a Presbyterian church known as Redeemer. The process of selecting that church's name had been elaborate and deeply concerned with discerning the Spirit's lead. When she tossed out the name in the New York meeting, consensus quickly formed—no drawn-out process needed.

Keller's curiosity enabled spiritual and intellectual formation by drawing on dozens of sources. This personality also facilitated Redeemer's rapid growth, with the help of zealous lay leaders who felt their input mattered. In less than thirty months, Redeemer attendance grew from zero to one thousand.[18] The church began with Sunday afternoon meetings for prayer and vision in the apartment of Dave and Diane Balch. Redeemer held its first service on Palm Sunday, April 1989, at 6:30 p.m. in the four-hundred-seat Church of Advent Hope, near Park Avenue in the Yorkville neighborhood, north of Hunter College on the Upper East Side. By the end of 1989, only half a year into the church's history, about 250 people were attending. Already the pace of change felt dramatic to the small group of twelve who had met together before the launch.[19] Redeemer particularized (ordained its own officers) in 1991, with a budget of $694,000 in expenses. That number jumped to more than $1 million for 1992, when attendance crossed one thousand. Even at this early stage, Redeemer allocated 15 percent of its budget to missions.[20] The foundation had been laid for Redeemer to expand down the road into a missional church network.

As they strained under the pressures of growth, the leaders assembled around Keller sensed that God was doing something that no merely human strategy could generate.

"It was so full of grace and so full of confidence that what was being done here was not of our hands but of God's hands," Hucks said. "In those days it was really like you were following after something he was doing, following him in something he had already mapped out."[21]

It was a revival. And everyone knew it, in part because Keller had prompted them to pray for it. For the rest of their lives, Redeemer members would long for it again.

"Those were foundational years for us," Barbara Ohno said. "When we spun out of Redeemer into the world, there was an ache in our heart, like we had left Narnia or Camelot. God allowed us to be part of a revival. God did this amazing thing."[22]

Edify and Evangelize

The growth of Redeemer confounded PCA leaders in the South as much as secular journalists in New York.

Kathy Keller assumed the role of director of communications. Over the years many mainstream journalists, including some Redeemer members, wrote about the church. Kathy commented to one of the journalists, "It's surprising that so many educated twenty- and thirty-somethings would attend a church that teaches against sex outside marriage." The journalist laughed. "Yes, that *would* be surprising." "No," Kathy clarified, "I'm saying that's what we actually teach." The journalist blinked a dumbfounded response.

In the fall of 1991, Tim Keller preached nine weeks on marriage, a series recalled by many early Redeemer members, most of whom were not yet married. It's the most downloaded content the church has ever released.[23] Keller knew he couldn't avoid talking about sex, because so many people who professed faith through Redeemer's ministry fell away when confronted with the commands against sex outside marriage between one man and one woman. Chastity wasn't even comprehensible to most New Yorkers. Many just laughed at the biblical ethic. Some diagnosed it as psychologically destructive.

Many PCA leaders from the South also visited Redeemer in the 1990s to discern the secret to the church's success amid these challenges. Maybe the church had discovered a new musical genre. Maybe they used video and clips from popular TV shows in this era of uber-popular New York sitcoms *Friends* and *Seinfeld*. Maybe in the city of Broadway they mustered the best evangelistic skits.

But that's not what visitors found at Redeemer. The simple and traditional service, which borrowed from Calvin's sixteenth-century church in Geneva, resembled PCA churches around the country. When one visitor from Scotland asked Keller where he kept the dancing bears (assuming there was some clever entertainment hook to lure people in), Keller didn't know how to respond. Outwardly the church didn't look any different. But inwardly the culture was unusual for churches. One artist described Redeemer's culture as irony, charity, and humility. Keller explained:

> They said Redeemer lacked the pompous and highly sentimental language they found emotionally manipulative in other churches. Instead, Redeemer people addressed others with gentle, self-deprecating irony. Not only that, but beliefs were held here in charity and with humility, making Manhattanites feel included and welcomed, even if they disagreed with some of Redeemer's beliefs. Most of all, they said, teaching and communication at Redeemer was intelligent and nuanced, showing sensitivity where they were sensitive.[24]

Keller may have been explaining these artists' impressions about Redeemer. But he could have been talking about himself. He may not have controlled every mechanism for administration in the church. He did, however, set the tone in character and communication.

Not surprisingly, he set that tone with an assist from church history, since he couldn't look back to his own experience in Hopewell for successful models of urban churches reaching secular people. When

Keller moved to New York City, only 6 percent of Americans claimed "no religious preference." By comparison that number was 30 percent in Manhattan. (Today the American number is nearly 24 percent, roughly equal to the number of Protestant evangelicals or Roman Catholics.[25])

So Keller looked to recent church history in Great Britain, closer in secularization to New York City than to the rest of the United States. He returned to a name he first heard at Bucknell, Martyn Lloyd-Jones, and reread his *Preaching and Preachers*. He listened to hundreds of sermons by Lloyd-Jones, who preached at Westminster Chapel in London from 1939 until 1968, the same year Keller started college. Lloyd-Jones aimed his morning sermons to build up Christians and his evening sermons to reach non-Christians. Both sermons, though, focused on the gospel of Jesus Christ and challenged listeners with biblical and theological insight.

Lloyd-Jones encouraged Christians to attend both services, even as he hoped they would bring friends, especially in the evening. Lloyd-Jones still argued against dividing too sharply between the audiences though. Both needed to be reminded of the gospel. Both needed spiritual depth.[26] Lloyd-Jones warned that when preachers target only believers, they tend to make Christians harsh, cold, and self-satisfied. When they don't evangelize in their sermons, preachers produce Pharisees.[27]

For the first seven years at Redeemer, Keller followed the Lloyd-Jones plan, though he reversed evening and morning, so that he preached more narrative portions of the Bible for nonbelievers in the morning.[28] Keller learned from Lloyd-Jones never to assume everyone is a Christian, and never assume Christians no longer need the gospel. "Evangelize as you edify, and edify as you evangelize."[29] As Keller lingered after the evening services to answer questions about the sermon, he knew that when non-Christians challenged him, he could model for Christians how to engage skeptics.

Early Redeemer members reported to Keller that they never wanted to be embarrassed when they brought their friends. Michael Green, in his book *Evangelism through the Local Church*, an early Redeemer favorite, warned pastors against "insider" language and appeals for money that repel non-Christians. Green said that when churches pray expectantly and welcome visitors warmly, Christians want to bring their friends along.[30] Keller delivered three-point sermons with the same straightforward simplicity as a *Business Week* article.[31] He quoted everyone from C. S. Lewis to Madonna, from Jonathan Edwards to Woody Allen.[32]

Visitors tried but couldn't pigeonhole the church. When Keller quoted Shakespeare and *The Village Voice*, liberals thought he was one of them. Then he'd confuse them with an explanation of the cross that would hearten any conservative evangelical. They had never heard a preacher rooted in the theology of John Owen, Martin Luther, Jonathan Edwards, and John Calvin who also read *The Village Voice* alongside *The Wall Street Journal*, *The New York Times* and *First Things*, *The Nation* and *The Weekly Standard*, *Wired* and *The New Yorker*.

Keller didn't dilute Redeemer's Reformed convictions in his preaching. He emphasized them in the context of this wide-ranging reading.[33] Keller found that if he didn't read broadly and deeply at the same time, his preaching grew stale and repetitive. Usually preaching beside a music stand, which he used to hold printed copies of quotes he intended to use, he addressed the congregation as "friends." His sermons felt less like stereotypical preaching and more like a good friend instructing you in the context of a small group. He didn't preach from notes, but rather memorized his sermons and only looked at papers for accurate quotation. He didn't come across as threatening or condescending. "His demeanor created the expectation that they knew him," said Cregan Cooke, a longtime Redeemer staff member.[34]

Lloyd-Jones himself often longed to see the kind of revival that broke out in New York during the last decade of the twentieth century.

"One of the most exhilarating experiences in the life of a preacher is what happens when people whom everybody had assumed to be Christians are suddenly converted and truly become Christians,"

Lloyd-Jones said. "Nothing has a more powerful effect upon the life of a church than when that happens to a number of people."[35]

Keller coined the phrase "ecclesial revivalist" to describe how he merged the unpredictable dynamics of spiritual renewal with biblical ordering for the local church.[36] He preached to the heart as he taught the mind. He expected much of church members—his view of revival still involved large binders full of training notes. Keller had previously been a seminary professor, after all. Mako Fujimura remembers Monday evening classes as a precious time. It was a major commitment for Fujimura to commute back and forth from his home in New Jersey for weekly classes that ran from 7:00 to 9:00 p.m.

"I was really excited to go," he said. "It was like sitting under a master."

Keller prepared some fifty pages of notes for each meeting. Fujimura pored over these notes on the train headed home to New Jersey at 10:30 p.m.[37] Keller's enthusiasm for the ministry carried these eager young leaders along.[38]

Wedding Sermon like No Other

Somehow in Keller's vision for Redeemer, Young Life, L'Abri, and Lloyd-Jones formed a coherent evangelistic strategy for a new church in a leading post-Christian global city. But he reached back into his Doctor of Ministry study of Reformed church diaconates to add another key element.

From his study and experience, Keller knew Redeemer needed to serve the city by meeting practical needs of their neighbors outside the church. Or, more broadly, he and other Redeemer members could just look to the streets of New York City in the late-1980s and early 1990s. They asked each other what the Good Samaritan would do with the drug-addicted, homeless, and poor of their neighborhoods.

He found one model in Philadelphia at Tenth Presbyterian, led at the time by James Montgomery Boice. When Redeemer first launched, Boice announced the church plant during a worship service and encouraged graduating students moving north to New York City to join. Tenth Presbyterian was the kind of church that Keller believed evangelicals should have built at the end of the nineteenth century when waves of immigration overwhelmed city services.

Until his experience with Tenth, Keller mostly associated urban churches with the poor. He wasn't familiar with the diversity of urban church expressions. Boice gave Keller a vision for a "city center" church that could serve the poor and evangelize young professionals at the same time.

Boice, who succeeded the renowned Donald Grey Barnhouse at Tenth, began to shift the church away from commuters attracted to the excellent preaching to instead engage with their more proximate neighbors in the city. Boice even encouraged Christians to move into the city for strategic ministry not just *in* the city but *for* the city. During a time of high crime risk in the 1970s and 1980s, young couples connected to Tenth began moving into Philadelphia. They started ministries for the poor, dialogues with Muslims, and outreaches to gays who cruised for sex on the same block as Tenth. Tim and Kathy served together on the board for Harvest, a ministry to the gay community. Even though his family continued to attend New Life, Keller began to serve Tenth in more formal capacities, preaching seven times for Boice in one year. Straining under growth in the fall of 1986, the church asked Keller to consult. He produced a hundred-page report in the spring of 1987 with twelve recommendations, many of which were adopted, with the exception of separate worshiping congregations.

Tenth wasn't the only city-center model for what Keller wanted from Redeemer. John Stott, likewise, showed that in London a city-center church could care just as much about mercy ministry as about expositional preaching. By starting nearly one hundred city-center New

York churches in twenty years, Redeemer could help pave the way for ministry that was as committed to teaching about justification and expiation as acts of justice and mercy.[39]

The woman who translated Keller's vision into reality is Yvonne Sawyer, who in 1992 became Hope for New York's first full-time staff member. Hope for New York recruits volunteers and raises money from churches on behalf of affiliated nonprofit ministries serving the poor and marginalized across New York. Her work was so integral to the life of Redeemer that when she got married to Rick Sawyer in 1998, the wedding was held in the middle of a Sunday morning service. The whole day was such a blur that Yvonne doesn't even remember the sermon.

But many others do. Because it was probably the most memorable sermon Keller ever delivered.

For his youthful church, Keller wanted to preach a wedding sermon that would not discourage singles who wanted to be married. For this wedding, he wanted to preach about a better Wedding to come, featuring a Spouse who will never let anyone down. He had recently been teaching through Genesis when he came across Leah, daughter of Laban, and "The Girl Nobody Wanted." Leah points us to Christ, who was also rejected. She looked forward to her descendant as a true and better Spouse than Jacob.[40]

It wasn't your typical wedding homily. Maybe that's why so many treasure it today. Keller explained that, contrary to what we might expect about family values, the Bible offers little sentimentality about marriage. "It is utterly realistic about how hard it is not to be married; and it is utterly realistic about how hard it is to be married."[41]

Keller, who had never combined a Sunday service and wedding before (or since), told the congregation that New York City is a tough town where everyone looks like they have their act together. But by dressing in expensive clothing they reveal their desperation. "They cannot imagine living without *apocalyptic* romance and love," said Keller, who attributed the phrase to Pulitzer Prize winner Ernest Becker.[42]

Appealing to one of his favorite commentators, Robert Alter, Keller observed that in waking up next to Leah instead of her sister Rachel, the deceiver Jacob had been deceived. Once he had fooled his father. Now his uncle had fooled him. It's poetic justice, Alter explained.[43] When Keller preached this message in 2001, he again cited Alter to identify Jacob's sexual impatience as the cause of his calamity.[44] Jacob thought he was going to be with the beautiful Rachel. He woke up with the "weak-eyed" Leah. Keller said:

> [Laban] wondered how he was going to get rid of her, how he was going to unload her. And then he saw his chance, he saw an opening, and he did it. And now the girl that Laban, her father, did not want has been given to a husband who doesn't want her either. She is the girl nobody wants.[45]

About this point in the sermon you might wonder what the bride and groom standing in front of Keller were thinking. What's the point of the story? Who's supposed to be the good guy of this twisted tale? Keller anticipated these objections: "I don't see any! What is going on here." Keller continued:

> The answer is: That is absolutely correct. You are starting to get it. You are starting to get the point of the Bible. What do I mean? The Bible doesn't give us a god at the top of a moral ladder saying, "Look at the people who have found God through their great performance and their moral record. Be like them!" Of course not! Instead, over and over again, the Bible gives us absolutely weak people who don't seek the grace they need and who don't deserve the grace they get.[46]

Leah hoped that by giving her husband sons, he would love her. But no, this is not a love story. Or at least not the kind of love story we expect. Through Leah we see the bigger Story, a deeper Love. Because

Leah eventually gave birth to Judah, her child of thanksgiving and praise, the son from whom Jesus descended. Leah may never have been loved by Jacob, but she knew the love of God, who would one day send his only Son to save the world.

In the late-1990s, at the same time he preached this wedding message, Keller taught a weeklong Doctor of Ministry course for Reformed Theological Seminary in Orlando with his longtime mentor Ed Clowney. He preached "The Girl Nobody Wanted" again, only this time to preachers. Clowney had never preached that passage. But if he did, Clowney told Keller, he'd preach it the same way. "It was one of the most comforting and encouraging statements I have ever received from anyone in my life."[47] Now they could die in peace, Kathy told Tim when she heard Clowney's compliment.[48]

When God Pushed Pause

Between Hope for New York, church planting, DMin lectures, growing boys, and a host of regular church responsibilities as Redeemer continued to grow, Keller reached the limits of his leadership capacity in the mid- to late-1990s. Though the evidence suggests otherwise, Keller often insists he's not a great leader. Mako Fujimura admired his entrepreneurial leadership. He saw him as a drum major coordinating the music and leading the band marching in the same direction.[49]

It's more accurate, then, to say that Keller has never been an effective manager.[50] "Tim likes to keep everybody happy," said Arthur Armstrong, an early Redeemer elder. "But when you're leading a big office, you can't keep everybody happy."[51]

In these years of growth pains, elders and staff pushed back hard on Keller, who knew virtually nothing about the dynamics of management. "He went through a long, hard struggle with not being liked, where he was failing," Katherine Alsdorf said of management struggles that continued for Keller into the mid-2000s. "That was painful and humbling, with a lot of his time spent on his knees in prayer."[52] Keller admitted as much himself in *Every Good Endeavor*, the book on work he coauthored with Alsdorf. "At times staff members have protested that my vision was outpacing my ability to lead it or their ability to implement it."[53]

Nothing in Keller's experience had prepared him for the crushing onslaught of organizational complexity at Redeemer. Not even his ninety-hour work ethic could save him. He was already approaching burnout by the end of 1993. While personally organized, Keller needed better managers to take over the operations at Redeemer.

When Dick Kaufmann arrived as executive pastor in 1994, the staff was in chaos. The Land of Yes had become the Land of Oh No. The movement dynamics that made the church so vibrant in its early days now threatened to undo the entire institution. Redeemer couldn't run like a mom-and-pop organization any longer.[54] If Kaufmann had not helped Keller shift from doing the ministry to leading the leaders—by equipping his whole staff to follow suit—Redeemer would have failed, or at least faltered. Right away, all staff began reporting to Kaufmann, who alone reported to Keller. Some leaders may have resented losing access to Keller, but he had no other option if he wanted relief from exhaustion.

Kaufmann not only contributed executive leadership, but in his shared influence under Jack Miller, he impressed Keller with his deep spirituality—so much so that Keller's book on prayer is dedicated to him. Near the end of his time with Redeemer, Kaufmann also cast the vision that would eventually become Keller's retirement plan from the church. He proposed, first, a multisite church that, second, would mature into a multiplying network of independent sister churches. When Keller stepped down in 2017, he followed the plan crafted by Kaufmann in 1997. Today the Redeemer network includes five churches—including one led by his son Michael—with others in the works.

It wasn't easy for Tim and Kathy to step back from so much in the church they started. But they didn't have any choice, especially when

Kathy got sick in the early 2000s with Crohn's disease, and when the church grew so rapidly after 9/11. "God pushed pause," said Cregan Cooke, senior director of media and communication at Redeemer.[55] Then, between 2003 and 2004, Tim battled thyroid cancer. He missed three months of preaching, his longest absence from Redeemer to that point.

Many of the earlier management problems recurred after 9/11. Kaufmann left to plant churches in San Diego. Kathy endured dozens of surgical procedures. Terry Gyger, who had taken over as executive pastor, began work on a church planting center that became Redeemer City to City. Between 2004 and 2006, Keller faced persistent criticism from his staff. This time the answer to prayer arrived in executive pastor Bruce Terrell. He didn't need to reorganize the church as Kaufmann had a decade earlier. But Keller needed a friend he could trust to run Redeemer. Terrell stayed on as chief operating officer through the end of Keller's tenure in 2017.

Church plants that grow often reach an inflection point where they struggle to transition into a stable institution. Many church planters can't grow into institutional leaders. Keller never became an effective manager. For the rest of his tenure at Redeemer, he discipled more through his preaching than in one-on-one or small-group relationships. As a result, sometimes his closest followers lived the farthest away. These church leaders listened to his sermons over and over and learned his instincts for interpreting and teaching the Bible.[56]

You won't find leaders close to Keller who idolize him. And that's not because they think he's fake. They know his weaknesses, his penchant to please people and avoid conflict. He's transparent about his sins. And they know from his teaching that it's not safe to idolize anyone or anything.

But they do admire him for his character.

"What makes Tim great is his humility," Yvonne Sawyer said. "He knows what he doesn't know and goes and finds the answer."[57]

Key to any successful Christian leader, Keller wrote, is character. No pastor will be good at preaching, counseling, and leading at the same time. Character, then, must make up for where leaders fall short in their gifting, Keller explained:

> The greatest factor in the long-term effectiveness of a Christian minister is how (or whether) the gift-deficient areas in his skill set are mitigated by the strong grace operations in his character. The leadership literature advises us to know our weaknesses, our gift-deficient areas. It usually tells us to surround ourselves with a team of people with complementary gifts, and that is certainly wise if you can do it. But even if you can, that is not sufficient, for your gift-deficient areas will undermine you unless there is compensatory godliness. . . . I continually observe that ministry amplifies people's spiritual character. It makes them far better or far worse Christians than they would have been otherwise, but it will not leave anyone where he was![58]

When leaders fall, it's usually because of character deficiency related to their family. That's why the apostle Paul, in Titus 1 and 1 Timothy 3, makes character in household leadership a prerequisite for church leadership. Redeemer leaders also trusted Keller because they knew his family. And the Kellers loved Redeemer for how the church's members loved their family.

Kathy Keller has often cited two factors in her three sons growing up with vibrant faith in Jesus Christ. They admired their father as a man of integrity and love, and they grew up surrounded by Redeemer members. Many believers coming to faith in the Redeemer revival were in their twenties when the Keller boys were teens. These excited Christians worked as actors and talent agents and opera singers. And as they hung around the Kellers, they modeled for the boys how to love the city and love Jesus even more.

When Keller taught on the power of community for evangelism, he wasn't just remembering his student days at Bucknell. He could point to his own sons:

The essence of becoming a disciple is, to put it colloquially, becoming like the people we hang out with the most. Just as the single most formative experience in our lives is our membership in a nuclear family, so the main way we grow in grace and holiness is through deep involvement in the family of God. Christian community is more than just a supportive fellowship; it is an alternate society. And it is through this alternate human society that God shapes us into who and what we are. . . . The real secret of fruitful and effective mission in the world is the quality of our community.[59]

He could also have been referring to his own younger brother.

Billy's Robe

For churches to grow, Christians need to come out of the closet.

That's what Keller wrote in *Center Church* about why so many churches struggle with evangelism. Christians are afraid to be known publicly as followers of Jesus. That's similar to the experience of gay people fifty years ago. Many skeptics living in cities know Christians; they just don't *know* they know Christians, so they persist in media-driven stereotypes.[60]

Meanwhile, their Christian friends shuffle off to church under the cover of Sunday slumber and brunch, as if they're Nicodemus at night.

Keller didn't make the comparison lightly. When he worked with AIDS victims in Philadelphia in the 1980s, he couldn't have known that his own younger brother would die of complications from AIDS in the 1990s. Keller has rarely spoken in public about his brother. And never in much detail. It would have been too easy to come across as exploiting his brother's story to advance his own credibility and agenda, especially in a city with the largest LGBTQ+ population in the United States.

In the Keller home back in Pennsylvania, Tim becoming a PCA pastor had been scandalous. But Billy coming out as gay in 1981 was another order of magnitude.[61] Five years younger than Tim, Billy spent more time with his parents in the Evangelical Congregational Church. His siblings never responded to an altar call. But Billy responded to every single one. He became so much like his mother that when his sister, Sharon, visited his apartments, she knew where to find everything in his kitchen.

Billy began to identify as gay while living in an art dorm at Penn State University. His parents paid for private education for Tim but would only allow Sharon and Billy to attend state schools. At Penn State, Billy found a welcoming, accepting, and philanthropy-minded community where being gay was not considered shameful. When Billy came out in 1981, his parents didn't tell even their closest friends.

It wasn't until 1992 that the family found out he had AIDS. Billy had tried to reconnect with his family at a beach reunion to take photos for his mother. The Kellers rented two cottages. Sharon's family stayed with Billy. Sharon asked him point-blank, "You don't have AIDS, right?" Billy tried to lie. His partner, Joachim, had contracted AIDS from unprotected sex prior to their relationship. At the time, Billy had been teaching classes on how to protect from AIDS.

William Christopher Keller died on May 22, 1998.

Tim and Kathy had met Joachim on numerous vacation trips south. They would always stop in Baltimore with their sons and go out to dinner with Billy and Joachim. And they visited Billy in Baltimore before he died. Billy entered hospice care in December 1997. Every day until Billy died, his parents sat by his bedside, singing and tending to his failing body.[62] Doctors didn't expect him to live long, as fungus ate into his brain. Two Baltimore-area pastors, Frank Boswell and Mark Gornik, visited him every week.

Their visits amazed Billy. It was his first glimpse of real Christian community. "He saw a vision of the church that we really didn't have growing up," Sharon Johnson said. By contrast, Billy's friends didn't visit him. And even before he died, his lawyer liquidated his assets to distribute to various gay causes.

When they visited, Tim and Kathy talked to him about the gospel. Billy struggled to understand grace. As they prayed together, he kept asking if he was doing the right thing. Tim tried to emphasize the difference between grace and the legalism of their childhood.

Tim Keller preached his only brother's funeral on June 8, 1998. No more than thirty-five or forty-five people attended. And Keller turned to Luke 15:23–32 for the occasion.

In his own life, Tim alternated between the tendencies of the older and younger brothers in Jesus' parable. When he fled his mother's expectations for the Evangelical Congregational Church, he was the younger brother. But as the Boy Scout, he tried to be the elder brother who set a good example of responsibility and obedience.

When his own younger brother strayed far from home, far from God, this elder brother went looking for him.

Tim explained at the funeral that he wanted to honor his brother in such a way that would strengthen the living. He described his brother as sympathetic, flexible, diplomatic, unselfish, sacrificial, and loyal. And he also said that most in the room would understand that Billy spent most of his life as a prodigal.

Why bring this up in a funeral? Tim explained that prodigals were attracted to Jesus, and Jesus was attracted to prodigals. That's the whole message of the parable: the younger, prodigal son was closer to the heart of the Father than the older brother who always obeyed God.

Sadly, many churches don't welcome prodigals, Tim admitted. They're more like the older brother, and the Pharisees and the teachers of the law, than they want to admit.

In general, Billy, like so many of his friends, avoided orthodox, believing Christians. Why? Not just because he disagreed with them, but because he felt rather beat-up and condemned by them. We learn here that if prodigals are not attracted to our graciousness and humility and understanding, we are like the older brother, not Jesus. Jesus had them coming in. We do not. We need to humble ourselves here. This is a way of honoring Billy.

Jesus shattered the world's categories when he said you don't come to God by obeying his law. Neither do you find God when you pursue your own truth to fulfill yourself. The world isn't made up of good people and bad people, Keller explained. Only the humble enter the kingdom of God. The proud are left out.

The prodigal son limped home in tatters. He had squandered his entire inheritance. And yet the father still gave him the best robe and threw him a feast with the fattened calf—the fattened calf that belonged to the older brother. In Jesus' parable, this bitter brother represents the Pharisees and the teachers of the law.

So what should the elder brother have done? What Jesus came to do.

Who is the *true* elder brother? Who is the one who *truly* obeyed the Father completely? Who *truly* has lost his robe so he put it on us? Jesus!

Jesus has done for us what we could not do for ourselves in fulfilling the law perfectly. In every other religion, God owes us blessing in exchange for our obedience. But in Christianity, we get Jesus' perfect record, so we owe him everything. This grace infuriated the elder brother.

"In fact," Tim explained, "the elder brother doesn't fail to go in to the father's feast *in spite* of his goodness, but *because* of it."

Prodigals, though, understand they can be saved only by humility and grace, by weakness and brokenness, through the cross.

When Billy entered hospice in December, he said to Tim, "My Christian family isn't going to come with me when I enter eternity, and neither are my gay friends. So I have to figure out what is on the other side of this life." They talked at length. Pastor Frank Boswell came to visit. Billy said he was thinking hard about what it means to be righteous in Christ. He had thought being a Christian meant cleaning up his life and making himself righteous. But Tim pointed to 2 Corinthians 5:21: "For our sake he made him to be sin who knew no sin, so that in him we might become the righteousness of God."

Finally, Billy felt God's love. The transformation was immediately evident. He even called his lawyer and told him to give his money to Mark Gornik's ministry instead.[63]

"To my joy, Billy latched on and got it," Tim Keller told the mourners. "Thus he went into the Father's feast."

Billy took the robe.

Keller explained that when you attend a memorial service for someone who took the robe, you're not in the end grieving but rejoicing. "Is Billy dead today?" Tim asked. "No, he's not!"

Dead is when you're trying to earn your salvation or designing your own, Tim said. Dead is when you never weep with joy over what God has done for you. Dead is when God is never more than an abstraction, an idea. The gospel humbles and emboldens and melts us with understanding what Jesus has done on the cross. Dead is when we don't know God as Father but only as boss or vague influence.

"Billy *was* dead, but now he's alive," Tim said. "He took the robe, and when you take the robe, then what happens to death? We laugh at death." He quoted George Herbert: "Death used to be an executioner, but the gospel made him just a gardener."[64]

Christians don't fall asleep when they die. That's when they finally wake up. Billy hasn't gone to the cold and dark, Tim said. He's gone into the warmth and life where he perceives God in all five senses, or maybe even a thousand or a million senses we can hardly fathom in the cold and dark of this fallen world. So those left behind don't wish Billy to come back. They ask God to prepare them to be with him and our true elder brother.

"We get ready to greet daybreak," Tim concluded, "when it will be a bright, sunny morning forever."

The Keller family never faced a greater tragedy than Billy's death. When all hope seemed lost, God welcomed this prodigal son home.

SIXTEEN

EVERYBODY WORSHIPS

September 11 and The Reason for God

On a day that assaulted the senses, it's the silence that everyone remembers.

No more tragic sounds have been heard in American history than two fully fueled airliners crashing into the Twin Towers of the World Trade Center on the morning of September 11, 2001. The cacophony of terror grew when the sirens of police cars, ambulances, and fire engines descended on Lower Manhattan from across the city. Then came the steady thuds from bodies that leaped some ninety stories to avoid an even worse demise from flames above the impact zone. Finally each tower collapsed in a deafening rumble of crushed concrete and steel.

Then, silence.

No commercial planes in the sky, because the nation's airlines had been grounded. No vehicle traffic through the most densely populated blocks in the United States. Only the muffled shuffle of ash-caked survivors headed home across the Brooklyn Bridge. And eventually, no more ambulances, when the fate of thousands had been sealed under matching mountains of rubble that had once dominated the New York skyline as symbols of the city's global might.

For a brief time after a snowstorm, New York grows eerily quiet as flakes cushion taxi tires and dampen their horns' honking. That's the only experience to which New Yorkers could compare the silence that descended on a day that began with plans to enjoy the bright blue skies and gentle fall temperatures and ended with everyone huddled inside, waiting for the next wave of attacks.

Tim and Kathy Keller had been scheduled on September 11 to take their youngest son to the hospital for surgery on his broken leg, sustained while playing soccer. That surgery was canceled, along with all other elective surgeries. Hospitals expected so many trauma cases that they even woke up patients who had been under anesthesia. When the towers fell, the demand never materialized. There were few injuries, only death.

From his usual spot watching the morning news in the kitchen, Tim Keller saw the live shot of United Airlines Flight 175 hitting the second tower of the World Trade Center. For days he watched from his apartment on Roosevelt Island as smoke rose from downtown. Watched, and waited for news of church members killed. Watched, and waited for new horrors this era of terror might hold for the city, the country, the world.

The attacks were over, but the stench lingered over the city for days. New Yorkers didn't talk about why it smelled unique. They didn't want to know.

They knew.[1]

The attacks changed everyone who watched, whether on TV around the world or from their balcony overlooking Manhattan across the East River. In the aftermath, Redeemer Presbyterian Church grew initially by thousands of visitors and then permanently by hundreds of members. Tim Keller and the church attracted international attention that never relented. And a bestselling book birthed later in the decade made Keller one of the most visible teachers and defenders of the Christian faith around the world.

They Stayed Put

You don't just shrug off the sight of a gunboat in the East River guarding the United Nations headquarters. But after the Tuesday attacks, Keller's thoughts quickly turned to Sunday. He suspended his series on the Old Testament prophet of Jonah and planned a sermon on the resurrection of Lazarus from John 11. The crowds on Sunday morning were so eager for a word of hope that they lined up around the block to secure a seat. But there wasn't nearly enough room. Keller announced that Redeemer would add another morning service to accommodate demand. Normally around 2,800, Redeemer's attendance spiked to 5,400 on September 16, 2001.[2]

Keller didn't attempt to answer why God allowed this tragedy to befall New York. But as Jesus wept over the death of his friend Lazarus, he wasn't helpless. He wouldn't leave the sisters Mary and Martha hopeless. He didn't ignore their plight.

> When somebody says to me, "I don't know that God cares about our suffering; I don't know that God cares about it at all," I say, "Yes, he does." They say, "How do you know?" Well, I'll tell you something. If I was in any other religion, I wouldn't know what to say. But what I can say is the proof is he was willing to suffer himself. I don't know why he hasn't ended suffering and evil by now, but the fact that he was willing to be involved and he himself got involved is proof that he must have some good reason, because he cares. He is not remote. He is not away from us.[3]

By declining to assign blame beyond the attackers and their planners, Keller didn't grab nearly as many headlines as Jerry Falwell and Pat Robertson on *The 700 Club* on September 13. Falwell and Robertson said the United States got what it deserved for tolerating abortionists, pagans, feminists, and homosexuals. When *The 700 Club* sent a truck to broadcast Redeemer's Sunday morning service, Kathy Keller chased the crew out of the building and told them never to return. She wasn't about to violate Redeemer's "zero publicity" policy for Robertson's news program, widely loathed in traumatized New York.[4]

Robertson and Falwell didn't represent the typical reaction from Christian leaders, however. The Kellers spent weeks answering prayerful, sympathetic phone calls from friends. Financial gifts poured in from churches around the world.[5] Redeemer had to hire an accountant to track it and a social worker to distribute two million dollars that appeared unsolicited.[6]

If any church could say it was prepared, it was Redeemer, led by the pastor who literally wrote the book on mercy ministry. While a few members died in the 9/11 attacks, the church also looked outward as they disbursed funds. One woman, Christina Ray Stanton, had been knocked unconscious as she stood on the balcony of her twenty-fourth-floor apartment, just six blocks from Tower Two when the second plane hit. Relocated to Battery Park, she left the island in a maritime rescue larger than the famed British evacuation of Dunkirk in June 1940. Like many others in the downtown trauma zone, she couldn't return to her apartment for months. She worried about her health after inhaling dust from the collapsed towers.

While still standing in Battery Park, Stanton wondered whether she would survive the day. And she began to reconsider her shallow faith.

"I didn't know where I was going if I did die," Stanton said. "I became painfully aware that I didn't possess a relationship with God, that I'd only ever lived for myself. It was a terrible acknowledgment—that throughout my life a Savior beckoned to me with open arms, and I'd never cared enough to respond."[7]

A friend told her that Redeemer could help, and she accepted the church's financial gift. She and her husband, Brian, became members. And then they both took jobs with the church, he as chief financial officer, she as missions director.

A pastor from Oklahoma City who provided counseling in the aftermath of the 1995 bombing warned Tim Keller that the city's emotional recovery would take longer than expected.[8] While the church welcomed new converts, heaviness lingered when Keller resumed his series on Jonah.[9] Mako Fujimura, who was living downtown during the attacks, remembers Keller encouraging New Yorkers not to abandon the city. "It was something God spoke to me," Fujimura said. "Love is sacrificial and painful at times."[10]

Glen Kleinknecht and other longtime Redeemer leaders believed the church helped stave off a mass exodus from New York. Looking back, they could see how God had prepared them for this moment through Rodney Stark's book *The Rise of Christianity*. The book became a kind of paradigm for church growth in New York after the tragedy.

Part sociologist and part historian, Stark set out to explain why Christianity triumphed in the Roman Empire. During a one-hundred-year tipping point, Christianity jumped from less than 8 percent of the Roman Empire to nearly 50 percent. Stark taught Keller that one of the biggest reasons was the Christian response to plagues that afflicted the empire from AD 165 to about 180, and then again from AD 251 until around 270. Cities suffered especially high losses. As the second plague raged, about five thousand people died each day—that's thirty-five thousand per week—just in Rome, whose population did not exceed one million. That's larger than the number who died in the first year of COVID in New York City. Put another way, up to 30 percent of everyone living in the entire Roman Empire died during the two plagues.

No one knew how to cure the disease, whether smallpox or measles or something else. They could see that it spread via contact though. So, anyone who could leave the city did, including doctors. Families left their own to die.

"But not the Christians," Keller told Redeemer Presbyterian Church in 1997. "The Christians stayed in the cities, and not only did they care for their own sick, but they had dynamic nursing services. They went out and brought in, and they cared for all sorts of the pagan sick. As a result, many, many of them died."

So why did the Christians stay and die while the pagans fled to live? If pagans knew what to expect from the afterlife, it wasn't necessarily good, according to their own beliefs. Christians, by contrast, believed that death would only deliver them to Jesus. It would have taken more bravery from the pagans, according to Stark, to risk death by treating the sick. The Christians could risk making this world a better place because they expected an even better one to come. In fact, the odds of recovering were about 50 percent if someone just fed you, warmed you, and gave you water. When Christians stayed to take care of one another, they outpaced pagans in numeric growth by three or four times. And when Christians cared for pagan family and neighbors, many professed faith in Jesus.

The Christians didn't act because they knew their numbers would triple so that eventually they would take over the Roman Empire, Keller explained. They acted because it's what their Savior taught them to do.

"As a result, from what we can tell, there was this tremendous upsurge in the growth of Christianity, biologically and through conversions," Keller said. "Ironically, the most absolutely practical thing Christians could have done was to do the most impractical thing. They stayed put."[11]

Ten years after the 9/11 attacks, Redeemer looked back and assessed the growth in evangelical church attendance since 1990. They found that it had tripled from 1 percent to 3 percent of the city.[12]

No Exceptions

Redeemer had always emphasized love for New York. The work of Jane Jacobs and her classic *The Death and Life of Great American Cities* circulated through the church. Redeemer sought to serve the whole city without undermining distinct neighborhoods with their broad range of residents. Keller warned:

> If this happens, a church can become a commuter church that no longer knows how to reach the kind of people who live in their immediate vicinity. Urban churches, then, should be known in their community as a group of people who are committed to the good of all their neighbors, near and far. It takes this type of holistic commitment from all residents and institutions to maintain a good quality of life in the city, and a church that is not engaged in this manner will (rightly) be perceived by the city as tribal."[13]

After 9/11, with the church's profile growing near and far, Keller tried to balance between original priorities and new reality. He had pushed the church to be ready for just this moment. Mako Fujimura was one of the youngest elders in 1993 when Redeemer had the option of meeting in an auditorium at Hunter College on the Upper East Side. The only trick was that it seated 2,200. It felt crazy to Fujimura to move to Hunter, with more than double Redeemer's attendance at the time between two sites. But it was the only option available after scouring the city for alternative spaces.

Soon afterward, the church grew quickly, especially among Asian Americans. "He told us, 'We only get one shot at this,'" Fujimura said. Keller's willingness to risk, to keep pushing the church in entrepreneurial ways, made an impression on Fujimura as he built his career as a painter and writer.[14]

By 2003, in the aftermath of the terrorist attacks, Redeemer was no longer mostly White. And it claimed more Asian Americans than any other church in the country. When Redeemer opened the $50 million W83 facility in 2012, it was the first new Manhattan church building in forty years.

Tim Keller almost didn't make it to that landmark though. The 9/11 attacks left behind a kind of collective depression on the city, even while everyone tried to project a brave front. Though Redeemer grew by nearly eight hundred members overnight, a subsequent recession in New York led to a critical budget shortfall and the first staff layoffs in the church's history. More work and fewer resources exacerbated the staff's deteriorating morale. At the same time, health problems plagued the Kellers. Kathy Keller had been diagnosed with Crohn's disease back in 1991. But the disease began to exact an especially painful toll in the late-1990s. In one year she endured seven surgeries. Finally, Tim was diagnosed in 2002 with thyroid cancer. It was one of the darkest times in their lives to that point. Even as the church grew, Tim considered stepping away from Redeemer and ministry altogether so he could care for Kathy.[15]

As he would do again when diagnosed with pancreatic cancer in 2020, Keller asked God for spiritual renewal. He had known since a 1999 study through the Psalms that he needed a deeper, stronger prayer life. Kathy recommended that they pray together every night, no exceptions. Tim remembered that she told him:

> Imagine you were diagnosed with such a lethal condition that the doctor told you that you would die within hours unless you took a particular medicine—a pill every night before going to sleep. Imagine that you were told that you could never miss it or you would die. Would you forget? Would you not get around to it some nights? No—it would be so crucial that you wouldn't forget. You would never miss. Well, if we don't pray together to God, we're not going to make it because of all we are facing. I'm certainly not. We *have* to pray. We can't let it slip our minds.

Even when Tim traveled in different time zones around the world, they didn't miss evening prayer—on the phone or in person.[16] Tim dabbled in classics about spirituality and spiritual disciplines, including those written by Catholic authors. But he returned to his trusted sources, especially Martyn Lloyd-Jones and Jonathan Edwards, to deepen his personal prayer life and found these sources still unsurpassed. John Owen gave him the most help for deeper prayer in "beholding the glory of Christ by faith."[17] Additional prayer support came in relearning the discipline of meditation from Richard Baxter and Martin Luther.

Nothing could substitute for more simple, steady exposure to the Psalms and extended time in prayer. Even as Redeemer's staff challenges persisted, along with the health crises, Kathy Keller observed more happiness in Tim than she'd ever seen before. God's love and presence overwhelmed Tim in new ways. The leadership mistakes had humbled Tim. He couldn't just preach sermons and cast vision. He needed to recognize his limits and the value of working in teams, not always having to be the main leader. As when he first moved to New York, Keller needed a reinvigorated spiritual life.

The Kellers needed God in prayer even more than they realized in their initial desperation. Little did they know, in the aftermath of 9/11, that many of their biggest changes still lay ahead.

Big Books

Before 9/11, the archetypal enemy of the United States was an atheist, usually a Communist from the Soviet Union or its allies. After 9/11, and especially into President George W. Bush's 2004 reelection campaign and second term, the enemy shifted. Now many Americans perceived the greatest threat to be conservative religious believers—Islamic fundamentalists like the Taliban, terrorists like al-Qaeda . . . or anyone else who takes faith so seriously that they believe it should shape private and public life.

The new plague on urban life is religion, so warned the New Atheists who dominated bestseller lists in the 2000s. Richard Dawkins, Sam Harris, Daniel Dennett, and Christopher Hitchens didn't want to make religion illegal. They didn't have the legal or political support for such a move. They aimed instead to make religion toxic, the greatest threat to all humanity. They wouldn't need to ban religion if they could just make it embarrassing to believe or practice.[18] In place, the New Atheists told adoring crowds and readers around the world to "believe science." Thanks to evolution, they said, no one needs religion any longer.[19]

Not even the combined book sales of the New Atheists, though, could match those of Dan Brown. He sold 80 million copies of his potboiler novel *The Da Vinci Code* in the 2000s and convinced dime-store skeptics that he knew the "real story" behind the growth of Christianity in the Roman Empire after the Council of Nicaea in AD 325. Published in 2003, *The Da Vinci Code* got an assist from *The Boston Globe*, whose reports on abuse cover-ups in the Catholic Church contributed to the overall mood against any organized religion. When the Indian Ocean tsunami of December 2004 left more than 250,000 dead, God got the bulk of the blame in ensuing essays on theodicy.

Writing in 2008, Keller noted the changing mood. "When I first came to New York City nearly twenty years ago, I more often heard the objection that all religions are equally true," he said. "Now, however, I'm more likely to be told that all religions are equally false."[20]

By 2008, when Tim Keller published his first bestselling book, *The Reason for God*, he had already invested several decades in listening to and answering common critiques of Christianity. Gabfests in Hopewell became the post-service Q and A in New York. "I want to thank the people and leaders of Redeemer Presbyterian Church, and especially the many inquirers, strugglers, and critics I have met there over the years," Keller wrote in *The Reason for God*. "This book is nothing but the record of what I've learned from them."[21]

With *The Reason for God*, Keller sought to rebuild the bridge between Christianity and science that the New Atheists had demolished. He cited his friend Francis Collins, author of *The Language of God* and head of the Human Genome Project. Like Keller, Collins was born in 1950 and read C. S. Lewis's *Mere Christianity* at a pivotal time before professing faith in Jesus. Collins was nominated in 2009 by President Obama to head the National Institutes of Health, where he would continue to serve under Presidents Trump and Biden.

Along with objections based on science, Keller tackled questions about history in *The Reason for God*. Keller never stopped adding "big book" pillars in his intellectual and spiritual development over the years. He read everything on apologetics he could find. During his treatment for thyroid cancer in 2002, Keller added N. T. Wright's award-winning eight-hundred-page apologetic *The Resurrection of the Son of God*. More than a decade later, Keller still said he didn't think Wright's book could be topped in its defense of the historical resurrection of Jesus.[22]

"It was not only an enormous help to my theological understanding but, under the circumstances, also a bracing encouragement in the face of my own heightened sense of mortality," Keller wrote. "I was reminded and assured that death had been defeated in Jesus, and that death would also be defeated for me."[23]

For Keller, intellectual and spiritual development could not be separated. They brewed together before bubbling over into his conversations with skeptics, preaching, and then finally books. His book *The Reason for God* helped Christians around the world answer objections that gained new traction after 9/11.

Two Shifts

Hundreds of thousands of readers met Tim Keller in *The Reason for God*. But the book reflected his long-standing interests and previewed new directions in his apologetic approach. Before 9/11, Keller was teaching apologetics to Redeemer's small group leaders, which included literary agent Nicole Diamond, whose parents were atheists and psychologists. Diamond herself had become a Christian at Yale. She first recommended that Keller turn the talks into a book.

After Diamond moved to Los Angeles and married, Keller connected through the church with another literary agent, who negotiated a contract with Penguin. From this auspicious start, Penguin asked Keller for a book every year. By this time in his mid- and late-fifties, Keller used the relentless publishing pace to expand his reading and knowledge on his books' subjects, whether prayer, suffering, marriage, idolatry, faith and work, or so on. He felt intellectually fresh at a time when he could have coasted on his earlier research.

Before 2010, most of the people who came forward to talk to Keller after services were New Yorkers and members of the church. He spent an hour in evangelistic or pastoral conversation after each service. But he noticed two shifts in the late-2000s. First, the questions shifted from science and history to morals and values. Doubt and incredulity shifted to anger and denunciation. The New Atheists framed Christianity as oppressive to women and racial minorities.[24] Compared to when he began preaching in 1975, Keller observed that the gospel message, especially the topics of hell and judgment, had become a hundred times more unpopular.

But he noticed another change that concerned him more. After *The Reason for God* reached number seven on *The New York Times* nonfiction bestseller list, the people asking the questions changed. Many of them were visiting New York as tourists. They wanted him to sign the book and take a picture. As a pastor who had devoted nearly twenty years to reaching skeptics in New York, he hated the change.[25] Keller finally brought on an assistant, Craig Ellis, whose job entailed saying no to outside requests, which came more frequently. Never again would he be known primarily as a New York pastor. But Ellis didn't see the newfound fame, however frustrating, change Keller. "The biggest compliment I can give to Tim is that the guy you think Tim would be by watching him on stage, that's actually who he is."[26]

Idol Addicts

Keller's growing popularity with Christians around the world jeopardized his ministry in New York through Redeemer. He wanted to work closely with skeptics, or at least with new Christians in the city who spent most of their time with non-Christians. Apologetics moves quickly, especially in such a tumultuous decade as the 2000s, which started with the worst terrorist attack in American history and ended with the Great Recession and the nation's first African American president.

Ted Turnau earned his MDiv and PhD from Westminster Theological Seminary and studied under Keller. His definition of apologetics captures Keller's aim in preaching and writing:

> Apologetics, then, has a dual focus: to keep an eye on our hope and remain true to it, and to keep an eye on what speaks to your listener, what connects with him or her at the level of desire (without manipulation). The job of apologetics is to build a bridge between hope and the non-Christian. This bridge-building will include "the facts" and narrowly logical argumentation, but the possible range of "reasons" could also include arguments about the beauty, goodness, justice, mercy, vitality, or peacefulness of the hope within us. We can use whatever will speak with relevance to the worldview context of those around us.[27]

Keller excelled less in philosophical apologetics, with its proofs of God, and more in cultural apologetics. He sought to connect the gospel of Jesus Christ with all of life, which is mediated by culture. Defined by

Turnau, culture is "human imaging of God's community, communion, and creativity by engaging and responding to the meanings inherent in God's creation (revelation) in order to create 'worlds' of shared meanings that glorify God, demonstrate love to other human beings, and demonstrate care for the rest of creation." To put it more simply, culture is a "fundamentally *religious* pursuit."[28]

Idolatry results when culture turns away from its God-glorifying purpose. Long seen by Keller as a key way to connect with contemporary skeptics, idolatry is the focus of his 2009 book *Counterfeit Gods: The Empty Promises of Money, Sex, and Power, and the Only Hope That Matters*. Keller variously attributed his inspiration for talking more about idolatry than the more common explanation of sin as offending God by breaking his laws. He credited Augustine's "disordered loves" in *Confessions*, which reveals the enslaving power of passions not rooted in God.[29] Former Augustinian monk Martin Luther appeared more often in Keller's early Redeemer sermons than anyone else except Jonathan Edwards.[30] Luther said that no one breaks the commandments against murder or theft or covetousness without first breaking the commandment against idolatry.[31] The uneasy Lutheran Søren Kierkegaard described sin as building identity on anything other than God.[32]

Ernest Becker helped Keller translate this theology into contemporary application. In *The Denial of Death*, Becker argued that Americans had shifted their search for meaning from God, family, and nation to romance. Idolizing a romantic relationship, though, doesn't end any better than worshiping your parents or the flag. Becker wrote:

> After all, what is it that we want when we elevate the love partner to the position of God? We want redemption—nothing less. We want to be rid of our faults, our feeling of nothingness. We want to be justified, to know that our creation has not been in vain.... Needless to say, human partners cannot do this.[33]

Such relationships last only so long as we imagine they meet our needs. The same goes for a job, apartment, or art exhibit—all good things that become idols when we expect them to fulfill us. Painful breakups follow when the job demands ninety hours per week. When we can't afford the apartment mortgage. And when the art exhibit gets negative reviews. Sometimes it takes failure to realize we've turned goods into gods. "Such grasping desire distorts the gift and bends it to a sinful purpose," Turnau wrote. "And we do this habitually, even compulsively. We are idol-addicts."[34]

Keller quoted widely from Luther, Augustine, and Kierkegaard in his sermons. But he especially loved when he could quote someone like Becker, who didn't follow Jesus but made Christian arguments. Along these lines, Keller first mentioned the novelist David Foster Wallace in a 2010 sermon. Wallace's 2005 commencement address at Kenyon College couldn't have better illustrated Keller's teaching on idolatry.

"Everybody worships," Wallace told the students. "The only choice we get is what to worship. And the compelling reason for maybe choosing some sort of god or spiritual-type thing to worship . . . is that pretty much anything else you worship will eat you alive."

There will never be enough money. Our bodies break down with age. Power corrupts, and we destroy others to hide our fear. Intellect fails and fades and reveals us as frauds. "But the insidious thing about these forms of worship is . . . they're unconscious," said Wallace, who committed suicide in 2008. "They are default settings."[35]

As an apologist citing the likes of Wallace and Becker, Keller employed a version of the presuppositional arguments of Cornelius Van Til, a founding professor at Westminster Theological Seminary. Such arguments work backward from reality to its supporting presuppositions. They seek the *why* behind the *what*.[36]

Thousands of New Yorkers after September 11, 2001, wanted to know the *why* behind *what* they had just witnessed—and smelled.

Tim Keller didn't give any definitive explanation. But he offered hope and meaning by pointing to a God who works miracles when you least expect them.

Everybody worships. You may as well worship the God who rises—and raises—from the dead.

SEVENTEEN

MAKING SENSE
OF GOD

Dogwood Fellowship

As soon as Tim Keller published his bestselling apologetics book, he knew it was already obsolete.

In answering the most common objections to Christianity in the West, *The Reason for God* doesn't even devote a single chapter to sexuality.[1] After the book released in 2008, sexuality was just about the only objection to Christianity that many skeptics wanted to discuss. But that wasn't the book's biggest shortcoming. Even the objections assumed a level of awareness and interest in Christianity that is quickly eroding across the West.

But Keller didn't discover the shortcomings in *The Reason for God* by talking with readers, who made the book an overnight success. He realized the problems in his own research and reading, which had begun to chart a different course in 2004. That's the year Keller joined the

Dogwood Fellowship, organized by University of Virginia sociologist (and committed Christian) James Davison Hunter, and named in honor of their shared Virginia roots. Between 2004 and the 2008 recession, Keller met about four times a year with Hunter, pastor Skip Ryan, and two business leaders, Don Flow and Jim Seneff. Drawing together the "overlapping capital" of theology, sociology, and business, Hunter organized the group to understand how the church should respond to their times and culture. Their conversations resulted in Hunter's groundbreaking book *To Change the World: The Irony, Tragedy, and Possibility of Christianity in the Late Modern World*, published in 2010 and dedicated, "For Dogwood."

In these discussions, Keller enjoyed his most intellectually and spiritually stimulating fellowship since Westminster and Gordon-Conwell. Hunter shared unpublished handouts and papers as Keller gained a vision for cultural change and renewal through networks of friends. As a student of revival, Keller sensed something of what it felt like to be part of the Clapham Sect in the eighteenth and nineteenth centuries.

The epochal experience for Keller was cribbing the reading list of Hunter, who taught about his understanding of culture's "deep structures." Through Hunter, Keller was introduced to the "big four" critics of secular modernity. From this time forward, Charles Taylor, Alasdair MacIntyre, Philip Rieff, and Robert Bellah became staples in Keller's thinking, writing, and teaching.[2] They provoked Keller to a deeper analysis of the problems besetting the post-Christian West in politics and culture.

Much of Christian apologetics, including *The Reason for God*, still operates within the confines of the Enlightenment. Christians offer rational explanations and provide empirical evidence for biblical events and claims. But what if the Enlightenment has run its course? What if it's a dead end for Western culture? What if the Enlightenment can't deliver the meaning, identity, purpose, and justice that Westerners continue to demand?

If Western secularism derived its values of tolerance and fairness from Christianity, then supposedly objective and empirical science and reason can't sustain moral idealism. The West wants to be relativistic and moralistic at the same time. And it's not working, as these four critics have argued for decades.[3]

Sociologist Christian Smith describes the post-Enlightenment dilemma as a spiritual project in pursuit of a sacred good:

> To make everything new, to leave behind the past, to be unbound by any tradition, to enjoy maximum choice, to be free from any constraint, to be able to buy whatever one can afford, to live however one desires—that is the guiding vision of modernity's spiritual project. It is spiritual (not merely ideological or cultural) because it names what is sacrosanct, an ultimate concern, a vision for what is most worthy in a sense that transcends any individual life. It is spiritual because it speaks to people's deepest personal subjectivities, their most transcendent vision of goodness, their definition of ultimate fulfillment. It is spiritual because as a deep cultural structure it occupies a position in the modern West homologous with salvation in God that was prized in the premodern Christendom that modernity broke apart. And it is spiritual because, by being sacred, it is worth protecting, defending, policing, fighting for, perhaps dying for, even killing for.[4]

So if the Enlightenment supplanted Christianity with this rival spirituality, how can the West return to the gospel? That's the question Keller has set out to answer in the last fifteen years.

Oxford Missions

Every three years, the Oxford Inter-Collegiate Christian Union (OICCU) hosts a six-day mission to evangelize more than twenty thousand students in this iconic English university town. The missions began in 1940, months before the Battle of Britain. Martyn Lloyd-Jones led the missions in 1943 and 1951. Other Keller heroes John Stott and Michael Green also led Oxford missions.

During his first Oxford mission in early February 2012, Tim and Kathy along with their son Michael and his wife, Sara, stayed in the Old Parsonage Hotel, a couple blocks north of the Oxford University campus. As the family returned one night through falling snow, they caught a glimpse of a traditional lamppost. The magic of Narnia lingered around Oxford.

In the evenings around a seventeenth-century fireplace, the Keller family debriefed the good and bad from Tim's evangelistic talks and the students' questions. The talks from 2012 became Keller's book *Encounters with Jesus: Unexpected Answers to Life's Biggest Questions*. Many of the book's themes can be found in earlier books such as *The Reason for God*, *Counterfeit Gods*, and *The Prodigal God*.

When Keller returned in 2015, he insisted on a topical approach in contrast to the expositional talks he was asked to deliver in 2012. He wanted to test what he'd been learning from the social critics Taylor, Rieff, MacIntyre, and Bellah. Os Guinness delivered the lunchtime talks, while Keller spoke in the evenings on meaning, identity, and justice. After each day, these good friends with shared love for Francis Schaeffer and L'Abri retreated to the fireside at the Randolph Hotel and talked late into the morning. Compared to 2012, Keller saw more encouraging responses from skeptical students in 2015.[5] On the spot during Q and A in this second mission, Keller conceived what became one of his most memorable illustrations.

He was responding to a question about the Christian view of homosexuality. Keller realized he couldn't answer without turning the tables and critiquing the concept of identity in the modern West. His response at the talk that summer ended up being included in his book *Preaching: Communicating Faith in an Age of Skepticism*.

Keller asked the Oxford students to imagine an Anglo-Saxon warrior in Britain in AD 800. Inside he feels the impulse to destroy anyone who disrespects him. That's the response his honor/shame culture demands, and so he does. But he also feels sexually attracted to men. His culture demands that he suppress those feelings, so he does not act on them. Now consider a man of the same age walking the streets of Manhattan in our day. He feels just like the Anglo-Saxon warrior. He wants to kill anyone who looks at him the wrong way. And he desires sexual relations with other men. Our culture sends him to therapy for anger management. He will identify publicly with his sexual orientation.

So what does this illustration teach us? Keller explains:

> Primarily it reveals that we do not get our identity simply from within. Rather, we receive some interpretive moral grid, lay it down over our various feelings and impulses, and sift them through it. This grid helps us decide which feelings are "me" and should be expressed—and which are not and should not be. So this grid of interpretive beliefs—not an innate, unadulterated expression of our feelings—is what shapes our identity. Despite protests to the contrary, we instinctively know our inner depths are insufficient to guide us. We need some standard or rule from outside of us to help us sort out the warring impulses of our interior life.
>
> And where do our Anglo-Saxon warrior and our modern Manhattan man get their grids? From their cultures, their communities, their heroic stories. They are actually not simply "choosing to be themselves"—they are filtering their feelings, jettisoning some and embracing others. They are choosing to be the selves their cultures tell them they may be. In the end, an identity based independently on your own inner feelings is impossible.[6]

Instead of responding directly to the question about homosexuality, Keller turned to the underlying assumptions of identity in Western culture, what Bellah termed "expressive individualism." First published in 1985, Bellah's *Habits of the Heart* observes, "Expressive individualism holds that each person has a unique core of feeling and intuition that should unfold or be expressed if individuality is to be realized."[7] Individuality may be the goal, but as Keller observes with the Anglo-Saxon warrior imagery, identity forms in community. And communities shape which values can contribute to our identity. No one is free to be anything they want, especially when the government imposes secular views of sexuality on law and public education. Power convinces everyone they're expressing their individual identity, while instead they're all doing the same thing.[8]

This tension between expression and community is the dynamite beneath the Enlightenment implosion. Bellah and his colleagues saw it coming long before same-sex marriage became law across the West.

> What we fear above all, and what keeps the new world powerless to be born, is that if we give up our dream of private success for a more genuinely integrated societal community, we will be abandoning our separation and individuation, collapsing into dependence and tyranny. What we find hard to see is that it is the extreme fragmentation of the modern world that really threatens our individuation; that what is best in our separation and individuation, our sense of dignity and autonomy as persons, requires a new integration if it is to be sustained.[9]

Informed by Bellah, Keller's 2015 Oxford talks contributed to his book released that fall, *Making Sense of God*. Compared to *The Reason for God*, *Making Sense of God* hasn't found a broad audience. But it's the apologetics book he would have written in 2008 if he had known then what he knows now. *Making Sense of God* aims to expose the assumptions behind the objections to Christianity, while also seeking to stimulate interest in Jesus by exposing the contradictions in Western efforts to find a viable alternative to the Enlightenment. So far at least, though, the audience with intellectual inclination and spiritual openness hasn't yet materialized outside highly select venues such as the Oxford missions, which Keller reprised in 2019.[10] Before his 2019 mission, OICCU adjusted the typical order and preceded Keller's talks with weeks of small group discussion rather than following up afterward. The result was even more encouraging than 2015 and led Keller to begin planning ways to adapt such a model for evangelism in the United States.

Cross-Pressured

Charles Taylor didn't appear in Keller's preaching at Redeemer until 2013, after Keller's first Oxford mission and five years after the Canadian philosopher published his seminal work *A Secular Age*. For Keller, Taylor summarized much of the critique of secularism and modernity he found in Rieff, Bellah, and MacIntyre. Keller read Taylor's book twice, line by line, over the course of two years. Thanks to Taylor, he began to see why so many deeply secular people don't respond to traditional evangelism and apologetics. According to Taylor, secularism doesn't only mean that people stop believing in God. As Keller explained in a sermon on Psalm 111, in our secular age, the view of God becomes thinner. God is remote. We don't need to obey him or depend on him moment by moment. In the pre-Enlightenment view, we exist for God and serve him. But in the modern view, Taylor observes, God only exists for our benefit.[11] Among the consequences of this shift, suffering becomes unbearable for us, because we can't trust God with a purpose beyond our understanding.

Keller relied on Taylor to puncture self-assured secularism. In an evangelistic talk at Redeemer in 2014, Keller introduced Taylor's description of the cross-pressures between belief and doubt.[12] Some may pose as never doubting God's existence. Others may pose as never doubting God's nonexistence. But the rest of us fall somewhere in the middle, either believing in God but doubting from time to time, or doubting God but believing from time to time.

As recently as 150 years ago, the average person never met someone who didn't believe in God. Usually, communities generally believed the same things about God. Now, nearly everyone who believes in God knows and loves people who don't. And they know many arguments against God, some of which they even find compelling. The reverse is true as well. No atheist can escape Christmas carols when shopping in December.

Through Taylor's concept of cross-pressures, Keller sought to level the playing field between doubters and believers. By acknowledging doubt, Keller cracked open the door for belief:

> The premise is that since none of us can prove or disprove our deepest beliefs, your deepest moral convictions about right and wrong, your deepest convictions about what people should be doing with their lives, belief whether there's a God or whether there's no God. . . . You can't prove God. You can't totally disprove God. That means all of us have beliefs we can't prove, and yet you can't live without those beliefs.[13]

Social critics such as Taylor gave Keller fresh ammo, but he already knew how to use the weapons. He learned to wield presuppositional apologetics at Westminster as he explained to his class on "Preaching Christ in a Postmodern World" taught through Reformed Theological Seminary:

> I got this presuppositional stuff and biblical theology—[Geerhardus] Vos and [Edmund] Clowney and [John] Frame and [Cornelius] Van Til, and all that—way back when everybody thought of it as, "What is this stuff?" Back in the '70s and '60s, it just was this little tributary in the evangelical world. The evangelical world was completely dominated by the systematic theology and evidence for the resurrection

and proofs of the existence of God and all that sort of stuff. And now that stuff looks so passé it's unbelievable.[14]

Passé, perhaps. But the more classical apologetics of *The Reason for God* sold better than the presuppositional apologetics of *Making Sense of God*. One reason is that apologetics tends to shore up Christian belief more than convince skeptics. Keller continues to search for ways to reach the most skeptical audiences, whether in Oxford or New York.

To the skeptics tuning out the cacophony of Manhattan streets, to the doubters trudging through fresh Oxford snow, Keller offers sympathy. Forming identity under the terms of expressive individualism is crushing.[15] But he also offers a solution. "If you believe the Gospel and all its remarkable claims about Jesus and what he has done for you and who you are in him, then nothing that happens in this world can actually get at your identity," he wrote in *Making Sense of God*. "Imagine, for a moment, what it would look like to believe this. Consider what a sweeping difference it would make."[16] With Jesus, you get invincible confidence in your worth. But you must trade your autonomous independence to get it. And you'll be required to serve God at the center of the universe.[17] "Through faith in the cross we get a new foundation for an identity that both humbles us out of our egoism yet is so infallibly secure in love that we are enabled to embrace rather than exclude those who are different."[18]

Keller's own grasp of this truth about tolerance would be tested in 2017.

Missionary Encounter

Hardly anyone could be more qualified than Tim Keller to receive the Kuyper Prize for Excellence in Reformed Theology and Public Witness. But the reaction from many Princeton Theological Seminary (PTS) students and alumni to his selection showed why Keller adjusted his approach from *The Reason for God* to *Making Sense of God*. In less than a decade, the culture in Western education had shifted from tolerance of homosexuality to intolerance of anyone who didn't affirm homosexuality. Keller's views on women's ordination and homosexuality run counter to the prevailing norms at PTS and other mainline seminaries, not to mention the broader culture. By this standard, Abraham Kuyper himself wouldn't have been eligible for the award named after him. Under pressure, PTS leaders rescinded the award to Keller.

Richard Mouw, who won the Kuyper Prize in 2007, was among several leading Kuyperians who protested PTS's decision. He wrote for *Christianity Today*:

> While many of us disagree with Keller's stance on the ordination of women, we admire him greatly. His ministry—Redeemer Presbyterian Church in New York City—has done so much to model the practical application of Kuyper's theology of culture to Christian engagement in business, the arts, politics, journalism, and other areas of cultural leadership in seeking obedience to the lordship of Jesus Christ over, to use Kuyper's oft-cited imagery, "every square inch" of creation.[19]

Even though he didn't receive the prize, Keller agreed to give the lectures. Enthusiastic, sustained applause greeted Keller when he stepped to the podium. PTS president Craig Barnes got the message again when he returned to dismiss the crowd for a post-lecture reception. In 2018, the Kuyper Prize, as part of the annual Kuyper Conference, shifted from PTS to Calvin University and Calvin Theological Seminary.

For twenty years, the Kuyper Conference had attracted a wide spectrum of Reformed thinkers. But Keller's rejection in 2017 showed how the pressures of the post-Christian West had further fragmented Protestants. Keller's lecture engaged with Lesslie Newbigin's 1984 Warfield lectures at PTS, which became Newbigin's book *Foolishness to the Greeks: The Gospel and Western Civilization*. Newbigin argued for a missionary encounter with Western culture, which had become post-Christian. Look no further for evidence of this shift than a Christian seminary rejecting a Christian pastor because he holds to Christian beliefs.

For Newbigin, the post-Christian West is the most resistant, challenging missionary frontier of all time. None of the most common Christian responses will suffice for an effective missionary program. Christians shouldn't withdraw like the Amish. They shouldn't seek political takeover as some evangelicals and fundamentalists advocate through the religious right. They mustn't assimilate like the mainline. The categories correspond to James Davison Hunter's *To Change the World*: "defensive against" (religious right), "relevant to" (mainline), and "purity from" (Amish). Hunter proposed "faithful presence within" as a better alternative, which Keller adopted as his own perspective in *Center Church*.[20]

At PTS, Keller acknowledged differences with Newbigin, a mainline Protestant. But Keller's missionary instincts owe much to Newbigin, combined with several other influences that create a unique synthesis.

In a missionary encounter, Christians must connect with and confront culture so they can convert the skeptical. The Christian must be prepared, according to 1 Peter 2:12, to suffer persecution but also see conversion growth. When Christians denounce the Western cultural idols of science, individualism, and consumerism, many will rage in protest, while others will weep in gratitude. As Keller explained at PTS, his missionary program for the post-Christian West follows seven steps, deeply informed by the neo-Calvinism of Kuyper and his allies.

The first step is *promoting incisive public apologetics*. Classic apologetic works such as N. T. Wright's *The Resurrection of the Son of God* are helpful. Even better for our time is Augustine's *City of God*, because it speaks to social aspirations and assumptions. Skeptics who no longer see the need for Christianity must be shown how their inclusivity has become exclusive. They need to know that right and wrong can't be differentiated apart from religion. They need to see that science is based on faith, as Keller argued in *Making Sense of God*:

> When secularists endorse human dignity, rights, and the responsibility in order to eliminate human suffering, they are indeed exercising religious faith in some kind of supranatural, transcendent reality. . . . To hold that human beings are the product of nothing but the evolutionary process of the strong eating the weak, but then to insist that nonetheless every person has a human dignity to be honored—is an enormous leap of faith against *all* evidence to the contrary.[21]

Second, *horizontal and vertical dimensions of the faith must be integrated*. The mainline can't just care about social problems. And evangelicals can't just care about spiritual problems. Justification must lead to justice.

Third, *a critique of secularism must emerge from within its own framework*, not from an outward construct. Borrowing from Daniel Strange, Keller calls this process "subversive fulfillment." It's a form of "active contextualization" in three parts: enter the culture, challenge the culture, then appeal to the gospel.[22] You can see this model in his preaching. Keller begins by using accessible or at least well-defined vocabulary to connect with skeptics. He cites respected authorities, especially outside the church, who support his views. Next, he acknowledges objections to the Christian view. He affirms critiques where Christians and the church fall short of ideals. Then he exposes the contradictions within the critique. He shows that apart from the gospel, skeptics can't realize their own desires. And finally, he shows how only the gospel of Jesus Christ can fulfill our most fervent hopes and surpass our wildest dreams.[23]

Fourth, *Christian community must disrupt the culture's social categories*. Thriving communities lend credibility to the transformative power of the gospel. Keller cites Larry Hurtado, author of *Destroyer of the gods: Early Christian Distinctiveness in the Roman World*. In this incisive study, Hurtado showed how the persecuted early Christian community wasn't just offensive to Jews and Greeks; it was also attractive.[24] Christians opposed abortion and infanticide by adopting children. They didn't retaliate but instead forgave. They cared for the poor and marginalized. Their strict sexual ethic protected and empowered women and children. Christian churches brought together hostile nations and ethnic groups. Jesus broke apart the connection between religion and ethnicity when he revealed a God for every tribe and tongue and nation. Allegiance to Jesus trumped geography, nationality, and ethnicity in the church. As a result, Christians gained perspective so they could critique any culture. And they learned to listen to the critiques from fellow Christians embedded in different cultures.[25]

Fifth, to achieve an effective missionary encounter in the post-Christian West, *laity must integrate their faith with their work.* Discipleship must extend from private to public. It can't be compartmentalized. Non-Christians must see the difference faith makes in day-to-day living.

Sixth, *the local church must be informed by the global church.* Nobody did this better than Lesslie Newbigin. His experience in India gave fresh perspective on cultural changes inside and outside the church in his native England. In his answer to Newbigin at Princeton, Keller admitted that conservative evangelicals in the United States put too much faith in their methodology and struggle to see the kingdom of God apart from American national interest.

Seventh, and finally, Keller encouraged PTS *not to miss the difference between grace and religion.* As Richard Lovelace first showed Keller in his study of revival, missionary encounters that produce social change depend on grace, not on the rules of religion. Only grace brings spiritual transformation. And apart from the Spirit of God, we're helpless to effect lasting change in our fallen world.[26]

Before the Kuyper Prize incident, Keller observed how the secular West had become one of the most moralistic cultures in history.[27]

The secular West imagines itself as a tolerant refuge from the restrictive Christian past. But wielding the power of exclusion against evangelicals has contributed to increased enmity, along with cultural and political polarization.[28]

"People who are passionate for justice often become self-righteous and cruel when they confront persons whom they perceive as being oppressors," Keller wrote in *Making Sense of God*.[29] Only the gospel can unite tolerance and justice. "The Gospel of Jesus Christ provides a non-oppressive absolute truth, one that provides a norm outside of ourselves as the way to escape relativism and selfish individualism, yet one that cannot be used to oppress others."[30]

By showing up the PTS administration and canceling his talk, Keller could have gained greater attention and support from his fellow conservative evangelicals. But Keller has been teaching Christian leaders for years that the gospel offers an alternative to the intolerance of secularism and tribalism of religion. He wrote in *Center Church* that "the Christian gospel turns people away from both their selfishness and their self-righteousness to serve others in the way that Jesus gave himself for his enemies."[31]

If Christians hope to evangelize their neighbors, they can't ignore or denounce them. They must show how the gospel changes everything. In Jesus, as Keller wrote in *How to Reach the West Again*, Christians find:

- a meaning in life that suffering can't take away, but can even deepen;
- a satisfaction that isn't based on circumstances;
- a freedom that doesn't reduce community and relationships to thin transactions;
- an identity that isn't fragile or based on our performance or the exclusion of others;
- a way both to deal with guilt and to forgive others without residual bitterness or shame;

- a basis for seeking justice that does not turn us into oppressors ourselves;
- a way to face not only the future, but death itself with poise and peace; and
- an explanation for the senses of transcendent beauty and love we often experience.[32]

How to Tell Time

When social justice became the hottest debate among evangelicals toward the end of the 2010s, Keller reached for help from another social critic recommended by James Davison Hunter. Keller claims that no one does a better job than Alasdair MacIntyre at explaining the Western confusion over justice. Author of *After Virtue: A Study in Moral Theory* and *Whose Justice? Which Rationality?* MacIntyre contrasts biblical, classical, and Enlightenment views of justice based on their philosophy of human nature and purpose, practical rationality, and morality.[33] The Enlightenment theory of justice taught by David Hume failed because morality and justice can't be determined by subjective feelings. MacIntyre argues that we can't decide if a wristwatch is good or bad unless we know if it's for telling time or hammering nails. When Hume disconnected justice from Christianity, the West forgot how to tell time.

The moral consensus of Christianity still hangs in the air, the residue of a civilization recently collapsed on itself. But why would this generation or any future one agree about good and evil? Why should anyone prefer Christian morality to its many historical alternatives? Friedrich Nietzsche admitted in the early twentieth century that without Christianity, equal rights and human dignity find no basis. We can assert our rights and claim them for others, such as the poor, but society can't agree on any reason why. Keller argues:

In a universe in which we just appeared, not for any purpose, through a process that is basically violent, we cannot talk about anything being deserved or right or wrong. The most that secular thinkers can ever argue for is that, on some cost-benefit analysis that murdering people or starving the poor is impractical for some agreed upon end. Yet, as MacIntyre points out none of the adherents of these views can avoid such talk. They unavoidably "smuggle" in language of morality and virtue that their own view of the world cannot support. That should tell them something.[34]

It should tell them that if they want justice, they need Jesus. Only he can reconcile individual dignity and freedom along with collective sacrifice and community. Only he can square the round pegs the post-Enlightenment West keeps trying to pound into the wrong holes. Keller identified this confusion in his 2018 book *The Prodigal Prophet*:

These modern beliefs—that we must all be committed to equal rights and justice but that there are no God-given moral absolutes—undermine each other. Modern secular education teaches every child that they must be true to themselves, that they must identify their deepest desires and dreams and pursue them, not letting family, community, tradition, or religion stand in their way. Then it calls for justice, reconciliation, and benevolence, all of which are basic forms of self-denial, even as it encourages self-assertion. It teaches relativism and calls people to be ethical. It encourages self-seeking and calls people to be sacrificial.[35]

In addition to pointing out these contradictions, with help from MacIntyre, Keller argued that secular views of justice reflect the privilege of modern middle-class life. Inspired by Howard Thurman of Boston University, who lectured at Harvard in 1947 on "Negro spirituals," Keller argued that you can only debate philosophy and ethics without reference to God when you're safe from real darkness.[36]

> Imagine how ludicrous it would have been to sit down with a group of early nineteenth-century slaves and say, "There will never be a judgment day in which wrongdoing will be put right. There is no future world and life in which your desires will ever be satisfied. This life is all there is. When you die, you simply cease to exist. Our only real hope for a better world lies in improved social policy. Now, with these things in mind, go out there, keep your head high, and live a life of courage and love. Don't give in to despair."[37]

These social critics helped Keller shake the foundations of social justice. But Keller also faulted the church when it fell short of the standards for biblical justice. He admitted that many younger Christians turn to secular justice because the church never taught them biblical justice.[38] As far back as *Center Church*, Keller argued, "If the church does not identify with the marginalized, it will itself be marginalized."[39] Keller himself had once been that skeptical young Christian—during the civil rights movement. He dismissed the church when older White Christians he knew showed no urgency to pursue justice for African Americans and even opposed their effort to secure civil rights. His view changed when he met Christians who applied their faith to the injustices of the late 1960s and early '70s. Still, he didn't know how God demands justice as the sovereign Creator and dispatched his prophets to condemn injustice. Only later did he realize how African American churches had appealed more to these biblical grounds for justice than to secular alternatives.[40]

When Keller reached seminary, debates over Black identity swirled around Gordon-Conwell as the school aimed to diversify. Elward Ellis, then a student and friend to Tim and Kathy, joined the InterVarsity staff in 1980. For seven years, he worked as the first director of Black Campus Ministries for InterVarsity. Across the kitchen table from Tim and Kathy in Massachusetts, he didn't hesitate to speak his mind—once the Kellers gave him permission to be honest. "You're a racist, you know," Ellis told the Kellers. "Oh, you don't mean to be, and you don't want to be, but you are. You can't really help it."

Ellis argued that many White people don't recognize their own cultural assumptions. "When Black people do things in a certain way, you say, 'Well, that's your culture.' But when White people do things in a certain way, you say, 'That's just the right way to do things,'" he told them.

The Kellers couldn't disagree. They had conflated culture with morality and judged other races.[41] But they learned the lesson. If we're saved by our good works, Tim Keller wrote in *Making Sense of God*, then the stronger and more privileged could boast in their accomplishment. Salvation by grace alone, however, favors the overlooked. Jesus, after all, didn't come to earth wealthy and powerful, but poor, born to a woman not yet married.

> If all this surprises you, it may mean that you have bought into a completely mistaken idea, namely that Christianity is about how those who live moral and good lives and consequently are taken to heaven. Rather, one of the main themes of the biblical story and stories is that even some of the ablest human beings who have ever lived, such as Abraham and David, could not rise above the brutality of their own cultures nor the self-centeredness of their own hearts. But by clinging to the wondrous promise that God's grace is given to moral failures, they triumphed.[42]

Keller couldn't know how *Making Sense of God* would be received when it released just before the 2016 presidential election. But the outcome of that election changed the tone and content of evangelical debates over racism and justice. Keller had long argued that the gospel humbles everyone to see themselves as part of the problem. He preached at Redeemer in the summer of 2001:

> If the gospel changes you, you will never see anybody else, anywhere else, as being the enemy, the real problem with the world. It makes you more able to cooperate with people, more able to make common cause with people, therefore, ultimately more pragmatic and more willing to compromise, more willing to do things with people. . . . Only self-righteousness makes you look at other people, saying, "The people over there are the bad guys. They're the real problem here."[43]

This mood of recrimination prevailed among many evangelicals after 2016. Writing in 2021, Kathy Keller said that many of their friends and colleagues left churches that only preached about social justice and not the gospel. "These are mature Christians who deliberately joined multi-racial congregations in order to advance the gospel by demonstrating its ability to break down barriers, but who now experience every kind of barrier against fellowship and conversation." At the same time, she and Tim were hearing from pastors who invited attack by the mere mention of justice. "So the question becomes," Kathy asked, "does the church want to be effective in changing hearts and making disciples, as Jesus commanded, or are we going to be content with preaching only to the already converted who agree with one another on the particular way they think gospel translates into social policy?"[44]

The problem, of course, is that justice is a partisan issue in the United States, with everything depending on whether you've lined up on the blue or red team. Christians realigned less because of their views on the gospel or theology and more on their politics. Churches that aligned with the blue team were tempted to ignore the vertical dimensions of personal conversion. And churches that aligned with the red team were tempted to ignore the horizontal dimensions of biblical justice and not evangelize outside their political tribe. Far from uniting to share Jesus with a world desperate for justice yet unable to even define it, American Christians had largely conformed by 2020 with the partisan battle lines.[45]

Keller didn't stop commending better alternatives though. He claimed it would be difficult to overstate the significance of Tom Holland's 2019 book *Dominion: How the Christian Revolution Remade the World*. Drawing on many of the same sources as Keller, Holland argued that the best achievements of the modern West come from Christianity, though few will admit it. Even secular critiques of the church depend on Christian beliefs. Christians can't be too disappointed if what the world really wants is for them to be more fully Christian—to act with integrity, to pursue justice for the poor. "If both sides would allow themselves to be chastened by Holland," Keller wrote in his review, "future conversations will be much more fruitful, and more tethered to reality."[46]

Keller also returned to the work of Dutch theologian Herman Bavinck, an associate of Abraham Kuyper in the late-nineteenth and early-twentieth centuries. Keller first read Bavinck at Gordon-Conwell in courses with Roger Nicole. Keller admired the balance of piety and theological depth, the nuance between Bible and dogmatics.[47] When James Eglinton published his critical biography of Bavinck in 2020, Keller described Bavinck as the greatest Reformed theologian of the twentieth century.[48]

Bavinck may have regarded Americans as too strong-willed to be Calvinists, but in the twenty-first century Keller found in the Dutch theologian a model of social criticism combined with Reformed dogmatics.[49] Eglinton wrote of Bavinck, "Western culture, he thought, was too deeply rooted in the Christian worldview to survive without it. To save Western culture from its eventual post-Christian demise, Bavinck insisted that Christ's lordship had to be brought to bear on every area of modern life."[50]

As a contemporary of Nietzsche, Bavinck could see that nihilistic theology had plunged Europe into a needless world war.[51] And like Keller, Bavinck preferred the both/and to the either/or. He combined eternal hope and holiness on one end of his denomination's spectrum with the world-transforming faith of the other.[52]

Not everyone, though, would read a Dutch theologian only recently translated into English. If thick dogmatics were beyond the patience of some, literature and film could help the post-Enlightenment West recover the best of its Christian past.

Babette's Feast

If you've watched the film or read the book *Babette's Feast*, chances are you got the recommendation from Tim Keller. One of his three favorite films, Keller featured *Babette's Feast* in the conclusion to his bestselling book *The Prodigal God*.[53]

Keller gave an extensive account of the story in a 1997 sermon at Redeemer. In the story written by Isak Dinesen, a Danish writer, two young sisters give up their dreams to sing and to marry. Their father wants them to stay and take over his Christian sect in their small community on the western coast of Jutland. The women grow up in a small, drab world with the graying members of their sect. One night, long after their father has died, a woman shows up at the door of their modest home in distress. They can't pay her to be a housekeeper, but she doesn't know where else to go. She has fled violence in France, and an opera singer who had trained the singing sister told her she'd be safe with them in Jutland. They take her in, and for years she cooks and cleans and becomes a beloved friend to the sisters.

One day, she receives notice that she won the lottery in France. But she surprises the sisters by not returning to live in France. She only visits to buy the makings of a marvelous feast. She insists on treating the

Danish villagers. They agree—on one condition. Among themselves they decide that their Christian convictions do not allow them to enjoy the food. They won't even taste it, they tell each other.

Joined by a military officer who had long ago courted one of the sisters, these Christian sectarians sit down to an extravagant meal beyond their imaginations. The meal recalls for the officer a restaurant he once enjoyed in Paris. He can't imagine how he could be enjoying a world-class feast in such a modest Jutland home. Eventually, the sectarians begin to share his enthusiasm for the gourmet delights.

Only later does everyone realize that Babette, the housekeeper, had been the chef of that Paris restaurant. She spent her entire lottery earnings on this one meal.

All she wanted to do was honor these women who had given her refuge and enjoy, for one last time in her life, the feeling of appreciation as a great artist. But in the end, all that's left is dirty dishes. And a return to bland meals of fish and bread.

Sensing Babette's disappointment, one sister embraces the chef in a trembling hug. She tells Babette, "'Yet this is not the end! I feel, Babette, that this is not the end. In Paradise you will be the great artist that God meant you to be! Ah!' she added, the tears streaming down her cheeks. 'Ah, how you will enchant the angels!'"[54]

The story pairs two of Keller's most important themes and suggests a way forward for the church in the twenty-first century and perhaps beyond. On the one hand, Dinesen exposes the joylessness of Christian obedience apart from the gospel of grace, which does more than save us from sin for eternity. Grace also prepares us to receive God's gifts here and now.

On the one hand, the gourmet feast symbolizes a kind of spiritual revival as the sectarians overcome their reluctance to enjoy the bounty of God's creation. Over food and wine, they grow more honest with each other and reconcile through forgiveness. Years of bitter feuds melt away over turtle soup. Keller explained in a 1993 sermon at Redeemer: "The message is if you can't enjoy a good feast, you are not ready for God's future. We will eat and drink and we'll sit down with Abraham, Isaac, and Jacob. God invented the physical. He became physical to redeem us."[55]

On the other hand, Dinesen reveals the futility of fleeting joy apart from eternity. If Jesus has not been raised, then the meal is nothing more than one last spectacular hurrah as Babette awaits the endless nothing of death. But if Jesus has been raised—if she believes as the sisters do—then an even more spectacular wedding feast of the Lamb awaits.[56] In the new heaven and the new earth, she may indeed glorify God and share her gifts with the angels in the company of the redeemed.

Dinesen's story borrows from the life and teaching of Søren Kierkegaard, the Danish existentialist philosopher from the nineteenth century. Kierkegaard grew up in Jutland and resented the stern Christianity of his father. His mother died in his childhood, and he lived in a profligate manner after he left home. He broke off an engagement in his late twenties. Kierkegaard's voice seems to come through in the story in the officer, who narrates the meaning of Babette's meal.

Keller explained to Redeemer in 1997 that Kierkegaard identified three ways to live before God: the aesthetic, the ethical, and the spiritual. We could summarize the aesthetic approach as, "Follow your dreams." This is the opera singer who sent Babette to the sisters. The ethical says, "Do your duty." This is how the sisters fulfill their father's wishes by staying home and overseeing the sect.

According to Kierkegaard, just about everyone looks for happiness either through duty or desire. Sometimes people switch between the two. Keller offered Russian novelist Leo Tolstoy as an example of switching from the aesthetic to the ethical. More often in New York City, Keller said, he finds the opposite. Raised in the ethical, many flee to find the aesthetic in New York.

Neither one works, Kierkegaard warned. Both the aesthetic Herodians and the ethical Pharisees miss the spiritual freedom and joy of the gospel.[57] A good feast can be a spiritual experience that draws us closer to God, because we catch a taste of what we'll enjoy forever in his presence.[58]

Kierkegaard isn't easy reading, especially if you don't know his context of Lutheran pietism in Denmark. But his spiritual approach to God resonated with Keller as the alternative to legalism and antinomianism. According to the *Stanford Encyclopedia of Philosophy*, Kierkegaard taught:

> The absurdity of atonement requires faith that we believe that for God even the impossible is possible, including the forgiveness of the unforgivable. If we can accept God's forgiveness, sincerely, inwardly, contritely, with gratitude and hope, then we open ourselves to the joyous prospect of beginning anew. The only obstacle to this joy is our refusal or resistance to accepting God's forgiveness properly.[59]

Advocating for a missionary encounter in global cities, Keller gravitated toward writers like Bavinck and Kierkegaard because they had already straddled the decline of Christendom with the rise of Enlightenment skepticism. In this transition, they didn't bemoan the loss of Christian privilege, in part because they had experienced and rejected legalism. They instead shared for their skeptical generations the wonders of grace in creative and faithful ways.

And that is the essential task still today. As the Enlightenment gives way to an uncertain future for the West, how do Christians present the gospel in compelling and intelligible ways?[60] Christians can't count on shared assumptions across the culture about God, morality, sin, or eternity. In fact, the post-Christian world poses a new challenge where the very idea of salvation threatens self-satisfied agnosticism.[61] Perhaps the biggest challenge is still underappreciated by many church leaders. A few hours scattered between teaching, singing, and chatting among other Christians can't compete with the 24/7 digital deluge.

"Our models of theological formation give us a firm grasp of biblical doctrine, which is indispensable," Keller wrote, "but they fail to deconstruct culture's beliefs and provide better, Christian answers to the questions of the late modern human heart."[62]

Typical for Keller, he doesn't suggest either/or but advocates both/and. Biblical doctrine and cultural criticism go hand in hand. During the last decade of his ministry at Redeemer, Keller traveled abroad two or three times each year for evangelism and training. In cities as diverse as Rome, Berlin, Paris, Hong Kong, and Beijing, and countries as different as South Africa, South Korea, Taiwan, and Poland, Keller saw how the DNA of *Center Church*—including biblical inerrancy and substitutionary atonement—led to different social and cultural conclusions. Keller had spent decades contextualizing for New York, but he gained fresh eyes on Scripture through these opportunities opened up by his book publishing and the expansion of Redeemer City to City.[63]

He brought these insights back to the senior pastors he trained to take over for him at Redeemer. In capital campaigns led by Bruce Terrell in 2005 and 2009, Redeemer prepared for a multisite church that would evolve into a network of independent churches when Keller stepped down within five or ten years.

Before he retired from the church in 2017 to work full-time for Redeemer City to City, Keller focused on training these pastors to read an increasingly hostile culture. No longer would evangelicals benefit from the umbrella of support provided by nominal believers, who still identified as Christians without personal zeal for the faith. Not only in New York City, but across the Western world, Christians would need to prepare for increased criticism of historical beliefs in the exclusivity of Christ, sexual ethics, and the Bible overall. For these pastors and others, through his Questioning Christianity series, Keller modeled apologetics that doesn't assume shared rational understanding.

Even as he dove into social criticism, however, Keller renewed his appreciation for the Reformation essentials that gripped him as a college student. When Michael Horton's two volumes on *Justification* appeared in 2018, many young Christian leaders had already been persuaded by N. T. Wright's criticism of the Reformers as overly individualistic. Though Keller didn't engage deeply in the New Perspective debates that raged during the 1990s and 2000s, he observed subtle legalism in alternatives to the Reformers.[64] Keller has often recommended Horton's works, which give the exegetical and historical background for the Reformers' views on justification while interacting with Wright and other critics.

Not long before he read Horton, Keller followed a plan that took him through John Calvin's *Institutes* five nights a week, with six or seven pages per day for twelve months. He found the experience not just edifying but even electrifying—profoundly devotional, moving him to praise and wonder of God. As a Reformed minister, he knew Calvin's work, but in this systematic reading, he marveled at how Calvin used citations of the Bible and church fathers to make his case. He did not find in Calvin a cold rationalist but instead a powerful advocate for the necessity of spiritual experience.

He also saw Calvin as the fountainhead of various Reformed schools that Keller devoted his ministry to holding together. Through Calvin, Keller found resources to resist the spiritual weakness and unhealthiness that results when Reformed churches separate piety and revival from cultural engagement and mission. These same churches need confession and history as well as community and sacraments in their theological vision.

If some Christians argue that we need more cultural analysis, and others insist that we need more gospel preaching, Keller answered that we need *both*. As Keller learned amid the success of *The Reason for God*, successive generations of Christian apologists and preachers will need to dive deeper into social criticism. Otherwise, they speak to a world that doesn't know it's supposed to be listening—and doesn't have ears to hear what God's Word tells them.

EIGHTEEN

RINGS ON A TREE

Conclusion

The closest Tim Keller has come to writing an autobiography is his 2008 book *The Prodigal God*. When he planted Redeemer in New York, he met many young adults who thought they could find a better path on their own, apart from family and church and their restrictive communities. That's how Keller himself felt in the ferment of 1968, when he doubted what his family and church taught him about religion, race, and sex.

If distrust of Christian community led him to crisis, Christian community also led him to faith. Keller wrote in *The Prodigal God* that "there is no way you will be able to grow spiritually apart from a deep involvement in a community of other believers. You can't live the Christian life without a band of Christian friends, without a family of believers in which you find a place."[1]

This book has introduced you to Keller's community—in books and in the flesh. We have cut open the tree of his life and ministry to examine the rings. In a 2014 conversation with D. A. Carson and John Piper, Keller explained why it's important to draw on multiple influences:

> I don't just mean multiple individuals. I think you have to have multiple sources. I would say if you don't appreciate any of the Puritan writers, you're missing out. There are some tremendous Puritan writers. But I also know people who only seem to care about the Puritans. They went into the Puritan forest, and they've never come out. It's the only thing they read. And when they speak, and when they preach, they start, "Methinks." I think the fact that you [Piper] and I have really learned so much both from C. S. Lewis and Jonathan Edwards, two people who almost certainly would not have gotten along, they're so different, I think that has corrected me at a number of places where I get too much into one guy and the other guy comes in and reminds me, "No, he's not the only way." It's almost like if you cut a person—a good minister, for example—like a tree, there should be a lot of rings. That gives that minister his own distinctive voice and perhaps really helps him listen to what God is calling him to be as a minister. Whereas if you only have one or two individuals or even kinds of sources, you really become almost a clone.[2]

From the inner ring of the gospel in his college conversion, Keller branched out for insight wherever he could find it. He grabbed from John Stott's preaching over here and Herman Bavinck's worldview over there. He reached for new urbanism from Jane Jacobs, and existentialist philosophy from Søren Kierkegaard. Long before he'd found even moderate fame, his rings grew to include Jack Miller and R. C. Sproul, Elisabeth Elliot and Barbara Boyd, Richard Lovelace and Harvie Conn, not to mention little-known pastors such as Kennedy Smartt.[3] Keller opted for synthesis over antithesis. When he added rings, he didn't subtract others.

Redeemer brought the entire vision together—small groups with vocational training with evangelistic preaching with mercy ministry. The church aimed to be intellectual but also pious, Reformed but not sectarian. Among his generation, no one did more than Keller to prepare evangelicals for the global, multicultural, urban future. He wouldn't warrant an obituary in *The New York Times* if not for this central theme. The closest parallel is John Stott from the previous generation. And yet for the first half of his life, Keller showed almost no familiarity with global, multicultural, or urban ministry. He didn't gain widespread recognition until relatively late in his career, during his fifties. Rising generations can do no better than to patiently build out their rings as they wait on the Lord.

We can trace the rings on Keller's tree only because he's so quick to credit his influences, with a prodigious gift for recall.[4] By citing so many others, Keller leaves the impression that he's not an original thinker. Rarely will you find an idea in Keller that you can't trace back to someone else. To understand Keller is to read his books' footnotes, where he shows the work of processing and wrestling with sources. He also leads others to underestimate his contributions because his story shows more continuity than discontinuity—in his theology, in his relationships, in his personality. He's added many rings to his tree of influences, but he's still recognizable today to the younger students he mentored at Bucknell. Classmates from Gordon-Conwell recognize his teaching style. Church members from Hopewell recognize his zeal for revival. Early Redeemer members recognize the simple packaging of his complex thinking.

Keller's originality comes in his synthesis, how he pulls the sources together for unexpected insights. Having one hero would be derivative; having one hundred heroes means you've drunk deeply by scouring the world for the purest wells. This God-given ability to integrate disparate sources and then share insights with others has been observed by just about anyone who has known Keller, going back to his college days. He's the guide to the gurus. You get their best conclusions, with Keller's unique twist. "That's part of Tim's genius," said Arthur Armstrong, an early Redeemer elder. "He simplifies the incredible depth and complexity of the gospel and the Word for consumption by modern human beings."[5]

As public intellectuals, pastors are not commonly known for citing their sources. In fact they're often explicitly discouraged in training from doing so, for fear of distracting the congregation with author and book names they won't remember. Keller breaks that mold. From Tolkien to Taylor, Clowney to Conn, Keller shows his work, so we can carry on his project. Future generations will honor Keller better by reading his library than by quoting him.

How ironic if the pastor who gathered from such varied tributaries became a solitary river flowing down through the years.

EPILOGUE

O ver the course of three years of interviews with Tim Keller for this book, one theme stood out above all. Tim never stopped pushing for a deeper experience of God's grace. Amid treatments for pancreatic cancer, Tim told me, "I'm not fighting my cancer; I'm fighting my sin." He wanted to rest in Christ by rejoicing in the hope of the resurrection, as he saw in John Owen's *The Glory of Christ*, written as the seventeenth-century theologian faced death. Tim also told me about John Newton's battle against inordinate attachments. The eighteenth-century British pastor provokes us to consider what we value too much in this world that prevents us from seeking the next. For Kathy, Tim explained, it's vacations, the places they've visited, especially in South Carolina and England. But for Tim, it's ministry accomplishments. Tim confessed:

> The other night we said, 'We really try to turn this world into heaven.' . . . And as a result of all that, we were always unhappy because you can't stay in England. You have to come home. You can't stay in South Carolina. . . . Meanwhile I was never enjoying my day because I was always thinking about tomorrow and all the stuff I have to get done and how I'm behind. . . . We can't make a heaven out of this earth because it's going to be taken away from us. . . . When

you actually make heaven *heaven*, the joys of earth are more poignant than they used to be. That's what's so strange. We enjoy our day more than we ever did.[1]

Tim himself anticipated that suffering would contribute to personal revival—stronger emotional engagement with friends, growing sanctification and focus, deepening prayer life. Writing in his 2013 book on suffering, Tim said that "one of the main teachings of the Bible is that almost no one grows into greatness or finds God without suffering, without pain coming into our lives like smelling salts to wake us up to all sorts of facts about life and our own hearts to which we were blind."[2]

Life changed for the Kellers in particularly personal ways in May 2020, just as the world was bracing for a prolonged COVID-19 shutdown. First through New York City's acute pandemic suffering, and then due to Tim's immunocompromised health, the Kellers experienced isolation unlike anything before in their people-packed lives. They watched from Roosevelt Island as friends and colleagues struggled to lead churches through sociopolitical division akin to the late 1960s and early '70s.

During this time, they returned to basics—to their formative influences. They spent more time together than they had since their friendship and eventual romance blossomed on the North Shore of Boston. They shared *life together*, that sense of spiritual community captured in the Dietrich Bonhoeffer classic. Tim Keller continued reading—more than ever before, even in the face of death, as he prepared for future writing projects he may never complete. Whether God gives him another month or another decade, he wants to connect with and serve younger leaders with an intentionality not shown in earlier, busier stages of life.

Above all Tim Keller returned to God in prayer, with greater length and depth, as he prepared for his faith to become sight.

POSTSCRIPT

I never found a parallel among biographies for this book, which has explored the influences *on*, more than the influence *of*, our subject, Timothy Keller. Future biographies, I trust, will seek to assess his enduring influence through Redeemer Presbyterian Church, The Gospel Coalition, Redeemer City to City, his books, and his sermons. I hope those biographers will find in this work much helpful and accurate source material.

I didn't write this book as a Keller clone. But I did, and do, write with much personal appreciation and a relationship that dates back to 2007. Since 2010, I've worked for The Gospel Coalition, cofounded by Keller. I admire his work, even though we differ in many ways. I'm about the age of his sons. I'm not Presbyterian. I live on the other end of America's cultural divide—in Birmingham, Alabama, somewhere near the buckle of the Bible Belt. I'm not a close friend of the family, and I only visited Redeemer in New York City a couple times when he preached.

Countless times since 2007—on the phone, over email, in New York, or during TGC events in the United States and abroad—I talked with Keller about what he's reading and what he's learning. I'm thankful that through this book others can listen in on those conversations and find inspiration to build their own community of friends, their own library, and their own theological vision for ministry in the twenty-first century.

ACKNOWLEDGMENTS

S o how long have you been working on the book?"
  I never know how to answer that question. On this book? For twenty-five years, in some ways. Or at least for sixteen years, since I met Timothy Keller. Or three years intensively, since the Zondervan Reflective publishing group invited me to be the author. Thank you to my longtime editor and friend Ryan Pazdur for his leadership in this project and his support for me along the journey.

To Tim and Kathy Keller, thank you for entrusting me with your story. Throughout the research and writing, I have felt the weight of responsibility, especially given Tim's health. Thank you for vouching on my behalf with your friends and family. I hope what you read in these pages will honor the God you serve and the love that you share with each other and your community.

Many pitched in with just the right help at the right time, and thereby answered prayers they didn't even know had been offered. Thank you, Louise Midwood, for collecting and sharing precious documents from your Gordon-Conwell days. Craig Ellis pointed me in the right direction and surfaced the message from Billy Keller's memorial service. Jake Petty offered analysis of sources quoted in Keller's Redeemer sermons. Gordon-Conwell Theological Seminary located and digitized Edmund Clowney's 1973 Staley lectures, which I trust will now inspire further generations. Yvonne Sawyer invited me into the fellowship of Redeemer's earliest members and leaders.

My colleagues at The Gospel Coalition deserve special recognition for their prayerful support. Apart from the leadership of Julius Kim I don't think this project could have ever moved from idea to print. The same goes for Michele Bullock and her counsel during my time of acute need. Thank you to Brannon McAllister for his help in tracking down the images for the photo insert.

The God-given beauty of my adopted home state of Alabama—especially Lake Martin and Mentone—offered inspiration during the most intense writing weeks. Thank you to my in-laws, Paul and Eileen Salter, for the generous use of your home, and to Beeson Divinity School for the generous use of office space. Back in my birth state of South Dakota, I know my parents, Randy and Julie Hansen, prayed that God would give me strength and stamina. I hope in this book you can see some yield from your loving sacrifices for more than forty years.

No one has offered such steadfast encouragement, through this project and every other stage of ministry, than my wife, Lauren. Even as she contributed counsel and practical support to this book, she also gave birth to our third child and began working in our church's women's ministry. Thank you for sticking with me and standing beside me through everything, Lauren. I see your beauty and joy in our three children—Paul Carter, Elisabeth Owen, and William Christopher.

This book is dedicated to the memory of my late grandfather, William Owen Daniel Jr., who passed to me an inheritance of faith, with the accent of Welsh revival. I pray that your namesake, William Christopher Hansen, will follow in your example.

INDEX

INDEX

INDEX

NOTES

Preface

1. Craig Ellis, interview with Collin Hansen, January 15, 2021.
2. Glen Kleinknecht, interview with Collin Hansen, February 12, 2021.

Chapter 1: Mom Competition

1. See Timothy Keller with Kathy Keller, *The Meaning of Marriage: Facing the Complexities of Commitment with the Wisdom of God* (New York: Dutton, 2011), 259–60, n. 17, chapter 4.
2. See Timothy Keller with Kathy Keller, *The Meaning of Marriage: Facing the Complexities of Commitment with the Wisdom of God* (New York: Dutton, 2011), 151.
3. Janet Essig, interview with Collin Hansen, January 27, 2021.
4. Timothy Keller, *Walking with God through Pain and Suffering* (New York: Dutton, 2013), xi.
5. Louise Midwood, interview with Collin Hansen, January 29, 2021.
6. Kathy Keller, email to Collin Hansen, January 7, 2021.
7. Sharon Johnson, interview with Collin Hansen, January 13, 2021.
8. Sharon Johnson, interview with Collin Hansen, January 13, 2021.
9. Kathy Keller, email to Collin Hansen, February 16, 2021.
10. Timothy Keller, *The Reason for God: Belief in an Age of Skepticism* (New York: Dutton, 2008), xi.
11. Timothy Keller, interview with Collin Hansen, May 20, 2022.

Chapter 2: The Absurd Man

1. Timothy Keller, interview with Collin Hansen, May 20, 2022.
2. Timothy J. J. Altizer and William Hamilton, *Radical Theology and the Death of God* (Indianapolis: Bobbs-Merrill, 1966).
3. John Robinson, *Honest to God*, 50th anniv. ed. (London: SCM Press, 2013), back cover.

4. See Timothy Keller, *Hope in Times of Fear: The Resurrection and the Meaning of Easter* (New York: Viking, 2021), 2–4.

5. See Timothy Keller, *The Reason for God: Belief in an Age of Skepticism* (New York: Dutton, 2008), xii.

6. Timothy Keller, *Generous Justice: How God's Grace Makes Us Just* (New York: Dutton, 2010), xv–xvii.

7. See Keller, *Reason for God*, 81–82.

8. See Keller, *Hope in Times of Fear*, 2.

9. See Keller, *Reason for God*, 97–98.

10. Timothy Keller, interview with Collin Hansen, May 20, 2022.

11. See Keller, *Reason for God*, xii–xiii.

12. Timothy Keller, *Jesus the King: Understanding the Life and Death of the Son of God* (New York: Penguin, 2013), xx.

13. Keller, *Jesus the King*, xxi.

14. Timothy Keller, interview with Collin Hansen, May 20, 2022.

15. Sharon Johnson, interview with Collin Hansen, January 13, 2021.

16. See Keller, *Reason for God*, xiii.

17. Keller, *Hope in Times of Fear*, 19–20.

18. Bruce Henderson, interview with Collin Hansen, January 21, 2021.

19. Janet Essig, interview with Collin Hansen, January 27, 2021.

20. Janet Essig, interview with Collin Hansen, January 27, 2021.

21. Sue Pichert, interview with Collin Hansen, January 28, 2021.

22. Jim Pichert, interview with Collin Hansen, January 28, 2021.

23. Janet Essig, interview with Collin Hansen, January 27, 2021.

24. Timothy J. Keller, "The Girl Nobody Wanted," in *Heralds of the King: Christ-Centered Sermons in the Tradition of Edmund P. Clowney*, ed. Dennis E. Johnson (Wheaton, IL: Crossway, 2009), 54, www.monergism.com/girl -nobody-wanted-genesis-2915-35.

25. Timothy Keller, "His Wonderful Light" (sermon, Redeemer Presbyterian Church, New York City, September 19, 2010).

26. Bruce Henderson, interview with Collin Hansen, January 21, 2021.

27. Sue Pichert, interview with Collin Hansen, January 28, 2021.

28. A. Donald MacLeod, *C. Stacey Woods and the Evangelical Rediscovery of the University* (Downers Grove, IL: IVP Academic, 2007), 19.

29. Bruce Henderson, interview with Collin Hansen, January 21, 2021.

30. Timothy Keller, interview with Collin Hansen, May 20, 2022.

31. Bruce Henderson, email to Collin Hansen, January 23, 2021.

32. Mako Fujimura, interview with Collin Hansen, March 4, 2021.

33. Dick Merritt was thirty-eight years old when Keller started at Bucknell in 1968. Tall and slightly overweight, Merritt's pastor voice drew listeners in. He and his wife, Florence (known to all as Flossie) lived next door to the church in the manse. A military man of firm routines, Merritt's interests ranged widely from

jazz music to fast-pitch softball to Mel Brooks films (*Young Frankenstein* was a particular favorite). Every day, except in hard rain, Merritt walked four blocks from the church to pick up the evening newspaper. The short walk nevertheless occupied sixty to ninety minutes because he talked to so many passersby in this college town of about 5,700. Merritt was less popular in his own presbytery, which led the Orthodox Presbyterian Church to attempt to convince him to switch to their more conservative denomination.

34. Bruce Henderson, interview with Collin Hansen, January 21, 2021.
35. Bruce Henderson, email to Collin Hansen, January 22, 2021.
36. Bruce Henderson, email to Collin Hansen, January 15, 2021.

Chapter 3: The Woman Who Taught Him to Study the Bible

1. Janet Essig, interview with Collin Hansen, January 27, 2021.
2. Janet Essig, interview with Collin Hansen, January 27, 2021.
3. Janet Essig, interview with Collin Hansen, January 27, 2021.
4. Kathy Keller, email to Collin Hansen, January 22, 2021.
5. Keith Hunt and Gladys Hunt, *For Christ and the University: The Story of InterVarsity Christian Fellowship of the U.S.A./1940–1990* (Downers Grove, IL: InterVarsity, 1991), 256.
6. Hunt, *For Christ and the University*, 265.
7. Timothy Keller, "Joshua and the General" (sermon, Redeemer Presbyterian Church, New York City, September 22, 1996).
8. Timothy Keller, interview with Collin Hansen, May 20, 2022.
9. Peter Krol, "The Bible Study Tim Keller Never Forgot," Knowable Word, December 10, 2014, www.knowableword.com/2014/12/10/the-bible-study-tim-keller-never-forgot.
10. Janet Essig, email to Collin Hansen, February 10, 2021.
11. Barbara Boyd, interview with Patricia Grahmann, Oral History Project, April 7, 2011, CD 007, InterVarsity Christian Fellowship Records, Collection 300, Billy Graham Center, Wheaton College, Illinois.
12. Janet Essig, interview with Collin Hansen, January 27, 2021.
13. Janet Essig, interview with Collin Hansen, January 27, 2021.
14. Boyd, interview with Patricia Grahmann.
15. Hunt, *For Christ and the University*, 208.
16. A. Donald MacLeod, *C. Stacey Woods and the Evangelical Rediscovery of the University* (Downers Grove, IL: IVP Academic, 2007), 12.
17. Hunt, *For Christ and the University*, 265.
18. Hunt, *For Christ and the University*, 264.
19. Kathy Keller, email to Collin Hansen, January 7, 2021.
20. Hunt, *For Christ and the University*, 303.
21. Hunt, *For Christ and the University*, 279.
22. Hunt, *For Christ and the University*, 303.

23. MacLeod, *C. Stacey Woods and the Evangelical*, 102–3.

24. MacLeod, *C. Stacey Woods and the Evangelical*, 161.

25. Timothy Keller, *Center Church: Doing Balanced, Gospel-Centered Ministry in Your City* (Grand Rapids: Zondervan, 2012), 79.

26. Timothy Keller, "Tim Keller speaks at John Stott's US Memorial" (eulogy, College Church, Wheaton, IL, November 11, 2011), www.youtube.com/watch?v=n3WkR0LPCxM.

27. Keller, "Tim Keller speaks at John Stott's US Memorial."

28. Hunt, *For Christ and the University*, 302.

29. Hunt, *For Christ and the University*, 272.

30. Hunt, *For Christ and the University*, 291.

31. Timothy Keller, email to Collin Hansen, May 6, 2021.

32. Gordon Govier, "InterVarsity alumni: Tim Keller," InterVarsity Christian Fellowship, October 6, 2009, https://intervarsity.org/news/intervarsity-alumni-tim-keller.

Chapter 4: Kathy the Valiant

1. Lyle W. Dorsett and Marjorie Lamp Mead, eds., *C. S. Lewis Letters to Children* (New York: Touchstone, 1995), 105.

2. Dorsett and Mead, *C. S. Lewis Letters to Children*, 109.

3. Dorsett and Mead, *C. S. Lewis Letters to Children*, 112.

4. Dorsett and Mead, *C. S. Lewis Letters to Children*, 113.

5. Nate Guidry, "Obituary: Henry R. Kristy /WWII pilot, Westinghouse Power exec," *Pittsburgh Post-Gazette*, May 30, 2005, 16.

6. Kathy Keller, email to Collin Hansen, February 16, 2021.

7. Louise Midwood, interview with Collin Hansen, January 29, 2021.

8. Gary Scott Smith, *A History of Christianity in Pittsburgh* (Charleston, SC: History Press, 2019), 64.

9. Sarah Pulliam Bailey, "C. S. Lewis's Pen Pal, Kathy Keller," Religion News Service, November 22, 2013, www.christianitytoday.com/ct/2013/november-web-only/cs-lewiss-penpal-kathy-keller.html.

10. Sue Pichert, interview with Collin Hansen, January 28, 2021.

11. Louise Midwood, interview with Collin Hansen, January 29, 2021.

12. See Timothy Keller with Kathy Keller, *The Meaning of Marriage: Facing the Complexities of Commitment with the Wisdom of God* (New York: Dutton, 2011), 40.

13. Kathy Keller, email to Collin Hansen, May 5, 2021.

14. Kathy Keller, email to Collin Hansen, May 5, 2021.

15. Kathy Keller, email to Collin Hansen, May 5, 2021.

16. Sharon Johnson, interview with Collin Hansen, January 13, 2021.

17. Kathy Keller, email to Collin Hansen, May 5, 2021.

18. Keller, *Meaning of Marriage*, 10.

19. See Keller, *Meaning of Marriage*, 30.

20. Keller, *Meaning of Marriage*, 216.

21. Kathy Keller, email to Collin Hansen, February 4, 2021.

22. Louise Midwood, interview with Collin Hansen, January 29, 2021.

23. Keller, *Meaning of Marriage*, 270, n. 28, chapter 6.

24. Timothy Keller, *Walking with God through Pain and Suffering* (New York: Dutton, 2013), 4.

25. See Keller, *Meaning of Marriage*, 186–87.

26. Timothy Keller, *Counterfeit Gods: The Empty Promises of Money, Sex, and Power, and the Only Hope That Matters* (New York: Dutton, 2009), 209.

27. Louise Midwood, interview with Collin Hansen, January 29, 2021.

28. Jim Pichert, interview with Collin Hansen, January 28, 2021.

29. Liz Kaufmann, interview with Collin Hansen, March 11, 2021.

30. See Timothy Keller, *The Prodigal Prophet: Jonah and the Mystery of God's Mercy* (New York: Viking, 2018), 229.

31. Keller, *Counterfeit Gods*, 210.

32. Keller, *Meaning of Marriage*, 171.

33. Louise Midwood, interview with Collin Hansen, January 29, 2021.

34. Timothy Keller, "Truth, Tears, Anger, and Grace," (sermon, Redeemer Presbyterian Church, New York City, September 16, 2001), www.youtube.com/watch?v=KkZqsZqiEIA.

35. See Keller, *Walking with God through Pain and Suffering*, 6.

36. Kathy Armstrong, interview with Collin Hansen, March 18, 2021.

37. Kathy Armstrong, email to Collin Hansen, March 18, 2021.

Chapter 5: True Myth

1. Mako Fujimura, interview with Collin Hansen, March 4, 2021.

2. See Timothy Keller, *Jesus the King: Understanding the Life and Death of the Son of God* (New York: Penguin, 2013), 6–7.

3. Timothy Keller with Kathy Keller, *The Meaning of Marriage: Facing the Complexities of Commitment with the Wisdom of God* (New York: Dutton, 2011), 74, italics in original.

4. Timothy Keller, "Service of Remembrance on 9/11," https://discover.redeemer.com/docs/service_of_remembrance.pdf.

5. Mako Fujimura, interview with Collin Hansen, March 4, 2021.

6. Timothy Keller, "Self-Control: Part 2" (sermon, Redeemer Presbyterian Church, New York City, April 15, 1990).

7. Collin Hansen, interview with Timothy Keller, May 20, 2022.

8. J. R. R. Tolkien, *The Return of the King* (New York: HarperCollins, 2004), 1148–49.

9. Keller, *Jesus the King*, 231.

10. Timothy Keller, *Preaching: Communicating Faith in an Age of Skepticism* (New York: Viking, 2015), 176, italics added.

11. Timothy Keller, "An Old Woman's Laughter" (sermon, Redeemer Presbyterian Church, New York City, September 14, 1997).

12. Timothy Keller, "The Joy of Jesus" (sermon, Redeemer Presbyterian Church, New York City, May 3, 1998), https://podcast.gospelinlife.com/e/the-joy-of -jesus-1630526615; https://lifecoach4god.life/2013/08/04/tim-keller-on-the -joy-of-knowing-jesus.
13. See Keller, *Preaching*, 308–9, n. 30.
14. Keller, "Joy of Jesus."

Chapter 6: Doubters Welcome

1. Charles E. Cotherman, *To Think Christianly: A History of L'Abri, Regent College, and the Christian Study Center Movement* (Downers Grove, IL: IVP Academic, 2020), 14.
2. Cotherman, *To Think Christianly*, 121.
3. Stephen J. Nichols, *R. C. Sproul: A Life* (Wheaton, IL: Crossway, 2021), 90–91.
4. Nichols, *R. C. Sproul*, 63.
5. Gary Scott Smith, *A History of Christianity in Pittsburgh* (Charleston, SC: History Press, 2019), 16.
6. Smith, *History of Christianity in Pittsburgh*, 12.
7. Sarah Pulliam Bailey, "C. S. Lewis's Pen Pal, Kathy Keller," Religion News Service, November 22, 2013, www.christianitytoday.com/ct/2013/november -web-only/cs-lewiss-penpal-kathy-keller.html.
8. Cotherman, *To Think Christianly*, 2.
9. Cotherman, *To Think Christianly*, 2.
10. Nichols, *R. C. Sproul*, 94.
11. Cotherman, *To Think Christianly*, 5.
12. Cotherman, *To Think Christianly*, 16.
13. Cotherman, *To Think Christianly*, 29.
14. Nichols, *R. C. Sproul*, 93.
15. Nichols, *R. C. Sproul*, 249.
16. Nichols, *R. C. Sproul*, 84.
17. Timothy Keller, email to Collin Hansen, March 4, 2021.
18. Nichols, *R. C. Sproul*, 102.
19. Timothy Keller, email to Collin Hansen, March 4, 2021.
20. Kathy Keller, email to Collin Hansen, January 7, 2021.
21. Timothy Keller, interview with Collin Hansen, May 20, 2022.
22. Timothy Keller, "Doubters Welcome," Redeemer Report, 2014, www.redeemer .com/redeemer-report/article/doubters_welcome.

Chapter 7: Theological Smorgasbord

1. George M. Marsden, *Reforming Fundamentalism: Fuller Seminary and the New Evangelicalism* (Grand Rapids: Eerdmans, 1987), 211–12; Justin Gerald Taylor, "John Piper: The Making of a Christian Hedonist," DPhil diss. (The Southern Baptist Theological Seminary, 2015), 127–29.

2. When the International Council on Biblical Inerrancy began in 1977, several of Keller's mentors were involved, including R. C. Sproul, Edmund Clowney, and Roger Nicole.

3. Louise Midwood, interview with Collin Hansen, January 29, 2021.

4. Timothy Keller, interview with Collin Hansen, May 20, 2022.

5. Commenting on Mark 14:34, when Jesus prayed in Gethsemane and said, "My soul is overwhelmed with sorrow to the point of death" (NIV),William Lane wrote, "Jesus came to be with the Father for an interlude before his betrayal, but found hell rather than heaven before him, and he staggered." For the verse, "My God, my God, why have you forsaken me?" (Mark 15:34), Lane concluded, "The cry has a ruthless authenticity which provides the assurance that the price of sin has been paid in full. Yet Jesus did not die renouncing God. Even in the inferno of his abandonment he did not surrender his faith in God but expressed his anguished prayer in a cry of affirmation, 'My God, my God'" (*The Gospel of Mark* [Grand Rapids: Eerdmans, 1974], 516, 573). Keller often returned to this Gethsemane experience in his writing and preaching. Keller cited his New Testament professor in his first bestselling book, *The Reason for God*. He wrote, "Christian theology has always recognized that Jesus bore, as the substitute in our place, the endless exclusion from God that the human race has merited" (*The Reason for God: Belief in an Age of Skepticism* [New York: Dutton, 2008], 29).

6. Mark A. Noll, *Between Faith and Criticism: Evangelicals, Scholarship, and the Bible in America* (Grand Rapids: Baker, 1986), 118.

7. After Keller's first year, Lane divorced his wife and left Gordon-Conwell.

8. Timothy Keller, email to Collin Hansen, July 18, 2022.

9. Timothy Keller, "Christ Our Head" (sermon, Redeemer Presbyterian Church, New York City, July 9, 1989), https://lifecoach4god.life/2013/10/27/sunday -sermon-dr-tim-keller-on-christ-our-head.

10. Timothy Keller, "Reconciliation" (sermon, Redeemer Presbyterian Church, New York City, June 29, 2003), www.youtube.com/watch?v=lcNIyJZ2bbU.

Chapter 8: Table Talk

1. Elisabeth Leitch, "Table Talk," *The Paper*, February 18, 1975.

2. See Timothy Keller with Kathy Keller, *The Meaning of Marriage: Facing the Complexities of Commitment with the Wisdom of God* (New York: Dutton, 2011), 270, n. 29, chapter 6.

3. Kathy Keller, email to Collin Hansen, February 4, 2021.

4. Kathy Kristy, quoted in Elisabeth Elliot, *Let Me Be a Woman: Notes to My Daughter on the Meaning of Womanhood* (1976; repr., Wheaton, IL: Tyndale, 1999), 50–51.

5. Elliot, *Let Me Be a Woman*, 16.

6. Elliot, *Let Me Be a Woman*, 40.

7. Kathy Keller, *Jesus, Justice, and Gender Roles: A Case for Gender Roles in Ministry* (Grand Rapids: Zondervan, 2012), 11.

8. Gary Scott Smith, *A History of Christianity in Pittsburgh* (Charleston, SC: History Press, 2019), 12.

9. Kathy Keller, *Jesus, Justice, and Gender Roles*, 42; see also Keller, *Meaning of Marriage*, 267–68, n. 14, chapter 6.

10. See Timothy Keller, *Walking with God through Pain and Suffering* (New York: Dutton, 2013), 174.

11. Smith, *History of Christianity in Pittsburgh*, 16.

12. Leitch taught at Gordon-Conwell from its inception to 1973, when cancer killed him. Previously he served as a professor at Pittsburgh-Xenia Theological Seminary as a professor until 1961, and from 1940 to 1946 as dean of men and college pastor at Grove City College in Grove City, Pennsylvania, halfway between Pittsburgh and Lake Erie to the north. Babbage left to return to his native Australia, and Lane ran away with his secretary.

13. Louise Midwood, interview with Collin Hansen, January 29, 2021.

14. Louise Midwood, interview with Collin Hansen, January 29, 2021.

15. Louise Midwood, interview with Collin Hansen, January 29, 2021.

16. Kathy Keller, "The Nestorian Threat to Christmas," Redeemer Report, December 2012, www.redeemer.com/redeemer-report/article/the_nestorian _threat_to_christmas.

17. John Palafoutas, email to Collin Hansen, February 15, 2021.

18. "The Issue of Biblical Authority Brings a Scholar's Resignation," *Christianity Today*, July 15, 1983, www.christianitytoday.com/ct/1983/july-15/issue-of -biblical-authority-brings-scholars-resignation.html.

19. Timothy Keller, *Center Church: Doing Balanced, Gospel-Centered Ministry in Your City* (Grand Rapids: Zondervan, 2012), 107, n. 8.

20. "Fuller Theological Seminary Professor David Scholer Dies at 70," *Pasadena Star-News*, August 27, 2008, https://blackchristiannews.wordpress.com/2008 /08/27/fuller-theological-seminary-professor-david-scholer-dies-at-70.

Chapter 9: Disagree without Being Disagreeable

1. Mark Dever, "Reflections on Roger Nicole," 9Marks, June 11, 2014, www.9marks.org/article/reflections-on-roger-nicole.

2. Dever, "Reflections on Roger Nicole."

3. John Muether, email to Collin Hansen, June 10, 2021.

4. Timothy Keller, interview with Collin Hansen, May 20, 2022.

5. Louise Midwood, interview with Collin Hansen, January 29, 2021.

6. Collin Hansen, "Carson, Keller, and Dever Remember Roger Nicole," The Gospel Coalition, December 11, 2010, www.thegospelcoalition.org/article/carson-keller -and-dever-remember-roger-nicole.

7. Sally Lloyd-Jones, *The Jesus Storybook Bible: Every Story Whispers His Name* (Grand Rapids: Zonderkidz, 2007).

8. Timothy Keller, *Center Church: Doing Balanced, Gospel-Centered Ministry in Your City* (Grand Rapids: Zondervan, 2012), 131, italics in original.

9. Timothy Keller, email to Collin Hansen, March 4, 2021.

10. Louise Midwood, interview with Collin Hansen, January 29, 2021.

11. Louise Midwood, interview with Collin Hansen, January 29, 2021.

Chapter 10: Pneumodynamics

1. Timothy Keller, "Cleansing of the Spirit" (sermon, Redeemer Presbyterian Church, New York City, March 23, 1997).

2. Timothy Keller, "The Book Tim Keller Says We Can't Do Without," The Gospel Coalition, August 24, 2020, www.thegospelcoalition.org/reviews /dynamics-spiritual-life-richard-lovelace.

3. Timothy Keller, *Center Church: Doing Balanced, Gospel-Centered Ministry in Your City* (Grand Rapids: Zondervan, 2012), 54.

4. Keller, *Center Church*, 55.

5. Keller, *Center Church*, 74.

6. Richard F. Lovelace, *Dynamics of Spiritual Life: An Evangelical Theology of Renewal* (Downers Grove, IL: InterVarsity, 1979), 101.

7. Keller, *Center Church*, 54.

8. Lovelace, *Dynamics of Spiritual Life*, 211–12.

9. Timothy Keller, *The Prodigal God: Recovering the Heart of the Christian Faith* (New York: Dutton, 2008), 54.

10. Timothy Keller, "The Sin of Racism," *Life in the Gospel*, Summer 2020, https://quarterly.gospelinlife.com/the-sin-of-racism.

11. Lovelace, *Dynamics of Spiritual Life*, 207.

12. Timothy Keller, *Generous Justice: How God's Grace Makes Us Just* (New York: Dutton, 2010), 68–75.

13. See Timothy Keller, *The Reason for God: Belief in an Age of Skepticism* (New York: Dutton, 2008), 168.

14. Keller, *Center Church*, 68, italics in original.

15. George M. Marsden, *Jonathan Edwards: A Life* (New Haven, CT: Yale University Press, 2003), 471.

16. Marsden, *Jonathan Edwards*, 464.

17. Marsden, *Jonathan Edwards*, 468.

18. Marsden, *Jonathan Edwards*, 470.

19. Marsden, *Jonathan Edwards*, 470.

20. Keller, *Generous Justice*, 183.

21. Marsden, *Jonathan Edwards*, 471.

22. Christopher Lasch, *The True and Only Heaven: Progress and Its Critics* (New York: Norton, 1991), 257.

23. See Timothy Keller, *Preaching: Communicating Faith in an Age of Skepticism* (New York: Viking, 2015), 160.

24. Keller, *Preaching*, 162.

25. Jonathan Edwards, "A Divine and Supernatural Light," in *Selected Sermons of Jonathan Edwards*, ed. H. Norman Gardiner (New York: Macmillan, 1904), 29, italics added.

26. Keller, *Preaching*, 165–66.

27. Timothy Keller, "Wise Relationships" (sermon, Redeemer Presbyterian Church, New York City, February 11, 1996).

28. Timothy Keller, *Jesus the King: Understanding the Life and Death of the Son of God* (New York: Penguin, 2013), 133.

29. See Timothy Keller, *Hope in Times of Fear: The Resurrection and the Meaning of Easter* (New York: Viking, 2021), 119–20.

30. Archibald Alexander, *Thoughts on Religious Experience* (Edinburgh: Banner of Truth, 1967), xvii.

31. Jonathan Edwards, "Heaven Is a World of Love," in *The Sermons of Jonathan Edwards: A Reader*, ed. Wilson H. Kimnach, Kenneth P. Minkema, and Douglas Sweeney (New Haven, CT: Yale University Press, 1999), 242–72.

32. See Timothy Keller, *Making Sense of God: An Invitation to the Skeptical* (New York: Viking, 2016), 169.

33. Edwards, "Heaven Is a World of Love," 252–53.

34. Timothy Keller, "The Counterintuitive Calvin," The Gospel Coalition, November 14, 2012, www.thegospelcoalition.org/reviews/counterintuitive-calvin.

Chapter 11: Chemical Capital of the South

1. Graham Howell, interview with Collin Hansen, February 1, 2021.

2. "Industrial Hopewell," *Washington Post*, October 2, 1989, www.washington post.com/archive/business/1989/10/02/industrial-hopewell/4d3af332-cc65 -443d-a405-04d72134c0e4.

3. Richard Foster, "Kepone: The 'Flour' Factory," *Richmond Magazine*, July 8, 2005, https://richmondmagazine.com/news/kepone-disaster-pesticide.

4. Bruce Henderson, interview with Collin Hansen, January 21, 2021.

5. Timothy Keller, interview with Collin Hansen, May 20, 2020.

6. "Fort Lee," MilitaryBases.us, www.militarybases.us/army/fort-lee.

7. Graham Howell, interview with Collin Hansen, February 1, 2021.

8. See Timothy Keller, *Generous Justice: How God's Grace Makes Us Just* (New York: Dutton, 2010), xx.

9. Laurie Howell, interview with Collin Hansen, February 1, 2021.

10. Laurie Howell, interview with Collin Hansen, February 1, 2021.

11. Timothy Keller, interview with Collin Hansen, May 20, 2022.

12. Nicholas Wolterstorff, "The AACS in the CRC," *Reformed Journal* 24 (December 1974): 9–16.

13. George Marsden, "Introduction: Reformed and American," in *Reformed Theology in America: A History of Its Modern Development*, ed. David F. Wells (Grand Rapids: Baker, 1997), 1–12.

14. Timothy Keller, interview with Collin Hansen, June 4, 2021.

15. Laurie Howell, interview with Collin Hansen, February 1, 2021.

16. Timothy Keller, interview with Collin Hansen, May 20, 2022.

17. See Timothy Keller with Kathy Keller, *The Meaning of Marriage: Facing the Complexities of Commitment with the Wisdom of God* (New York: Dutton, 2011), 102.

18. Timothy Keller, interview with Collin Hansen, May 20, 2022.

19. Laurie Howell, interview with Collin Hansen, February 1, 2021.

20. Graham Howell, "How God Is Making Me into Who I'm Meant to Be," Life in the Gospel, Spring 2020, https://quarterly.gospelinlife.com/how-god-is-making-me-into-who-im-meant-to-be.

21. Graham Howell, interview with Collin Hansen, February 1, 2021.

22. Timothy Keller, Facebook post, January 9, 2021, www.facebook.com/TimKellerNYC/posts/3837664312940093.

23. Timothy Keller, *Preaching: Communicating Faith in an Age of Skepticism* (New York: Viking, 2015), 211–12.

24. Keller, *Preaching*, 211–12.

25. Timothy Keller, interview with Collin Hansen, May 20, 2022.

26. Timothy Keller, *Generous Justice: How God's Grace Makes Us Just* (New York: Dutton, 2010), xvii–xviii.

27. Laurie Howell, interview with Collin Hansen, February 1, 2021.

28. Timothy Keller, *Center Church: Doing Balanced, Gospel-Centered Ministry in Your City* (Grand Rapids: Zondervan, 2012), 370.

29. Laurie Howell, interview with Collin Hansen, February 1, 2021.

30. Laurie Howell, interview with Collin Hansen, February 1, 2021.

31. Laurie Howell, interview with Collin Hansen, February 1, 2021.

32. Timothy Keller, interview with Collin Hansen, May 20, 2022.

33. Laurie Howell, interview with Collin Hansen, February 1, 2021.

34. John Piper, interview with Collin Hansen, March 2, 2021.

35. "John Owen had at least as many afflictions in his life as did Paul. He had eleven children and outlived every one of them, as well as his first wife. In the 'Great Ejection' of 1662 he, along with other Puritan ministers, was turned out of his church and employment" (Keller, *Hope in Times of Fear*, 188).

36. The Gospel Coalition, "Get More Rings in Your Tree," *Vimeo* video, 11:33, July 9, 2014. https://vimeo.com/100309192

37. Timothy Keller, interview with Collin Hansen, May 20, 2022.

38. John Hanford, interview with Collin Hansen, March 5, 2021.

39. Sarah Eekhoff Zylstra, "Has Global Religious Freedom Seen Its Best Days?," The Gospel Coalition, May 25, 2021, www.thegospelcoalition.org/article/religious-freedom.

Chapter 12: Unfolding Drama

1. Timothy Keller, "Finding Our Identity in Christ—Part 1" (sermon, Redeemer Presbyterian Church, New York City, October 29, 1989), https://podcast.gospelinlife.com/e/finding-our-identity-in-christ-part-1/2.

2. Timothy J. Keller, "The Girl Nobody Wanted: Genesis 29:15–35," in *Heralds of the King: Christ-Centered Sermons in the Tradition of Edmund P. Clowney*, ed. Dennis E. Johnson (Wheaton, IL: Crossway, 2009), 54.

3. Kathy Keller, email to Collin Hansen, January 7, 2021.

4. D. Clair Davis, interview with Collin Hansen, June 8, 2021.

5. Dennis E. Johnson, "Preface," in *Heralds of the King*, 11.

6. Edmund P. Clowney, *The Unfolding Mystery: Discovering Christ in the Old Testament* (Phillipsburg, NJ: P&R, 1988), 11.

7. Clowney, *Unfolding Mystery*, 13.

8. J. I. Packer, foreword to Clowney, *Unfolding Mystery*, 8.

9. Timothy Keller, foreword to Alec Motyer, *A Christian's Pocket Guide to Loving the Old Testament: One Book, One God, One Story* (Ross-Shire, Scotland: Christian Focus, 2015), xi–xii.

10. Keller, foreword to Motyer, *Christian's Pocket*, ix–xii.

11. D. Clair Davis, interview with Collin Hansen, June 8, 2021.

12. Kathy Keller, email to Collin Hansen, January 7, 2021.

13. Keller, "The Girl Nobody Wanted," 54–55.

14. Edmund P. Clowney, "The Lord and the Word" (lecture, Gordon-Conwell Theological Seminary, South Hamilton, MA, March 26, 1973).

15. Edmund P. Clowney, "The Sufferings of Christ and the Glory" (lecture, Gordon-Conwell Theological Seminary, South Hamilton, MA, March 27, 1973).

16. Timothy Keller, *Jesus the King: Understanding the Life and Death of the Son of God* (New York: Penguin, 2013), 157–58.

17. Edmund P. Clowney, "The Fullness of Christ" (lecture, Gordon-Conwell Theological Seminary, South Hamilton, MA, March 28, 1973).

18. Edmund P. Clowney, "The Praise of Christ" (lecture, Gordon-Conwell Theological Seminary, South Hamilton, MA, March 30, 1973).

19. Edmund P. Clowney, "The Salvation of Christ" (lecture, Gordon-Conwell Theological Seminary, South Hamilton, MA, March 27, 1973).

20. Clowney, "Fullness of Christ."

21. Clowney, "Salvation of Christ."

22. Julius J. Kim, "Rock of Ages," in *Heralds of the King*, 56.

23. Edmund P. Clowney, "The Wisdom of Christ" (lecture, Gordon-Conwell Theological Seminary, South Hamilton, MA, March 29, 1973).

24. Clowney, "Salvation of Christ."

25. Timothy Keller, *Preaching: Communicating Faith in an Age of Skepticism* (New York: Viking, 2015), 60.

26. Timothy Keller, "What Is Gospel-Centered Ministry?" (lecture, The Gospel Coalition National Conference, Deerfield, IL, May 23, 2007), www.thegospel coalition.org/conference_media/gospel-centered-ministry.

27. Timothy Keller, "Born of the Gospel" (sermon, Redeemer Presbyterian Church, New York City, February 11, 2001).

28. Keller, "What Is Gospel-Centered Ministry?"

29. Clowney, "Wisdom of Christ."

30. Timothy Keller, *The Prodigal God: Recovering the Heart of the Christian Faith* (New York: Dutton, 2008), xiii.

31. Kathy Keller, email to Collin Hansen, January 7, 2021.

32. Timothy Keller, "Second Lost Son (and the Dance of God)" (sermon, Redeemer Presbyterian Church, New York City, January 25, 1998), https://podcast.gospel inlife.com/e/second-lost-son-and-the-dance-of-god.

33. Keller, *Prodigal God*, 15–16.

34. Timothy Keller, "First Lost Son (and the Kiss of God)" (sermon, Redeemer Presbyterian Church, New York City, January 18, 1998).

35. D. Clair Davis, interview with Collin Hansen, June 8, 2021.

36. The counseling approach Tim Keller learned at Gordon-Conwell tended toward integration between secular psychology and Christian insight. But he and Kathy, who earned her degree in counseling from Gordon-Conwell, preferred the approach they learned from Jay Adams at Westminster in 1971. After counseling according to this method in Hopewell, however, Tim Keller came to view Adams's approach as behavioristic—"If you do right, you will feel right"—in Keller's experience. It did not reach the heart by properly engaging motivations and emotions. He saw too much of Cornelius Van Til's antithesis in Adams's rejection of modern psychology and its treatment of emotions and motivations. Keller wanted to allow for common grace—the truth that nonbelievers could be inconsistent in their worldviews and therefore speak wisdom and insight better than they understood. For Keller, David Powlison and Ed Welch offered a corrective for biblical counseling through CCEF by engaging the heart, with its loves and motives. CCEF director John Bettler, who like Powlison also served on the Westminster faculty, recommended that his counselors read secular psychologists such as Alfred Adler on "individual psychology." Adler taught that every person has a motivational drive that propels them to believe if they get something, their life will be well. This desire defines reality and orders emotions. Bettler recognized how this psychological insight on idolatry cohered with biblical teaching about the heart and human propensity toward approval, power, comfort, and control. See Timothy Keller, "Worship Worthy of the Name," in *Changing Lives through Preaching and Worship* (New York: Moorings, 1995), 178–85, www.christianitytoday.com /pastors/2007/july-online-only/013006a.html.

37. Ron Lutz, interview with Collin Hansen, June 14, 2021.

38. See David Powlison, "Idols of the Heart and 'Vanity Fair,'" *Journal of Biblical Counseling* 13, no. 2 (Winter 1995): 35–50, www.ccef.org/wp-content/uploads /2009/10/Idols-of-the-Heart-and-Vanity-Fair.pdf.

39. Keller, *Prodigal God*, 134–35.

40. Steve Arcieri, interview with Collin Hansen, February 2, 2021.

41. Craig Ellis, interview with Collin Hansen, January 15, 2021.

42. Keller, *Preaching*, 41.

Chapter 13: "Moulded by the Gospel"

1. Edmund P. Clowney, "Moulded by the Gospel," *Presbyterian Guardian* 38, no. 5 (May 1969): 55, www.opc.org/cfh/guardian/Volume_38/1969-05.pdf.
2. Clowney, "Moulded by the Gospel," 55.
3. Clowney, "Moulded by the Gospel," 56–57.
4. Clowney, "Moulded by the Gospel," 57
5. Clowney, "Moulded by the Gospel," 58.
6. Clowney, "Moulded by the Gospel," 58.
7. D. Clair Davis, interview with Collin Hansen, June 8, 2021.
8. Ron Lutz, email to Collin Hansen, June 14, 2021.
9. Timothy Keller, interview with Collin Hansen, May 20, 2022.
10. Timothy Keller, *Generous Justice: How God's Grace Makes Us Just* (New York: Dutton, 2010), xviii–xix.
11. Harvie M. Conn, *Evangelism: Doing Justice and Preaching Grace* (Grand Rapids: Zondervan, 1982), 13.
12. D. Clair Davis, interview with Collin Hansen, June 8, 2021.
13. Timothy Keller, *Center Church: Doing Balanced, Gospel-Centered Ministry in Your City* (Grand Rapids: Zondervan, 2012), 103.
14. Keller, *Center Church*, 120–21.
15. Keller, *Center Church*, 89.
16. Keller, *Center Church*, 109.
17. Keller, *Center Church*, 125.
18. Keller, *Center Church*, 121.
19. Keller, *Center Church*, 20.
20. Keller, *Center Church*, 151.
21. Harvie M. Conn and Manuel Ortiz, *Urban Ministry: The Kingdom, the City and the People of God* (Downers Grove, IL: IVP Academic, 2001), 87.
22. Conn and Ortiz, *Urban Ministry*, 224.
23. Conn and Ortiz, *Urban Ministry*, 408.
24. Timothy Keller, "An Evangelical Mission in a Secular City," in *Center City Churches: The New Urban Frontier*, ed. Lyle E. Schaller (Nashville: Abingdon, 1993), 34.
25. Keller, *Center Church*, 172.
26. Matthew Bowman, *The Urban Pulpit: New York City and the Fate of Liberal Evangelicalism* (New York, Oxford University Press, 2014), 110.
27. Timothy J. Keller, *Resources for Deacons: Love Expressed through Mercy Ministries* (Lawrenceville, GA: Christian Education and Publications of the PCA, 1985).
28. Kathy Keller, email to Collin Hansen, February 4, 2021.
29. Conn and Ortiz, *Urban Ministry*, 17.
30. Conn and Ortiz, *Urban Ministry*, 21.
31. Michael Green, *Evangelism through the Local Church: A Comprehensive Guide to All Aspects of Evangelism* (Nashville: Oliver-Nelson, 1992), 101.

32. See Timothy Keller, *The Prodigal Prophet: Jonah and the Mystery of God's Mercy* (New York: Viking, 2018), 38.

33. See Keller, *Prodigal Prophet*, 92–93.

34. Keller, *Center Church*, 215.

35. Keller, *Center Church*, 272–73.

36. See Keller, *Prodigal Prophet*, 197–98.

37. Keller, *Center Church*, 21, italics in original.

38. Keller, *Center Church*, 47–48.

39. See Keller, *Generous Justice*, 141.

40. Jonathan Edwards, "Christian Charity: The Duty of Charity to the Poor, Explained and Enforced," in vol. 2 of *The Works of Jonathan Edwards*. ed. Sereno Dwight (Carlise, PA: Banner of Truth, 1998), 164.

41. Keller, *Generous Justice*, xiii.

42. Keller, *Generous Justice*, xiii.

43. Keller, *Generous Justice*, 189.

44. Steve Preston, interview with Collin Hansen, February 16, 2021.

45. Four years later, Tom Hanks would win the Academy Award for best actor in his portrayal of a gay lawyer in *Philadelphia*.

46. Keller, *Center Church*, 21.

47. Timothy Keller, "Our Place in the Story: Part 2," Redeemer Report, November 2014, www.redeemer.com/redeemer-report/article/our_place_in _the_story_part_2.

48. Timothy Keller, interview with Collin Hansen, May 20, 2022.

49. Keller, *Center Church*, 56–57.

50. Timothy Keller, endorsement for Michael A. Graham, *Cheer Up! The Life and Ministry of Jack Miller* (Phillipsburg, NJ: P&R, 2020).

51. Timothy Keller, "Dear Children" (sermon, Redeemer Presbyterian Church, New York City, April 14, 1991), https://podcast.gospelinlife.com/e/dear -children.

52. Graham, *Cheer Up!*, 177–78.

53. Liz Kaufmann, interview with Collin Hansen, March 11, 2021.

54. Liz Kaufmann, interview with Collin Hansen, March 11, 2021.

55. Graham, *Cheer Up!*, 45–46.

56. Timothy Keller, "Foreword," in Sinclair Ferguson, *The Whole Christ: Legalism, Antinomianism, and Gospel Assurance—Why the Marrow Controversy Still Matters* (Wheaton, IL: Crossway, 2016), 11.

57. Timothy Keller, interview with Collin Hansen, May 20, 2022.

58. Thomas Kidd, "Why Do We Say 'Gospel-Centered'?," The Gospel Coalition, April 21, 2021, www.thegospelcoalition.org/article/why-say-gospel-centered.

59. Graham, *Cheer Up!*, 204.

60. Timothy Keller, email to Collin Hansen, March 18, 2021.

61. D. A. Carson, email to Collin Hansen, March 17, 2021.

62. Michael Luo, "Preaching the Word and Quoting the Voice," *New York Times*,

February 26, 2006, www.nytimes.com/2006/02/26/nyregion/preaching-the
-word-and-quoting-the-voice.html.

63. Keller, *Center Church*, 260.

64. Keller, *Center Church*, 48.

65. Keller, *Center Church*, 48, italics in original.

66. Timothy Keller, email to Collin Hansen, January 24, 2021.

67. Richard Lints, *The Fabric of Theology: A Prolegomenon to Evangelical Theology* (Grand Rapids: Eerdmans, 1993), 83.

68. Keller, *Center Church*, 19.

69. Lints, *Fabric of Theology*, 316–17.

70. Keller, *Center Church*, 17.

71. Keller, *Center Church*, 19.

72. "Foundation Documents: Theological Vision for Ministry," The Gospel Coalition, www.thegospelcoalition.org/about/foundation-documents/#theological -vision-for-ministry.

Chapter 14: Masters of the Universe

1. Ray Bakke, *The Urban Christian: Effective Ministry in Today's Urban World* (Downers Grove, IL: InterVarsity, 1987), 41.

2. Nicholas Goldberg, "Column: The Urban Legend of Kitty Genovese and the 38 Witnesses Who Ignored Her Blood-curdling Screams," *Los Angeles Times*, September 10, 2010, www.latimes.com/opinion/story/2020-09-10/urban -legend-kitty-genovese-38-people.

3. "New York Crime Rates 1960–2019," www.disastercenter.com/crime/nycrime .htm.

4. Timothy Keller, *Center Church: Doing Balanced, Gospel-Centered Ministry in Your City* (Grand Rapids: Zondervan, 2012), 164, n. 12.

5. Lora Gaston, interview with Collin Hansen, February 16, 2021.

6. Kenneth A. Briggs, "Decline in Major Faiths' Influence in City Reflects Last 10 Years of Urban Change," *New York Times*, August 18, 1975, www.nytimes.com /1975/08/18/archives/decline-in-major-faiths-influence-in-city-reflects-last-10 -years-of.html.

7. Matthew Bowman, *The Urban Pulpit: New York City and the Fate of Liberal Evangelicalism* (New York: Oxford University Press, 2014), 15.

8. Bowman, *Urban Pulpit*, 34.

9. Tom Wolfe, *The Bonfire of the Vanities* (New York: Picador, 1987), 9.

10. Wolfe, *Bonfire of the Vanities*, 11.

11. Wolfe, *Bonfire of the Vanities*, 12.

12. Wolfe, *Bonfire of the Vanities*, 13.

13. Wolfe, *Bonfire of the Vanities*, 16.

14. Jordan Belfort, *The Wolf of Wall Street* (New York: Bantam, 2007), 3.

15. Peter Donald, "Sermons and Soda Water: A Rich Philadelphia Widow Wants to Save New York Society," *New York*, November 7, 1988, 55.

16. Donald, "Sermons and Soda Water," 56.
17. Donald, "Sermons and Soda Water," 57.
18. Donald, "Sermons and Soda Water," 57–58.
19. Donald, "Sermons and Soda Water," 58.
20. Laura Fels, interview with Collin Hansen, February 16, 2021.
21. Harvie M. Conn and Manuel Ortiz, *Urban Ministry: The Kingdom, the City, and the People of God* (Downers Grove, IL: InterVarsity, 2001), 379.
22. See Conn and Ortiz, *Urban Ministry*, 379–80.
23. Timothy Keller, "An Evangelical Mission in a Secular City," in *Center City Churches: The New Urban Frontier*, ed. Lyle E. Schaller (Nashville: Abingdon, 1993), 31–32.
24. See Timothy Keller, *The Reason for God: Belief in an Age of Skepticism* (New York: Dutton, 2008), xiii–xiv.
25. Keller, "Evangelical Mission in a Secular City," 32.
26. William Gurnall, *The Christian in Complete Armour* (London: Thomas Tegg, 1845), 3.
27. Sue Pichert, interview with Collin Hansen, January 28, 2021.
28. Kathy Keller, interview with Collin Hansen, January 23, 2021.
29. Bruce Henderson, interview with Collin Hansen, January 21, 2021.
30. D. Clair Davis, interview with Collin Hansen, June 8, 2021.
31. Timothy Keller with Kathy Keller, *The Meaning of Marriage: Facing the Complexities of Commitment with the Wisdom of God* (New York: Dutton, 2011), 244.
32. Marlene Hucks, interview with Collin Hansen, March 10, 2021.
33. Kathy Keller, interview with Collin Hansen, January 23, 2021.
34. Kathy Keller, interview with Collin Hansen, January 23, 2021.
35. Jackie Arthur, email to Collin Hansen, February 18, 2021.
36. Even if Keller had wanted to plant a church to gather like-minded Christians, he couldn't have found enough of them. They hardly made a dent in the city. Evangelicals accounted for less than 1 percent of Manhattan residents, and only 5 percent attended any kind of Protestant church, compared to 25 percent nationwide.
37. Craig Ellis, interview with Collin Hansen, January 15, 2021.
38. Jim Pichert, interview with Collin Hansen, January 28, 2021.
39. Kathy Armstrong, interview with Collin Hansen, March 18, 2021.
40. Timothy Keller, email to Collin Hansen, May 6, 2021.
41. Jackie Arthur, interview with Collin Hansen, February 16, 2021.
42. Jim Pichert, interview with Collin Hansen, January 28, 2021.
43. Glen Kleinknecht, interview with Collin Hansen, February 16, 2021.
44. Keller, *Center Church*, 101–3.

Chapter 15: Land of Yes

1. Yvonne Sawyer, interview with Collin Hansen, February 2, 2021.

2. Yvonne Sawyer, interview with Collin Hansen, February 16, 2021.

3. Tim Lemmer, interview with Collin Hansen, February 2, 2021.

4. Kathy Keller, email to Collin Hansen, February 16, 2021.

5. In the church's first two or three years, 50 percent of attenders had not come from a different church. They were either unbelievers or unaffiliated Christians. And like a student ministry, about 33 percent of the church turned over every September. The average age of a church member during the mid-1990s was thirty, and 75 percent were single. Less than half, about 45 percent, were White.

6. Timothy Keller, "An Evangelical Mission in a Secular City," in *Center City Churches: The New Urban Frontier*, ed. Lyle E. Schaller (Nashville: Abingdon Press, 1993), 33.

7. Timothy Keller, email to Collin Hansen, June 6, 2021.

8. Lane Arthur, interview with Collin Hansen, February 16, 2021.

9. Timothy Keller, *Center Church: Doing Balanced, Gospel-Centered Ministry in Your City* (Grand Rapids: Zondervan, 2012), 350.

10. Lorraine Zechmann, interview with Collin Hansen, February 4, 2021.

11. Lane Arthur, interview with Collin Hansen, February 16, 2021.

12. See "Manhattan Center City 2019," PowerPoint presentation via Zoom, A Journey through NYC Religions Data Center, October 2, 2020.

13. See Keller, *Center Church*, 73.

14. C. John Miller, *Outgrowing the Ingrown Church* (Grand Rapids: Zondervan, 1986, 1999), 98–101.

15. Katherine Leary Alsdorf, interview with Collin Hansen, February 2, 2021.

16. Kathy Keller, interview with Collin Hansen, January 23, 2021.

17. Marlene Hucks, interview with Collin Hansen, March 10, 2021.

18. Keller, "An Evangelical Mission in a Secular City," 31.

19. When Redeemer added a 10:00 a.m. service, many members begged Keller to keep the 6:30 p.m. service, since so many of them had jobs in entertainment that kept them out until two or three in the morning. Attendance had jumped again to 350 by June 1990, and to 600 by the fall, with 100 members. In January 1991, Redeemer prepared to move away from PCA support and particularize with its own officers by June. When 1991 ended, Redeemer reported 275 members, with 950 in attendance. Nearly half came to the 6:30 p.m. service.

20. Keller, "An Evangelical Mission in a Secular City," 36.

21. Marlene Hucks, interview with Collin Hansen, March 10, 2021.

22. Barbara Ohno, interview with Collin Hansen, February 2, 2021.

23. See Timothy Keller with Kathy Keller, *The Meaning of Marriage: Facing the Complexities of Commitment with the Wisdom of God* (New York: Dutton, 2011), 11.

24. Timothy Keller, *The Reason for God: Belief in an Age of Skepticism* (New York: Dutton, 2008), 43–44.

25. Ryan P. Burge, *The Nones: Where They Came From, Who They Are, and Where They Are Going* (Minneapolis: Fortress, 2021).

26. D. Martyn Lloyd-Jones, *Preaching and Preachers* (Grand Rapids: Zondervan, 1972), 151.

27. Lloyd-Jones, *Preaching and Preachers*, 152–53.

28. Timothy Keller, email to Collin Hansen, April 27, 2021.

29. Keller, *Center Church*, 79.

30. Michael Green, *Evangelism through the Local Church: A Comprehensive Guide to All Aspects of Evangelism* (Nashville: Oliver-Nelson, 1992), 320.

31. Arthur Armstrong, interview with Collin Hansen, March 18, 2021.

32. Barbara Ohno, interview with Collin Hansen, February 2, 2021.

33. Timothy Keller, "An Evangelical Mission in a Secular City," 33.

34. Cregan Cooke, interview with Collin Hansen, February 3, 2021.

35. Lloyd-Jones, *Preaching and Preachers*, 152.

36. Keller, *Center Church*, 315.

37. Mako Fujimura, interview with Collin Hansen, February 4, 2021.

38. Katherine Leary Alsdorf, interview with Collin Hansen, February 2, 2021.

39. Timothy Keller, "Our Place in the Story: Part 2," Redeemer Report, November 2014, www.redeemer.com/redeemer-report/article/our_place_in_the_story_part_2.

40. Timothy J. Keller, "The Girl Nobody Wanted," in *Heralds of the King: Christ-Centered Sermons in the Tradition of Edmund P. Clowney*, ed. Dennis E. Johnson (Wheaton, IL: Crossway, 2009), 55.

41. Keller, "The Girl Nobody Wanted," 57.

42. Keller, "The Girl Nobody Wanted," 61, italics in original.

43. Robert Alter, *Genesis: Translation and Commentary* (New York: Norton, 1996), 155.

44. Alter, *Genesis*, 154.

45. Keller, "The Girl Nobody Wanted," 63.

46. Keller, "The Girl Nobody Wanted," 64–65.

47. Keller, "The Girl Nobody Wanted," 56.

48. Timothy Keller, interview with Collin Hansen, June 11, 2021.

49. Mako Fujimura, interview with Collin Hansen, March 4, 2021.

50. Lorraine Zechmann, interview with Collin Hansen, February 4, 2021.

51. Arthur Armstrong, interview with Collin Hansen, March 18, 2021.

52. Katherine Leary Alsdorf, interview with Collin Hansen, February 2, 2021.

53. Timothy Keller with Katherine Leary Alsdorf, *Every Good Endeavor: Connecting Your Work to God's Work* (New York: Dutton, 2016), 92.

54. Liz Kaufmann, interview with Collin Hansen, March 11, 2021.

55. Cregan Cooke, interview with Collin Hansen, February 3, 2021.

56. Craig Ellis, interview with Collin Hansen, January 15, 2021.

57. Yvonne Sawyer, interview with Collin Hansen, February 2, 2021.

58. Timothy Keller, *Preaching: Communicating Faith in an Age of Skepticism* (New York: Viking, 2015), 196–97.

59. Keller, *Center Church*, 311.

60. Keller, *Center Church*, 284.
61. Sharon Johnson, interview with Collin Hansen, January 13, 2021.
62. Kathy Keller, interview with Collin Hansen, June 24, 2021.
63. Sharon Johnson, interview with Collin Hansen, January 13, 2021.
64. Paraphrased from George Herbert, "Time": "For where thou onely wert before an executiner at best; thou art a gard'ner now, and more," www.ccel.org/h /herbert/temple/Time.html.

Chapter 16: Everybody Worships

1. John Starke, "New York's Post-9/11 Church Boom," The Gospel Coalition, September 7, 2011, www.thegospelcoalition.org/article/new-yorks-post-911 -church-boom.
2. Starke, "New York's Post-9/11 Church Boom."
3. Timothy Keller, "Truth, Tears, Anger, and Grace" (sermon, Redeemer Presbyterian Church, New York City, September 16, 2001), www.youtube.com/watch ?v=KkZqsZqiEIA.
4. Kathy Keller, interview with Collin Hansen, June 24, 2021.
5. Liz Smith, interview with Collin Hansen, February 16, 2021.
6. Kathy Keller, interview with Collin Hansen, June 24, 2021.
7. Christina Ray Stanton, "God Sustained Me in COVID-19, as He Did on 9/11," The Gospel Coalition, April 28, 2020, www.thegospelcoalition.org/article/god -sustained-me-911.
8. Timothy Keller, interview with Collin Hansen, June 24, 2021.
9. See Timothy Keller, *The Prodigal Prophet: Jonah and the Mystery of God's Mercy* (New York: Viking, 2018), 2.
10. Mako Fujimura, interview with Collin Hansen, March 4, 2021.
11. Timothy Keller, "Heaven" (sermon, Redeemer Presbyterian Church, New York City, June 8, 1997), https://gospelinlife.com/downloads/heaven-5931.
12. Starke, "New York's Post-9/11 Church Boom."
13. Timothy Keller, *Center Church: Doing Balanced, Gospel-Centered Ministry in Your City* (Grand Rapids: Zondervan, 2012), 175.
14. Mako Fujimura, interview with Collin Hansen, March 4, 2021.
15. See Timothy Keller, *Walking with God through Pain and Suffering* (New York: Dutton, 2013), 6.
16. Timothy Keller, *Prayer: Experiencing Awe and Intimacy with God* (New York: Dutton, 2014), 9–10.
17. John Owen, *The Glory of Christ*, abridged ed. (Carlisle, PA: Banner of Truth, 1994), 7.
18. See Timothy Keller, *The Reason for God: Belief in an Age of Skepticism* (New York: Dutton, 2008), 244–45, n. 2, chapter 1.
19. See Keller, *Reason for God*, 84.
20. Keller, *Reason for God*, 9.
21. Keller, *Reason for God*, 241.

22. Timothy Keller, *Hope in Times of Fear: The Resurrection and the Meaning of Easter* (New York: Viking, 2021), xiii–xiv.

23. Keller, *Hope in Times of Fear*, xi.

24. Keller, *Reason for God*, 109.

25. Timothy Keller, interview with Collin Hansen, January 25, 2021.

26. Craig Ellis, interview with Collin Hansen, January 15, 2021.

27. Ted Turnau, *Popologetics: Popular Culture in Christian Perspective* (Phillipsburg, NJ: P&R, 2012), 38.

28. Turnau, *Popologetics*, 58–59.

29. Keller, *Center Church*, 126–27.

30. Luther gave Keller a way to apply the gospel to the heart instead of simply appealing to the will to obey the law. Luther showed him that our hearts naturally seek salvation through works, but the gospel brings Christians back to depend on grace alone.

31. Timothy Keller, "How to Talk about Sin in a Postmodern Age," The Gospel Coalition, May 12, 2017, www.thegospelcoalition.org/article/how-to-talk-sin-in-postmodern-age.

32. Keller, *Reason for God*, 275–76.

33. Ernest Becker, *The Denial of Death* (New York: Free Press, 1973), 167.

34. Turnau, *Popologetics*, 58–63.

35. "This Is Water by David Foster Wallace (Full Transcript and Audio)," Farnham Street (*fs*), accessed August 8, 2022, https://fs.blog/david-foster-wallace-this-is-water.

36. Turnau, *Popologetics*, 239.

Chapter 17: Making Sense of God

1. Craig Ellis, interview with Collin Hansen, January 15, 2021.

2. Several books stand out: Philip Rieff's *Triumph of the Therapeutic* and *Freud: The Mind of the Moralist*; Robert Bellah's *Habits of the Heart* and *The Good Society*; Alasdair MacIntyre's *After Virtue* and *Whose Justice? Which Rationality?*; and Charles Taylor's *Sources of the Self* and *A Secular Age*.

3. Timothy Keller, email to Collin Hansen, June 11, 2021.

4. Christian Smith, *To Flourish or Destruct: A Personalist Account of Human Goods, Motivations, Failure, and Evil* (Chicago: University of Chicago Press, 2015), 269–70.

5. Timothy Keller, interview with Collin Hansen, June 24, 2021.

6. Timothy Keller, *Preaching: Communicating Faith in an Age of Skepticism* (New York: Viking, 2015), 135–36.

7. Robert N. Bellah et al., *Habits of the Heart: Individualism and Commitment in American Life* (Berkeley: University of California Press, 2008), 333–34.

8. See Timothy Keller, *Hope in Times of Fear: The Resurrection and the Meaning of Easter* (New York: Viking, 2021), 197.

9. Bellah et al., *Habits of the Heart*, 286.

10. Craig Ellis, interview with Collin Hansen, January 15, 2021.

11. Timothy Keller, "God at Work" (sermon, Redeemer Presbyterian Church, New York City, August 25, 2013).
12. Timothy Keller, "Hope That Transforms" (lecture, Redeemer Presbyterian Church, New York City, February 20, 2014).
13. Keller, "Hope That Transforms."
14. Timothy Keller, "Session 1 Question and Answer" (lecture, "Preaching Christ in a Postmodern World," Reformed Theological Seminary, Orlando, Florida, September 8, 2008).
15. See Timothy Keller, *Making Sense of God: An Invitation to the Skeptical* (New York: Viking, 2016), 131.
16. Keller, *Making Sense of God*, 139.
17. See Keller, *Making Sense of God*, 142.
18. Keller, *Making Sense of God*, 147.
19. Richard J. Mouw, "From Kuyper to Keller: Why Princeton's Prize Controversy Is So Ironic," *Christianity Today*, March 27, 2017, www.christianitytoday.com/ct /2017/march-web-only/kuyper-keller-princeton-seminary-ironic.html.
20. Timothy Keller, *Center Church: Doing Balanced, Gospel-Centered Ministry in Your City* (Grand Rapids: Zondervan, 2012), 244.
21. Keller, *Making Sense of God*, 48–49, italics in original.
22. Keller, *Center Church*, 120.
23. See Keller, *Preaching*, 103–20.
24. Timothy Keller, *How to Reach the West Again: Six Essential Elements of a Missionary Encounter* (New York: Redeemer City to City, 2020), 29.
25. Timothy Keller, "Justice in the Bible," Life in the Gospel (Fall 2020), https://quarterly.gospelinlife.com/justice-in-the-bible.
26. Timothy Keller, "Answering Lesslie Newbigin" (lecture, Princeton Theological Seminary, Princeton, NJ, April 6, 2017).
27. See Keller, *Making Sense of God*, 179.
28. Keller, *Making Sense of God*, 181.
29. Keller, *Making Sense of God*, 210.
30. Keller, *Making Sense of God*, 301, n. 30.
31. Keller, *Center Church*, 235.
32. Keller, *How to Reach the West Again*, 20–21.
33. Timothy Keller, "A Biblical Critique of Secular Justice and Critical Race Theory," Life in the Gospel (Special Edition), https://quarterly.gospelinlife.com/a-biblical -critique-of-secular-justice-and-critical-theory.
34. Keller, "Biblical Critique."
35. Timothy Keller, *The Prodigal Prophet: Jonah and the Mystery of God's Mercy* (New York: Viking, 2018), 199–200.
36. See Keller, *Making Sense of God*, 172.
37. Keller, *Making Sense of God*, 158.
38. Keller, "Biblical Critique."
39. Keller, *Center Church*, 224.

40. Timothy Keller, *Generous Justice: How God's Grace Makes Us Just* (New York: Dutton, 2010), xv-xvii.

41. Keller, *Generous Justice*, xvii.

42. Keller, *Making Sense of God*, 208–9.

43. Timothy Keller, "Arguing About Politics" (sermon, Redeemer Presbyterian Church, New York City, July 15, 2001), www.youtube.com/watch?v=U79 Eef6U9nw.

44. Kathy Keller, "The Great Commission Must Be Our Guide in These Polarizing Times," Life in the Gospel (Spring 2021), https://quarterly.gospelinlife.com/the -great-commission-must-be-our-guide-in-these-polarizing-times.

45. Keller, "Justice in the Bible."

46. Timothy Keller, "Nietzsche Was Right," The Gospel Coalition, September 23, 2020, www.thegospelcoalition.org/reviews/dominion-christian-revolution-tom -holland.

47. James Eglinton, "Dutch Inspiration for Tim Keller," trans. Nelson D. Kloosterman, *Nederlands Dagblad*, July 11, 2011, https://cosmiceye.wordpress .com/2011/07/12/dutch-inspiration-for-tim-keller.

48. James Eglinton, *Bavinck: A Critical Biography* (Grand Rapids: Baker Academic, 2020), i.

49. Eglinton, *Bavinck*, 311.

50. Eglinton, *Bavinck*, 150.

51. Eglinton, *Bavinck*, 275.

52. Eglinton, *Bavinck*, 215.

53. Timothy Keller, *The Prodigal God: Recovering the Heart of the Christian Faith* (New York: Dutton, 2008), 127–31.

54. Isak Dinesen (Karen Blixen), *Babette's Feast and Other Stories* (New York: Penguin, 2013), 68.

55. Timothy Keller, "Death of Death" (sermon, Redeemer Presbyterian Church, New York City, May 16, 1993).

56. Timothy Keller, "The Finality of Jesus" (sermon, Redeemer Presbyterian Church, New York City, January 5, 1997).

57. Keller, "Finality of Jesus."

58. Timothy Keller, "Death and the Christian Hope" (sermon, Redeemer Presbyterian Church, New York City, April 4, 2004).

59. William McDonald, "Søren Kierkegaard," *Stanford Encyclopedia of Philosophy*, November 10, 2017, https://plato.stanford.edu/entries/kierkegaard.

60. Keller, *How to Reach the West Again*, 4.

61. Keller, *How to Reach the West Again*, 7.

62. Keller, *How to Reach the West Again*, 9.

63. What began as the Church Planting Center led by Terry Gyger within Redeemer evolved into Redeemer City to City with its own board. The ministry helps national leaders around the world plant churches in their biggest cities. The goal was to begin a global movement of gospel-centered, missional, and

doctrinally sound churches. It worked. By 2022, Redeemer City to City had helped plant more than one thousand churches in up to eighty cities with eight global affiliates of indigenously led church networks. *Center Church* lays out the DNA of the movement of gospel-centered, missional, and doctrinally sound churches.

64. Timothy Keller, interview with Collin Hansen, June 10, 2022.

Chapter 18: Rings on a Tree

1. Timothy Keller, *The Prodigal God: Recovering the Heart of the Christian Faith* (New York: Dutton, 2008), 125.
2. The Gospel Coalition, "Get More Rings in Your Tree," *Vimeo* video, 11:33, July 9, 2014, https://vimeo.com/100309192.
3. Keller, *Prodigal God*, 135.
4. Craig Ellis, interview with Collin Hansen, January 15, 2021.
5. Arthur Armstrong, interview with Collin Hansen, March 18, 2021.

Epilogue

1. "Tim Keller on Reformed Resurgence," *Life and Books and Everything* podcast audio, January 25, 2021, https://lifeandbooksandeverything.sounder.fm /episode/27.
2. Timothy Keller, *Walking with God through Pain and Suffering* (New York: Dutton, 2013), 80.